W9-CHB-402

THE REVOLUTIONARY MASTERS & JOHNSON APPROACH TO A NEW SEXUALITY

Headlines were made when the scientific research team of Masters and Johnson published their startling findings on the nature of male and female sexuality. Less well known, however, are the methods they have developed to treat heretofore "incurable" cases of male sexual inadequacy through the use of "surrogate wives"—otherwise known as "in-bed therapists."

Today, in St. Louis, these sexual laboratory methods are proving of enormous worth to sexually troubled men of all kinds. Valerie X. Scott is one of the extraordinary young women who have taken on the task of this still controversial method of therapy. Here, for the first time, she describes the methods and effects of her experiences through actual case histories of patients she treated. This truly important book charts a bold new course in one of the most vital areas of the human condition.

SURROGATE WIFE

"VALERIE X. SCOTT"
as told to
HERBERT d'H. LEE

A DELL BOOK

Published by
Dell Publishing Co., Inc.
750 Third Avenue
New York, New York 10017
Copyright © 1971 by "Valerie X. Scott" and
"Herbert d'H. Lee".
All rights reserved. No part of this book may be
reproduced in any form or by any means without the
prior written permission of the Publisher,
excepting brief quotes used in connection with reviews
written specifically for
inclusion in a magazine or newspaper.
Dell ® TM 681510, Dell Publishing Co., Inc.

Printed in Canada
First printing—October 1971

For "Gail"

A man without passion is only a
latent force, only a possibility, like
a stone waiting for a blow from the
iron to give forth sparks.

—Henri-Fréderic Arniel, *Journal*

SURROGATE WIFE:

The Story of a Masters & Johnson therapist and the nine cases she treated

FOREWORD

As co-authors of *Surrogate Wife,* we feel an obligation to pay tribute to Dr. William H. Masters and Mrs. Virginia E. Johnson for their pioneering work in the study of human sexuality, as described in their now-renowned books *Human Sexual Response* and *Human Sexual Inadequacy*. So basic to human well-being has been their contribution that, in but a few short years, these books have made their authors internationally famous, both among learned professionals and the general public.

While some have adjudged their methods and conclusions to be controversial, this is not unusual in cases of original research and original researchers. Freud's contemporaries made caustic comments too. The fact that many universities are beginning to teach the ideas of Masters and Johnson testifies to the value of their work. Indeed, their books must be considered as required reading for medical students, psychologists, and others studying in this area.

In their clinical work, Masters and Johnson alleviate suffering that too often in the past has been ignored or hidden. And while so doing, they scrupulously protect the anonymity of their patients. We have done the same: All personal names in *Surrogate Wife* (including our own) have been changed except for those of Dr. Masters and Mrs. Johnson. The individual identities are, after all, irrelevant. What matters is the good work of Masters and Johnson and their Reproductive Biology Research Foundation.

Authors, teachers, researchers, therapists—these terms aptly describe Masters and Johnson. But perhaps, most of all, they are compassionate human beings. This we, the authors, felt strongly in our roles of surrogate wife and patient. Compassionate therapists who have saved marriages and sent individuals back to sexual adequacy and joy in life.

This book shows how nine such individuals were helped.

"VALERIE X. SCOTT"

and

HERBERT d'H. LEE

PROLOGUE
by Herbert Lee

It was remarkably mild for an evening in late February, but then again, this was St. Louis. Mild or not, the weather wasn't responsible for the thin film of perspiration on my forehead. I was standing in front of the Forest Park Hotel, waiting for my "date." I enquote the word because in all my forty-five years I had never met a woman under such circumstances—nor, I can say with certainty, have more than a relative handful of people, all of them patients of Dr. William H. Masters and Virginia E. Johnson in their world-famous St. Louis clinic for the treatment of sexual inadequacies.

I had been told to watch for a white Camaro with black roof, driven by a woman, that would arrive at the hotel entrance at seven P.M. I was to approach and identify myself—common enough procedure for a blind date, or a setup with a member of the oldest profession. But I hadn't traveled a thousand miles, invested several thousand dollars in medical fees—plus air fare, hotel and living expenses—for anything like that.

I had come for treatment, a new and unique kind of treatment to be found only at the Reproductive Biology Research Foundation. I was a patient. The woman I was

waiting to meet was my therapist—my sexual therapist—
someone who would treat my ailment not in a hospital,
not in a doctor's office or clinic, not on an analyst's
couch—but in *bed*.

It began two months before, when as a last desperate
measure I sought the help of a psychiatrist. I was, to put
it bluntly, no longer able to function as a man with
women, no longer sexually capable. The analyst suggested I look into the Masters and Johnson Foundation.
I placed a long-distance call, spoke to a Dr. Spitz, and
was given several pieces of information. First, at age
forty-five, I had a good chance to be treated successfully.
Second, it was *not* necessary, as I had thought, either to
be married or to bring a female partner with me for
this special kind of therapy. And third, I would have to
be referred to Dr. Masters by a doctor, a therapist, or a
member of the clergy—someone who knew me and my
problem in a professional sense.

The referral was made by my doctor. I received a long
questionnaire from the Foundation, which covered not
only my basic medical and personal history but also my
approaches and opinions on sexual matters. But all this
was still not remarkable. What *was* was the idea of a
"wife surrogate." If, after an initial interview with Dr.
Masters, I was accepted for treatment by the Foundation, I would be assigned a female therapist. She would,
for the length of my stay in St. Louis—two weeks—and
for purposes of my treatment, take the place of a wife.
In other words, I would be sexually involved with her
during the treatment period.

About a month later, I took a jet from New York to
St. Louis, checked into a room at the Forest Park Hotel,
and spent a very nervous Sunday night thinking ahead to
my morning appointment with Dr. Masters. I had read
as much as I could about Masters and Johnson—articles
in several national magazines—and had struggled through
their book *Human Sexual Response*. I say "struggled,"
because it is written in language so heavily scientific that
even doctors have difficulty getting through it. And *why*
this is so is part of what impressed me about these two
sex researchers and helped bring me to them.

In 1947 Dr. Masters, a gynecologist, began research

into the problems of conception, treating couples who were having difficulty having babies. In 1952 he began working on contraceptive physiology, aware of the growing problem of population control. In 1954 he began his research into human sexual response, establishing a laboratory with the help of Washington University in St. Louis. By this time he was beginning to be known to the medical fraternity because of his twenty-five published papers, many of them on hormone-replacement therapy for postmenopausal women. He also taught obstetrics and gynecology in Washington University's medical school.

But it was the work in human sexual response that was to bring him, and the assistant he acquired soon afterward, Mrs. Virginia Johnson, national repute—along with a degree of criticism, some of it based on nothing more than the critic's moral and ethical preferences, but much of it vituperative. For this reason, Dr. Masters decided that a degree of secrecy was necessary, at least until he could publish his findings and inform the scientific world of the full extent of his motives, and his information.

Masters and Johnson were dealing with sexual performance. *Human* sexual performance, for so long ignored outside the psychiatric profession by doctors and laymen alike as a subject for serious investigation or treatment, because of blue-nose and Victorian attitudes.

Kinsey had gathered statistics, some of them shocking, all of them valuable and revealing, on American sexual practices. His reports had raised a hue and cry that almost buried the scientific value of his research. How, then, would the nation as a whole treat *laboratory observation* of human sexual performance? For this was what Masters and Johnson were engaged in.

At first they recruited subjects within the school, people they knew and trusted. Later, as word got around about the project, and as the need for a wider variety of subjects became necessary, they began accepting volunteers—but only those they felt were physiologically and psychologically able to undertake the work.

Just what was the work these subjects were doing?

It all came out in 1966, with publication of *Human*

Sexual Response. The work was men and women engaging at times in sexual intercourse, and being observed, both by the researchers and by testing equipment. At other times, female subjects used an artificial penis, made of transparent plastic material, that not only brought them to orgasm but also photographed and recorded their actual internal responses.

For the very first time in human history, a mass of scientific data was gathered on the procreative process. Myths were revealed as myths. For example: Women do *not* ejaculate any sort of fluid corresponding to the male's semen, but they *do* have an orgasmic reaction that is physiological, not just mental. Advancing age *does* have an effect upon the physiological response of men and women engaging in sexual intercourse, but it does *not* end ability or pleasure in sex, as proven by subjects in their seventies and eighties. Penis size varies far less in full erective state than mythology and literature suggest; furthermore, size matters little in satisfying the female.

The local news media in St. Louis knew what was going on, but in a rare example of altruism and public service, they did *not* publicize the project. Masters and Johnson could have gone on perhaps another two years, gathering data, and planned on at least one more year, if a medical man had not blown the whistle by publishing an adverse article about the project in a nonmedical magazine. So the book had to be written and put out before certain work on cardiorespiratory physiology was completed.

Because of the criticism, and because the public tended to consider sexual experience in published form prurient and pornographic matter, Masters and Johnson decided to make their book almost unreadable for the layman. In other words, they were going to give up their chance to reach vast numbers of the public, in order to reduce the risk that the scientific world might question their motives. Their book would inform only a few scientifically sophisticated people of a breakthrough in sexual research.

That's what they *thought*. They chose a publisher beyond reproach; the book was clothed in a sedate brown-paper jacket; the first printing was limited to

15,000 copies. But *Human Sexual Response* began to sell heavily, and has sold over 300,000 copies to date. Obviously, the nation—its scientific and informed lay establishment—was hungry for information about the real, the factual, after history's long state of the merely speculative.

But that was not why I was in St. Louis, not what had made my psychiatrist recommend Masters and Johnson for my own specific problem, and made my family doctor agree they might be able to help me.

For the past year, magazines had been running articles about the *new* Masters and Johnson book, due out in just a few months. (It was, in fact, in galley proofs when I paid my first visit to the Foundation Monday morning, and I glanced at this copy lying on a conference-room table, after Dr. Masters pointed it out.) The book was called *Human Sexual Inadequacy* and was the result not only of observations made during the laboratory experiments which led to *Human Sexual Response,* but also of observations and experience gained treating sexually dysfunctional men and women from 1959 on. This treatment had not been publicized nationally, or at least not in such a way that the average person seeking help for a sexual problem would be likely to become aware of it.

For obvious reasons, most patients who went to the Foundation were married. The male or female, or both, would have a sexual problem, and the marriage would begin to falter and die because of this problem. The family doctor, the marriage counselor, and often the clergyman caring for the couple would look for ways to save the marriage. If the doctor, counselor, or clergyman knew of Masters and Johnson, and was sophisticated enough to understand their work, the couple might then be referred to the Foundation. There, they would be interviewed separately by Dr. Masters and Mrs. Johnson, as well as having round-table discussions of the problem. Their problems ranged the full spectrum of male and female dysfunction—but most were based on, and therefore treated as, fear-induced psychological disorders. The *mind,* not the body, was creating the problem. *Fear* of dysfunction was causing the dysfunction itself. (In those few rare cases where a real physical disability existed, it was quickly defined in the medical-examination portion of the Foundation's services, and then treated in whatever way was indicated. But these were an infinitesimal fraction of the Foundation's cases.)

What are the common male and female dysfunctions? First the male:

Primary Impotence: The man who has never in all his life been able to gain or maintain an erection and so has never been able to engage in sexual intercourse. Thirty-two men were treated for this relatively rare form of impotence. Eleven of them were married, and had been married for from seven months to eighteen years without engaging in sexual intercourse with their wives.

Secondary Impotence: The man who *has* been able to gain and maintain an erection and engage in sexual intercourse at least once, and often hundreds of times, but who fails for one reason or another on a particular occasion, and who then begins *fearing* failure and therefore fails over and over again. Two hundred and thirteen cases of secondary impotence were treated at the Foundation.

Premature Ejaculation: The male who has his orgasm too quickly, before his partner can have hers, which often leads to unnatural strain upon the male to lengthen his coital period, and then to failure and secondary impotence. One hundred and eighty-six men were treated for premature ejaculation.

Ejaculatory Incompetence: The male who cannot ejaculate—"come"—while his penis is in his partner's vagina. Apparently rare, since only seventeen men were treated in eleven years.

As for the women:

Primary Orgasmic Dysfunction: The woman who has never in all her life had an orgasm—often because her partner is a premature ejaculator or impotent. One hundred and ninety-three women were treated for this.

Situational Orgasmic Dysfunction: Women in this category have had at least one and probably many more orgasms, and then either because of early psychopathology or because of a dysfunctional husband or partner, begin to fail.

Vaginismus: The virtual closing, due to psychosomatic

illness, of the woman's vaginal opening, making penetration by the partner's penis totally impossible or so uncomfortable as to delay unnaturally and sometimes defy coitus.

Dyspareunia: Painful intercourse, which destroys all pleasure for the female. This is often an excuse by women who want to avoid sexual intercourse, but as in other cases of psychosomatic illness, it causes very real discomfort and pain. Can also be caused by infections, scar tissue, brutal entry (as in gang rape).

(Far more rare is Dyspareunia in males, but it can be caused by lack of cleanliness in the uncircumcised penis, or irritation caused by chemical birth-control agents or harsh douches used by the female.)

For both males and females, the problem of *aging* is often very real, because of fear that they are no longer able, nor should they seek to be able, to involve themselves in sex play and intercourse. Masters and Johnson feel that their work with those of sixty and above is of the utmost importance, since it reverses these myths and proves that men and women can have sexual intercourse well into their eighties, given good health and willing partners.

And the treatment for this variety of sexual maladies? Well, in general, and skipping for the moment specific techniques which will be mentioned later, it can be summed up as *nondemand.* To eliminate the *need* to perform, on the parts of both male and female, to lessen the tension that leads to an "examination-time" approach to sex, to get away from the my-God-I-have-to-come-through feeling that leads to fear of failure and then to actual failure. And through this, to reverse a history of failure and establish a habit pattern of success, all within a two-week period.

All very well. All offering much hope to couples coming to the Foundation—couples who would work together, in the privacy of a hotel room, according to Masters and Johnson's instructions. But I wasn't a couple. I was a single male, and I was going to be given a single female, a strange female, one who would be part of my life only for that time in which we worked together. How much hope of success did *I* have?

The figures spoke of forty-one men being treated by thirteen surrogates over a period of eleven years, with better than an eighty-percent success factor.

Okay. The odds were in my favor. But I felt very little hope of success. Because I would still have to deal sexually with a woman, even though this time her title was not girl friend or sweetheart or lover, but wife surrogate. And women had become more pain than pleasure to me. That was why I was here, beginning to pace nervously in front of the Forest Park Hotel. And that was why I froze when the white Camaro Dr. Masters had described at my morning interview session, my first session that Monday in February, pulled up to the curb. I froze, and stared, and finally stepped forward, surprised at a weakness in my legs.

The car had stopped a distance away from the lighted hotel entrance; the driver was hidden in shadows; I was at the open window before I actually saw her. "Good evening, my name is Herbert Lee."

She nodded, smiled, said, "I'm Valerie. Have you had dinner yet?"

I got in the car, and said no. We discussed various kinds of restaurants—French, Italian, Spanish, Chinese—and she drove and mentioned points of interest. And even though I looked, reacted, laughed, spoke, joked, I wasn't concerned with anything I was doing. I was sitting beside a girl who was now revealed to me as a lovely redhead of perhaps twenty-six with long legs showing to mid-thigh under her tan mini and open short coat; a girl whose bust swelled dramatically; a girl whose face and body made me want her instantly. A girl who belonged to me; whom I had in effect purchased at the clinic two days ago; who would be mine in every way that a man wants a desirable woman. When and how would I have to prove myself with this beautiful woman?

I'm a professional writer. A little over two years before meeting Valerie, while researching European locales for a projected novel, I was stricken with prostatitis, an infection that is actually a breakdown of the prostate gland. It and other prostate conditions are among the most common ailments afflicting the American male.

Prostatitis is usually manageable via massage, antibiotics, and twice-yearly checks by a urologist. But I didn't know what was wrong at the time. I was in a restaurant in Bergen, Norway, sitting with a lovely girl, and suddenly my groin—or more specifically, my penis—was on fire.

Any veteran of the U.S. armed forces remembers the films warning against venereal disease. Men are shown with sweet, lovely, girl-next-door types (to prove that you can trust absolutely *no one*), laughing, drinking, and walking into darkened rooms together . . . and then fade-out, time passes, and suddenly these same men are in agony, horrible eruptions on their genitals; or as one World War II film had it, running for a bus and dropping dead of a syphilis-induced heart attack.

These films had a purpose, and there is no doubt that they served it. They also had side effects on some of the more sensitive G.I.s—long-range inhibition.

I was sitting with a sweet, lovely, girl-next-door type in Norway. I had already drunk with her, laughed with her, and walked through darkened doorways with her . . . five nights running. And even if it was too soon for this particular girl to have given me some horror, there were others—in London, in Paris, and back in the States.

That night I walked through no darkened doorway. The pain diminished, but my fears of venereal disease didn't. The thought of making love to my Norwegian companion—or any other woman—was suddenly repellent. I was about to join a huge and unhappy fraternity—those men who, for one reason or another, first reduce and then eliminate their own sexuality.

In New York I learned that my fears of venereal disease were baseless, and that I had something new to worry about—prostate problems. That a specialist said it need not interfere with my normal sex life meant nothing: my own mind had been at work for the three weeks it had taken me to complete my European trip and get to see a doctor; it continued to work, destructively, substituting the prostate for the syphilis bug.

Treatment for prostatic infection includes, besides medication and warm baths, painful prostate massages, which to me were debasing and traumatic. I had to bend over while the doctor inserted a rubber-tipped finger deep into my anus, for what seem like a half-hour and was actually a moment or two. The first doctor, the so-called specialist who gave this treatment, was also unnecessarily rough and callous, having no time and no inclination to discuss the whys and wherefores of his treatment. Like many successful urologists, he ran an assembly-line office, with three or four booths in which patients disrobed and waited for his not-so-gentle ministrations. Again, like many successful urologists, he had little or no knowledge of the latest research into sexual dysfunction, Kinsey as well as Masters and Johnson being nothing but names to him. And so I was left to my own inquisitor brain.

I sought more personal treatment, with my own family physician, and this led to my being pronounced cured after five weeks. But the festering infection of the mind was far from cured. I kept working, I lost myself in my characters—I tried not to think of women.

Two months after returning from Europe, I was on a date in Manhattan. The girl was lovely and very much the type that had always turned me on—not too tall, not too lean, and not too cool. We had dinner and danced— close, intimate dancing. I wanted her, and she knew it, and during the early part of the evening everything was fine. But then we got to her apartment house, and it began to change for me.

I'd had only a little pain since completing my treatment, and that diminished to nothing as time passed, but I was still *aware* of my genitals as I had never been before. I was *concentrating* on them, not with joy or lust, but with worry, some of it subconscious. "I'm fine," I kept telling myself. "I've never had trouble with girls, so no sweat."

But sweat I did—during the session on the couch; during the kisses and caresses and slow undressing that revealed a full-breasted, richly curved body; with her moans in my ears. I sweated—and for the first time in my life failed to maintain an erection during the sex act. One minute I was a man, mounting a beautiful and passionate woman; the next minute I was without the means to satisfy her.

My humiliation and suddenly magnified fears are difficult to describe. It's much easier to treat such a scene humorously than to face it realistically and squarely. And with help from the girl, that's just what I did. She'd been around, and it evidently had happened to her before. Also, hadn't I literally been panting for her right up to the moment of truth? So a surprised look, a little giggle, an "I didn't know you were so tired," and we were off to a club for a late drink. Yes, *very* tired I told her over martinis. Much work lately—this no lie. For work is an antidote to mental stress. (How many superactivated businessmen, I wonder, are trying to forget sex problems? With recent figures indicating that perhaps half the marriages in the United States are in trouble sexually, and with projected figures indicating the same percentage holds true for the unmarried, one might almost *correlate* the admired American go-getter with personal-sexual problems!)

I dated the same girl the very next week. I drank during the social part of the evening, but not too much, just enough to relax. Only I didn't relax. Was it pain I felt in my genitals? Was it a return of the infection? I wasn't sure. But the suspicion that I was impaired— physically impaired—was well rooted.

Again I failed to maintain an erection. And this time there were no giggles, no easy assumptions that I was simply tired. The girl ran from the bedroom to the bathroom. She didn't return, and I felt she was waiting for me to follow and offer some sort of explanation. I didn't follow. I understood she was bound to suspect it was *her* fault; that she'd failed to excite me; that she was lacking somehow as a woman. And cruel though it was, I preferred this to speaking the truth. Never before had I willfully allowed a friend to suffer, but I was now entering a very different world from any I'd ever known. Lifelong confidence was crumbling. What the Spaniards term *machismo* was being destroyed. I was caught up in a deepening nightmare of male failure, what every man secretly fears.

I dressed quickly and slipped out. I never saw the girl again, and only through this book will she learn the truth.

Later, at two that morning, I went to the typewriter. I had begun a new novel, and now I threw myself into it frantically. I worked like a demon for five solid weeks, barely pausing for meals and sleep. Then, emotionally exhausted, I had to have a break. I went to a party, met a desirable and very willing young woman, and that same evening was in her apartment. The opportunity was there, but I kept putting off the moment of truth. When it finally arrived, on the couch before the hi-fi set, I seized upon the natural (though purely formal) resistance of a new sex partner, and backed away.

The aborted moment of truth with this new friend was replayed a week later, and this time I never even got close to feeling passion.

Back to the doctors; four of them. Examinations and discussions, and it all boiled down to what one of them said while attempting to comfort me.

"You *seem* all right. Nothing physical, at least that I can tell. You might be overworking. You might be depressed . . . generally. And then, of course, there *does* come a time in a man's life when the sex urge declines. Quite normal, you know. For some it comes sooner, for others later. . . ."

So my body was ailing, or aging, sexually. Either way, I was convinced I was finished as a sexual being.

And yet, convinced though I was, I fought to regain the joys, the delights, of a good sexual response. I sought ever younger and ever prettier sex partners, reasoning that if I found one that satisfied every erotic dream I'd ever had, I'd certainly respond. Or, if I failed with the epitome of my desire, I would at least end the uncertainty and know just where I stood.

I was luckier than most. I had had a long history of successful sex, and because of this I was able, over the next few months, to have an occasional complete experience. But they became more and more widely spaced, despite a truly exciting trio of partners.

So began a two-year history of failure and joyless coitus—joyless because of the tension and fear accompanying it. Total lack of erection. Partial erection. Partial coitus. Coitus without orgasm. A rare, hard-won full act. And visits to new doctors, "specialists" and "experts" most memorable for the size of their fees.

I worked, and concerned myself with "more important

things." After all, I told myself, who can worry about sex when there's Vietnam, the population explosion, racial tension, the Middle East, chance of nuclear war, and so on and so forth. Who indeed?

Well, *I* for one!

I went to more doctors, and received more advice about involving myself in other interests, and from one kindly soul the following: "Since nothing, obviously, can be done about this decline, why not forget it?"

Sure, but how!

And, of course, there was repeated advice to seek psychiatric treatment. This last I considered very seriously. But my instincts warned me against starting something that might take forever to complete. I could be all through with hangups . . . by eighty!

I had, however, a few preliminary sessions with a friend who was also an analyst. The results were, at best, inconclusive, but it was he who gave me the best piece of advice I've ever had from a doctor, he who told me to look into Masters and Johnson's Reproductive Biology Research Foundation in St. Louis.

And so I came to St. Louis and the Forest Park Hotel and, on a gray Monday morning, to the modern medical building on Forest Park Boulevard.

Dr. Masters has been described by many writers, and his picture has graced the nation's newspapers and magazines: a medium-sized man with a square face, strong features, and piercing grayish-green eyes, quite bald. His voice is pleasant, neither too loud nor too soft, and despite my having close to fifty-percent loss of hearing in the right ear, I never, in all our sessions, missed a single word he spoke.

All right. A nice doctor. I'd seen many nice doctors in the past year and a half, and they hadn't done a thing for me. What was this one going to do, graft a new penis onto me?

What he did almost immediately was to shake my hand. Then he pointed out a microphone on his desk and explained that every word I spoke would be recorded, but not simply as a record. He and Mrs. Johnson would go over the interviews and search out key areas. Also,

Mrs. Johnson would be able to know what had gone on at this interview, and he would be able to know what took place during my interview with her. It is part of the Masters-Johnson method to subject all patients to both the male and female therapist, thus bringing out hidden areas of thought, of response. What the male can't get, the female will; and the other way around.

We talked. He explained that I would see him for about an hour each day of the two weeks that I was there, with a day or two off if and when he deemed it useful. Then he led *me* to talk, a basic ploy of the therapist. Only this time the questions, the talk, were all directed to one area of my life—my sexual history. And, it became obvious in later sessions, that everything we discussed would be aimed at illuminating my sexual background and my sexual malaise, or "dysfunction" as Masters and Johnson prefer to call it. So instead of an open-end analysis, a long-range and ever-expanding examination of my life and psyche—with the possible attendant necessity of *years* of therapy—we were entering a short-range and limited examination. As Dr. Masters put it, some of his patients might very well be neurotics in need of broad-spectrum analysis, but if their impotence could be cleared up within two weeks, they would be happier! (He has also stated that he would not attempt to treat anyone who was obviously psychotic, so sick in mind as to present a danger to himself and others. And the Foundation does, indeed, turn down a considerable number of applicants.)

I was now starting on my two weeks of therapy. Description of mental therapy can be found in a hundred books. Suffice it to say that I discussed everything from my first masturbation, through my active sex life as an Air Cadet, to the last failure back in New York a few weeks before. And I continually referred to the medical fact of my prostatitis and stated my belief that I'd had a breakdown in the *physical,* not mental, area.

Masters nodded and said we would soon determine whether that was true, but it was plain from his manner that he doubted it. Nevertheless, I would have a complete examination, and this from what is probably the foremost sexual physician in America, working with the

Missouri Chemical and Biological Laboratory developed by Masters and Johnson, certainly one of the most complete sexual testing facilities in the world, all of its testing equipment fully automated. I was yearning to get the damned examination over with, and yet dreaded its results. My dread had time to grow, because I didn't receive the examination that day.

I had lunch at a nearby restaurant, returned to my suite in the hotel, and tried to read a magazine. Everything in it, articles and ads, proclaimed sex and the joys to be derived from sex. I called my agent about a pending film offer (it was still pending), wrote a few letters . . . and then, as is my habit with whatever I'm experiencing, made a few notes on my impressions of the hotel, the Foundation on Forest Park Boulevard, and Dr. Masters. At that moment, the thought occurred to me that I might be acquiring material for future projects. Everything is grist for a writer's mill, including (or rather *especially*) his own anguish.

I checked the time, and was appalled to see that it wasn't quite two P.M. What could I do with the remainder of this day? I wasn't here for sightseeing; but then I remembered the large manila envelope handed me before I entered Masters' office. It contained, the receptionist had told me, a list of good restaurants and various suggestions for what to do in St. Louis.

Part of the Masters-Johnson technique is to have the patients relax between interview-therapy sessions and bed-therapy sessions by enjoying all there is to enjoy about St. Louis. This was part of the cure—to unwind and get away from tensions.

I went out into the street. The hotel is only a block or two away from Forest Park, and there I could find a museum, zoo, ice-skating rink, planetarium, and opera house. But the weather was still gray, cold, and grim, and I didn't feel like doing anything but walking. Somehow, I chose to go away from the park, through city streets. And somehow I was led to approach a girl waiting at a bus stop and to ask directions of her to a local movie house. And this in turn led her to accompany me, and we saw the movie together.

Well, this was obviously some sort of reaction to tension and *against* the program of treatment I was about to enter. I don't pretend to understand every twist and turn of my own mind. I only know that of all the girls I'd met since my problem began, and at this most inopportune time, I was most strongly attracted to this lovely little citizen of St. Louis (whom I'll call Gail). And she, in turn, was quite obviously interested in me. But even though I was invited to her apartment, and even though my feelings told me *this* girl could become a truly important part of my life, fear of sexual failure made me leave her rather abruptly. Still, I had her name, address, phone number. . . .

Tuesday was crystal-clear, bright, sunny, and I enjoyed the three-block walk to the Foundation. I presented myself in the ground-floor waiting room, sat for less than five minutes, and was summoned upstairs. Another short wait, and I was ushered into Virginia Johnson's office. She is dignified and scholastic . . . and somehow also sexy. We talked; she had listened to the tape of my interview with Masters; she questioned me about many things, among them my profession. She was very interested in writing—professionally so—and I later learned that she is the literary half of the Masters-Johnson bookwriting team.

It was nice chatting with her, just as it had been nice chatting with Dr. Masters. I have never been shy about discussing sex with women, and so discussing it with her neither opened new avenues of thought nor, I'm afraid, closed old avenues. I repeated again my conviction that a breakdown in the genital area was behind all my problems, and she said much the same as Masters had—that we'd soon find out. I asked, rather testily, just when was soon. She said the next morning.

Another long day to kill, and despite the nice chats with the sex experts, I hadn't accomplished a thing.

But leaving the office, I found myself thinking: *Except. Except* that I had a feeling of confidence in these two low-keyed people that kept building.

Not that there wasn't also fear. In-bed therapy—my wife surrogate and I would soon be in bed together! Yet the very purpose of our going to bed together was to eliminate fear.

Both Dr. Masters and Mrs. Johnson had touched upon the nondemand concept during our interviews, and I was beginning to form a clear picture of what was supposed to happen when I got into bed with my wife surrogate. Most importantly, I was not to think of sexual intercourse, because for one thing I would not be allowed that for several meetings. I was to concentrate on touching my partner, at first in nongenital areas, and later all over her body, and I would be touched by her, the same way. I was going to reestablish my feelings of tactile delight, of play without an end goal (coitus), of communication with a woman's body and with my own body. I was going to cease thinking ahead to exam time, cease having to prove something. I was going to stop watching myself and grading my reactions and performances. In-bed therapy was going to reverse the two-year pattern of tension, watching myself, fear, and failure, by the simple method of nondemand touching, nondemand sexual play, and an eventual return to normal or instinctive sexuality. And my partner, my wife surrogate, would be a woman specially trained to aid me in this therapy.

With another long, empty day ahead, I first phoned and then visited Gail, the girl I'd met yesterday. We went a little further in our kissing and petting, but again I ended the meeting abruptly. It wasn't just fear that stopped me this time. I realized I was breaking one of the two social rules under which I was operating as a patient at the Foundation. Dr. Masters had told me I wasn't to have more than two drinks per evening, and I was to have no women at all except the one that would soon be supplied me. (Nor was I to indulge in masturbation.)

"See you soon," Gail said as I walked out her apartment door.

I nodded, but I wondered if I would *ever* see her. Perhaps after my two weeks with Masters and Johnson. . . .

By then I'd have confirmed my fears of physical disability.

By then I'd have no more use for Gail, or any other woman.

The physical exam the next morning took about an hour and a half, without the usual time spent waiting around. Everything was done quickly and efficiently. There were quite a few blood tests, including the standard ones for venereal disease, urine analysis, and a very complete and very personal examination by Dr. Masters. After which I was told to dress and go to his office.

We talked again. He said I appeared to be in excellent physical condition, but that we'd have the laboratory results when I returned tomorrow. For once I had nothing to say. I was beginning to switch areas of fear. For if I was really in excellent physical condition, then it was my *mind* that was making me fail. But I couldn't believe I was robbing myself of the very thing I most wanted in life. A trained mind like mine? Impossible!

The doctor had paused and was looking at me. I began to rise, thinking the interview over. He said that tonight I was going to meet Valerie, my wife surrogate. I sank back down. He added that it was just to get acquainted, have dinner and a drink or two. She wouldn't come up to my room. I would meet her in front of the hotel, and she would leave me there.

His deep-set eyes regarded me with what seemed to be compassionate humor, and he began asking me questions about my work. I was relieved to have a chance to talk writing. I hadn't failed at writing. As we went on, I heard myself saying that I found my experience here quite interesting in a professional as well as personal sense. Then I stopped, realizing that it *could* sound as if I was here to do an exposé type of book and that my enrolling as a patient was simply a mask.

"I mean," I said, "I never seem to know where I leave off as a person and begin as a writer."

Quietly, he said they were aware of that, and that there was obviously some risk in treating a writer, but that they couldn't automatically reject someone who came to them for help because he *was* a writer. He said he believed my complaints were legitimate, but also that I was stimulated by the experience of being here.

And that's where we left it.

I walked half the day, going through the art museum and zoo, and seeing the show at the planetarium. I returned to the hotel at five, bone-tired and thoroughly relaxed, and ran a tub. Before it was filled, my phone rang. It was the hotel switchboard, informing me of a call I'd had earlier: "Please call Gail after five-thirty."

I glanced at the time. Ten to six.

I began to reach for the phone, and then thought again of Dr. Masters' rule: *No other women.*

Masters and Johnson had taken years to develop their method of treatment. Once refined, this treatment had succeeded, as previously stated, with over eighty percent of their patients, the vast majority of them married. Valerie was, for the next two weeks, my wife. I'd have to be crazy to allow Gail or any other woman to get in the way of what might be my last chance to regain my manhood, my joy in sex. Besides, another girl friend would probably mean another failure. Valerie wasn't another girl friend, and was far from just another girl.

Masters and Johnson had faced a problem during the early days of the Foundation—what to do about all the *single* men and women who wrote in requesting help for some sexual dysfunction or other. The Foundation was originally set up to assist only *couples*. In some cases, men and women who weren't married but who had a long-established relationship came to the Foundation together. For purposes of their treatment, they were considered husband and wife. But for those who had no partners, it was either let them suffer or develop some sort of program of surrogate partners.

In 1958 a decision against providing male surrogates was reached for several reasons, one a general inability —determined by long-established social mores—for most women to accept a stranger, a noninvolved male, as a sex partner. "Nice" girls in general don't copulate with strangers. Nice girls with sex problems were even less likely to be able to copulate with strangers, even if those strangers were sexual therapists. Also, there was the obvious danger of a male failing to attain or retain an erection under demand conditions with an *assigned* partner, no matter how effective he might be with women of his own choice. And what would such a failure do to a woman with an already fragile sexual identity! So, any single woman who could provide her own partner was accepted. The others had to be turned away.

As for male patients, they were more fortunate, society having established that men could, without loss of standing or self-esteem, have an occasional toss in the hay, an occasional quick affair—and so a surrogate partner wouldn't be shattering any deep-rooted tradition. But that didn't mean that it would be easy for the sex researchers to find the type of women who could carry through the wife-surrogate program.

With the help of a woman physician, who volunteered as a surrogate, a methodology was established and certain requirements formulated. Naturally, women physicians would be hard to come by, and, in fact, only that one ever took part in the program. Including her, thirteen women were accepted from among thirty-one volunteers, up until the time I was there. All but two of the thirteen surrogates had been married, but none was married at the time they performed surrogate duty for the Foundation. They had treated forty-one men, and most didn't handle more than one case a year—which should answer insinuations that these women in any way resembled prostitutes.

One of the first requirements for a potential surrogate was *motivation*. The woman had to *want* to serve in this capacity. No attempt was ever made to persuade a woman to become a surrogate. Those volunteers who hesitated or voiced undue worry about the work were eliminated. Nine of the thirteen volunteers had experienced sexually dysfunctional males in their private lives and had a strong desire to help other men solve similar problems.

The training program wasn't rigid; it depended on the knowledge, education, and personal history of the particular surrogate. But all were subjected to a complete course of instruction in the manner in which a male functions, physiologically and psychologically. They were also given information on male fears of performance, the part the spectator role can play in dysfunction, the stresses and strains the breadwinner can face in daily life, self-expectation of the male *(machismo)*, how to place the male at ease both socially and physically, and so on. In effect, as much sociosexual information as possible was fed to each and every surrogate.

Once assigned a patient, the surrogate was given a complete dossier of his life and psychosexual background, and then the details of his specific problem. From there on, she checked in day by day, receiving instructions from either Dr. Masters or Mrs. Johnson, and also reporting on the time spent with the patient.

As close a match as possible was made in terms of social and chronological values between patient and surrogate. In view of the results—approximately the same eighty-percent success factor as with the married cases— the selection of surrogates was handled effectively.

So I didn't call my charming little friend. Instead, I bathed and dressed, and went outside to meet my wife surrogate.

Valerie and I had dinner at the Spanish Pavilion (since closed) in downtown St. Louis. She was knowledgeable about food, and before the evening was over I realized she was also knowledgeable and sophisticated about other matters. New York was no romantic Shangrila to her, as it was to Gail. She had been there a number of times, and liked the Boston and Los Angeles areas, among other places, equally well, though she had only visited these areas, never lived in them.

By the time we were halfway through dinner, I wanted to say, "What's a nice girl like you . . . ?" I wanted to ask exactly how long she'd worked at the Foundation. I wanted to know exactly how many patients she'd handled. I wanted to talk to this girl, not about *my* life, but about *hers*.

But she was skilled at leading me to talk about my difficulties. Several times she murmured in her husky voice, "That's common enough," and later, "I think we'll be able to take care of that."

We went to a cocktail lounge, a cozy, English-style place with roaring fire and pianist-vocalist. I had my two drinks. Valerie continued to gentle me into talking about myself. We touched hands several times; she seemed to be relaxing, and I felt I was too. I opened up, talking about the grim beginnings, both emotionally and economically, of my writing career. I described my first triumphs, and the attendant triumphs as a male. I went into my recent sexual failures, and the reasons I had attributed to those failures. She then used a phrase I remembered Dr. Masters using at our session that morning.

"You've become a spectator at your own matings. You're watching every move you make," she continued. "The unthinking, *natural* quality of sex is lost. You wait for yourself to go soft, and so you do. But let's not go into that yet."

I asked if she'd heard the tapes of my meetings with Masters and Johnson. She hadn't—"But, of course, I've been briefed about you. I really don't think we'll have too much trouble."

I wasn't as hopeful as she was. Only bed could tell the story, and bed was the arena in which I'd been failing. I was looking at her face, her bust, and her legs, and I was excited. I was also looking into her eyes, wondering what she was, in a personal and private sense, and I was far more excited by these questions. At the same time, I couldn't help wondering where Gail was.

It was getting confusing. I wasn't keeping it simple, wasn't concentrating on the goal Masters had set for me: to have a successful sex act—period. And was all this confusion only another method my inquisitor brain had developed to block solution to sexual failure?

We didn't return to the hotel until after one A.M. Forgetting Masters' instructions, I asked Valerie to come up to my suite. She shook her head. I began to open the door. She said, "Herb," and when I turned, she kissed me gently on the lips.

Touched, I murmured, "You're a very nice person."

She looked away. "Am I, Herb? I sometimes can't help wondering whether I'm more hooker than therapist."

Perhaps her barriers had come down a little more than she'd realized. Perhaps she'd reacted to talking with a writer—as many people do—by speaking frankly.

But while this turned out to be true, I did not guess the main reason for her frankness, which was that, after almost four years, she had reached a point where inner pressures would soon make it impossible for her to continue as a surrogate wife.

The next morning I was ushered into Dr. Masters' office. (I never did see Mrs. Johnson again, so I presume the evaluation made was that Masters and Valerie could do the job between them.)

Masters began by saying that his examination and the lab results had convinced him that there was absolutely nothing wrong with me. Yes, I had a history of prostatitis, as described by my own physician in a letter to the Foundation. And yes, there could be further "infections" if I didn't consult a urologist on a regular basis. And certainly, I could experience occasional pain. But none of this could be considered a physical deterrent to coitus. My mind was the villain.

I believed him. I hadn't believed anyone else, because no one else had gone about the process of determining what was wrong in so complete a manner; and no one else had this man's track record, his reputation, his personality, all absolutely necessary when dealing with the mind embroiled in self-deceit and self-destruction. It was as if one could be analyzed by Freud, at the time when Freud was considered the one and only source of help, the unchallenged master in his field.

Without knowing it, I had taken a giant step forward.

Dr. Masters said that tonight Valerie would come to my suite. We could have dinner in or out, a drink or two, and we would then undress and go to bed—not to engage in sexual intercourse, but to explore each other, to play, to *touch*, to reestablish my sense of sexual pleasure. Tonight, and in the nights to come, I would begin to lose my role as spectator at my own matings; begin to regain a natural approach to sex—as natural as breathing. The doctor felt, from his own observations and from Valerie's first report to him, that I should progress at a rapid pace.

I nodded. I was still absorbing the fact that I was not sick physically. I was beginning to feel happy about it, because I was beginning to feel that Valerie could help me break through the barriers I'd set up for myself.

The day passed slowly, and by midafternoon I was thinking of Gail again. Unlike Valerie, she was someone I'd met on my own, someone who had responded to Herb

Lee the person and not the patient. Not someone who
had no choice *but* to go to bed with me.

But I had to stop thinking in this way, or I'd ruin everything! (And somewhere deep back in my mind, I knew
I was beginning to do just that; beginning to fight Valerie
and the impersonal method of my using her and her using me. At the same time, I struggled not to abort my
treatment, not to get in the way of the system Masters
and Johnson had developed for the very purpose of helping men like Herb Lee.)

By seven I was as uptight as could be . . . and Valerie
appeared at my door. I didn't know quite how to greet
her, but she leaned forward and we kissed lightly. I then
helped her off with her coat. She was wearing a far more
exciting outfit than she had the night before: a knit
mini-dress of pale yellow that hugged her body. She
smiled, said, "Hi," and waited. I dropped her coat on a
nearby chair and put my hands on her bare arms. I
looked at her, trying to see beyond the pale blue eyes,
to search out resistance, revulsion, or perhaps passion—
to find the *woman* behind the wife surrogate. Her smile
remained natural and convincing. I could read nothing
negative in her eyes. I drew her closer, ready to let go
at the first sign that I was doing something she didn't fully want. I brought her up against me and kissed her. A
second or two, and her mouth opened, her body moved.

Then she slipped away and said, "Don't I get a drink?"

I had a bottle of Canadian and went to the kitchen for
glasses and ice. She followed, looking around, commenting on the suite. I handed her a drink, we touched glasses,
she said, "Here's how," and laughed a little.

I said, "Yes, that *is* the toast of the hour, isn't it?" My
own laughter wasn't quite as convincing.

We went into the living room and sat on the couch.
Her dress rode up; she gave it a purely ritualistic tug
downward; I said, "Thank heavens for the mini." She
drank and smiled and looked at me. I moved closer. I
wanted to feel excitement, passion, lust with this beautiful
woman, but what I was feeling mainly was . . . confusion.

She asked me what I thought of St. Louis. I spoke
about Forest Park and the planetarium and the weather.

Somewhere between Forest Park and the weather, she put her hand on my thigh, lightly enough, and moved it back and forth, gently enough. But I knew it was there.

She was leaning into me, and my arm went around her shoulders, and we kissed. Her hand moved up and back, higher now on my thigh. The confusion began dissipating; excitement began building. I reached to cup a breast. She grew still. I looked at her and then remembered Dr. Masters' instructions this morning. Nongenital touching, he'd said. But the breasts?

"Isn't it allowed?" I asked, taking my hand away.

"Not usually. Tonight is nongenital touching, as you were instructed. We include the breasts, so as to get away from all demand-type situations. If you touch the breasts, you might feel . . ." She shrugged, and smiled. "I really shouldn't talk this much. It's touching we want, not talking. But you seem verbal enough, Herb." Again she smiled. "I think it'll be all right—touching the breasts, I mean."

Her mouth returned to mine; my hand returned to her breast. She had made a decision, and I was later to learn that Masters and Johnson gave Valerie considerable leeway in handling her patients. But at the moment, all I knew was that I wanted to tear the clothing off this woman!

I didn't have to do any tearing. She said, "We should have dinner."

"I'm not hungry. Are you?"

She shook her head, rose, and walked through the archway into the bedroom. I followed, and suddenly all the excitement was gone. It was exam time again. It was fish-or-cut-bait time again.

Except that, as she drew her dress up over her head, she said, voice slightly muffled, "You understand, Herb, that it can't lead to any real lovemaking." Then the dress was off, and she stood looking at me. "Help me, please?"

No lovemaking. No exam tonight. The pressure was off. I couldn't have this woman tonight, even if I went down on my knees and begged. The rules of the Masters-Johnson game. Valerie wouldn't break them.

I came to her, and she turned her back. I unhooked her brassiere, and then knelt to pull down her panties. The aroma of her body was good and clean, and I pressed my lips to her waist and then to those long, creamy-white cheeks. Her flesh was smooth, somewhat cool, but it warmed rapidly under my stroking hands. When I tried to slide one hand between her legs, she said, "Uh-uh," and turned. I was still kneeling, and looked up, and the size of those breasts really surprised me. I'd known they were big, but somehow Valerie was more slender, more delicately boned than she appeared in clothing, and those large breasts seemed even larger by contrast to her general body build. Not awkward or extreme—just wonderfully large. I began to rise, and on the way up I kissed her belly and then those breasts, one at a time, and then handled them, one at a time. When I next looked at her face, her eyes were closed, her lips parted, her breath coming fast. If she was acting, she was a consummate artist!

One thing was sure, *I* wasn't acting. I got rid of my clothes as quickly as possible, and pressed against her. She moaned, and with good reason. Then she led me to the bed, and made me lie down on my back, and got in beside me. Her hands stroked my face and neck and shoulders and arms, then my chest and belly, then jumped to my thighs and down along my legs.

She kissed my cheek, my chest. She ran her hands more quickly over me, up and down, always skipping that now-pulsing, now-urgent area of the genitals.

I finally pulled her against me. We kissed, and my chest felt those large, firm globes of flesh. When she moved away, murmuring, "Not tonight, dear," I found her breasts with my hands, with my mouth. And I begged her to touch me *"there,* just once, please," and kept begging until, suddenly, her hand closed on me, squeezing, bringing on the fire, bringing on the desire I hadn't felt in almost two years!

I wanted her on her back, legs spread! I wanted to take her, quickly, before the marvelous fury could leave. I said so, and even as she repeated the strictures handed down by Masters and Johnson, I knew that it was *because*

I was certain she wouldn't let me have her that I was so certain I wanted her. If she were suddenly to say yes, to grab me and want me . . . then what? I hadn't changed overnight. It couldn't be that simple. And once this thought intruded, another thought did too. It was Gail I wanted. It was Gail I would seek out and be with. . . .

The confusion was back. Senseless, wasn't it, to think of anyone else when with this beautiful woman, this therapist who knew what was best for me? Senseless and dangerous—and the kind of rebellion that had always led me away from the easily attainable; that had, in fact, led me to become a writer.

I felt discomfort, near-pain. I looked down, and Valerie was squeezing my penis, using thumb and two fingers to dig in under the glans. In a moment, I was limp. I said, "Why . . . ?" and she kissed me and murmured, "To show you it can go away and come back, again and again."

"No, once it's gone, it never . . ."

She silenced me with her lips and with her touches, and I went back to her breasts, her body, touching and enjoying. Again, the simple fact that I couldn't have her, couldn't fail with her, took over. A while later, she pulled away and stood up and walked to the foot of the bed. "Look at yourself," she said, smiling. "Just look."

I looked.

"Rampant," she said. "Isn't that the word, Mr. Lee?"

It was, indeed, just the word.

"Let's have dinner," she said, and left the room.

I took Valerie to a nearby steak house, where we both ate exceedingly well. And where she said, "I had a hunch this case was going to be easy, Herb."

It was one of her few errors in judgment.

This, then, was the beginning of my therapy. Valerie takes over from here, to talk about her four years as a wife surrogate and her nine patients, the eighth being myself. She taped her story, which has been edited for length and to protect the identity of her patients and other persons involved in her personal and professional life; and of course to protect Valerie herself. At several meetings, in New York and St. Louis, additional material was gathered, and last-minute developments added.

I've reserved an epilogue for myself, in order to complete my version of our relationship—and thereby afford the reader a unique opportunity to see a case of sexual rehabilitation from both the therapist's and the patient's point of view.

VALERIE'S STORY

1

I know you want my personal history, Herb, but before I give it I'm going to go right into the first case, the first time I played wife to a patient of Masters and Johnson. I promise I'll go back, when I feel warmed up to it. It's hard talking about the cases, but it's even harder talking about myself and why I became a surrogate wife. And then to have to bring in my childhood, my parents, my divorce. . . .

I know you've told me over and over that you never considered me anything near a prostitute, and that I shouldn't feel that way, and I don't, *really*. Only when I'm low. And, of course, now that I'm forced to relive the last four years. But there's always been some shame connected with it for me. I think there must necessarily be some shame connected with it for any girl brought up as I was—solid middle-class home and church and all the rest—this in spite of a very early introduction to sex. But let me hold off on that, *please*.

It's really incredible, now that I'm out of it and going over it this way, to think I actually did it! And I wasn't sure I *would* do it, even after I'd promised Gini—that's Mrs. Johnson—that I would, one day in late October. I guess I might as well say something right now, since it'll become clear when I go into my personal history. From the time I got out of college at twenty, I was always struggling for money. There's my mother, who needed medical attention for many years. And then there was the death of my father, which left me, the only child, squarely on the spot. So when mention was made of reasonable payment for my services, I simply had to listen. My job provided just the barest essentials, after Mother's nursing bills, and anything extra was always welcome.

There, it's something I dreaded saying! Money was the most important reason, at least initially, though Dr. Masters and Mrs. Johnson didn't know it. There were other reasons, of course. I respected what Masters and Johnson were doing. Gini and I had talked several times about my entering the program, and I knew how much trouble they were having getting the right kind of people. I must admit I was flattered that they thought I was qualified—intellectually, I mean. I was a college graduate with some paraprofessional experience in hospital work. I had a good basic knowledge of psychology, having minored in it in college, and as good a knowledge of human anatomy —male and female—from school and hospital work. Still, Bill and Gini were terribly selective in choosing surrogates, and I felt their accepting me was real kudos.

But at that time, when I'd agreed to join the program and was sitting in Gini's office, it was the desperate need for immediate money that decided the issue. One other factor—and an important one—was the recent end of my marriage.

But there too I'll hold off.

Even so, as I said, I wasn't certain I'd actually be able to go through with it. And I almost got up and walked out of the office when they described the patient. They said he was distinguished, quite attractive . . . and in his early sixties.

There I was, a twenty-four-year-old girl who'd always had her share of eligible men, some more mature than others, but still, a man over sixty? *Older* than my father would have been, had he lived, by at least ten years!

It threw me, and Gini saw it. She lectured me, rather sternly as I remember, on age not being the deciding factor in a man's eligibility and attractiveness. She said this man, Glenn, was wealthy, successful, president of his own firm in Boston, and more that I can't remember. She stressed that he was *young* for his age. I felt vaguely ashamed, almost as if I'd shown prejudice of a particularly nasty and naïve sort. But let me tell you, when I left the office, committed to meeting Glenn that night, I was a very shaken young lady!

I should mention that I'd talked to Gini about the wife-surrogate program a number of times—on procedure, methodology, what I was to do. And despite my knowledge of psychology and biology, I was given several indoctrination sessions in both subjects, as related to the male.

I'd first met Dr. Masters while I was still a student, working part-time in the hospital. He was well known, and very well liked, and I simply happened to be at someone's desk or in someone's office when he came by. The introduction was made, and I reacted to the name, remembered it and remembered him, so that the next time we came across each other I greeted him by name. He surprised me by remembering mine, and afterward we would exchange a few words, sometimes chat, and I simply *grew* to know him, and then Gini, over a number of years. That's why, by the time I was ready for the surrogate program, they knew quite a bit about me; didn't have to interview me in quite the same way as they may have other volunteers. We were old friends.

During this first briefing on my first patient, Dr. Masters and Gini both spoke to me. I was told that, after each session with Glenn, I was to phone in (special night numbers were given to me, where I could reach either one of them), and that I would be instructed step by step on how to proceed. Of course, I would also be able to use my own judgment—but less so on this very first case than later. Much would depend on what the interview sessions, the taped analyses, showed was happening. However, there was a *general* procedure we would follow, a little different during those early cases, and later I would be given considerable latitude in making changes according to the needs of the individual patient.

I was to meet Glenn at his motel in the Forest Park area at seven-thirty. (Except in the cases of local patients, the hotels and motels are always in that area, so that the patient can walk to the Foundation each morning for his interviews.) He had been given a name for me, not my own; I think it was Barby. I went home at five. The woman who took care of my mother had agreed to return at seven, as she usually did when I had a date. She left, and I tried to relax. I didn't succeed. I was still so nervous when she returned that she said, "This must be a very *special* one, Miss Valerie!" So special that I was shaking as I drove from our apartment in West County into St. Louis proper. I'd been told a great deal about my patient, because Gini and Dr. Masters—I sometimes call him Bill, but not often—felt that this would create such a strong sympathy and desire to help that it would overcome my own hangups about the whole thing. And I *did* feel sympathy, and I *did* want to help . . . but at the same time, I couldn't escape all sorts of pictures coming into my mind. An old man with withered, putrescent body and limp penis. And I knew, from my discussions at the Foundation, that I'd eventually have to use every means at my disposal to give this man erections and orgasms. That was the name of the game—to prove to him he was capable with me, and therefore with his wife and any other woman.

Glenn was married. He came of lower-middle-class parents, had worked in a series of factories, first as a machinist, then as a foreman, and finally he'd bought a plant of his own and built it into quite a success. But he hadn't bought it entirely with his own money. He'd been helped by his wife's father. Glenn had married above his station, as my mother would put it; from the working class into an old family, a proper Bostonian family. He was a far greater success, in money terms, than his wife's family had ever been, but neither his in-laws nor his wife would allow him to forget his humble beginnings. The wife alluded at times to his "vulgarity" and joked that he would never have been able to get into the right country club without her help.

Five years ago Glenn had begun to have occasional failures with his wife, whom he described as "beautiful but cold." She wasn't *really* cold, because even though she said he was "a dirty old man" for trying to grab her ass around the house, or for wanting to go to bed sometimes on an afternoon instead of waiting for night "as all decent people do," she would begin to respond once they were doing it. Or rather, she would be still and unresisting during most of the sex act, but as she approached orgasm she would begin to take off. As Glenn told Dr. Masters, when she was coming, she would use every four-letter word in the book. Later she would seem to be unaware that she had let loose that way. It seemed to me that she had as much of a problem as he did!

The wife was always caustic about Glenn's financial success, equating it with his vulgarity—like the gentry mocking those in "trade"—so there was just no way he could win with her. And after that first failure to maintain an erection, she began to be caustic about his manhood, even in front of their children. She managed to be subtle about it, but *he* knew what she was saying, and he was humiliated—especially if his younger daughter was present. That daughter meant the world to him. He was really crazy about her. She was twenty-two, going for a graduate degree, and played "fantastic tennis." Another daughter, married, visited regularly, and she too heard the mother take off on Glenn.

A classic pattern, and he carried out his part of it classically. He began to fail more and more often, and finally took a young mistress, a secretary who worked for one of his assistants at the plant. He moved her into his own office as his private secretary, with a healthy raise. He also gave her a car and an apartment in a good part of town. She repaid him by exciting him all day at the office so he would be hot for it at night. She wore micro-minis to show lots of leg, bent over in front of him at every opportunity, and after they'd been making it awhile, would regularly handle his organ and even suck it right there in his office. So for three months he performed beautifully with her twice a week—his "poker nights" as his wife was led to believe. But then morality got in the way. He wanted to be honest, wanted to be "normal," wanted to make love to his wife and feel at ease in front of his daughters.

This was obviously not a swinger. This was a man who had one goal—to be happily married, to play his role of husband and father completely above board.

So guilt began to kill the relationship with his secretary;

and besides, she started angling for bigger stakes—Glenn himself. She asked him to get a divorce.

He couldn't face anything like that. Divorce for Glenn meant divorcing not only his wife, still admired and desired, but his children, worshiped as well as loved. And so he began to fail with the secretary. For a while she overcame this by, as he put it, "marvelous skill with her mouth." She blew him for as long as two hours at a time—poor girl! But even this eventually failed. And so a cash gift and she was in another office in another plant and Glenn was looking for a new outlet. But first he tried the wife again—and failed—and the wife put him down harder than ever.

He failed with two more young girls, and panic set in. For three years he had no sex life beyond a rare masturbation.

He began analysis, and continued it throughout the years of impotency. He also continued to see a urologist at regular intervals. Neither course of treatment helped him achieve and maintain an erection with a woman, and when he mentioned Masters and Johnson to the two doctors, they both agreed it might be worth a try.

This was the man who opened the door of a St. Louis motel at seven-thirty. He *did* have a nice face, but he was also an old man, at least as I saw it then. He was about five-six, and that pot belly I'd envisioned was right there. He had small, even features, and his expression was stern—the executive look, as I thought of it. The look changed when he saw me. I can only say that he seemed relieved. I was relieved too, since anything was better than the images of age and decomposition I'd been feeding myself! I mean, a man would have had to be ninety, and dead at least a month, to fit what I'd built up in my mind!

His voice, when he spoke, was the least attractive part of him. It was loud, booming, and while the accent was Boston, it was far from cultured. "Well, *hello!* Come on *in!*" he said, and I felt that everyone up and down the corridor was going to join us.

I entered quickly. It was rather chilly that last week in October, and I was wearing a coat, and under that a rather simple skirt and blouse. Earlier, while dressing, I'd chosen a sexy pair of black lace panties and a black net brassiere, and then changed my mind and put on simple white stuff instead. I don't know why. Gini hadn't gone into the question of dress at all. Neither she nor Bill ever has. I guess I didn't want to draw too much attention to my body, my sexuality—which is contradictory and ridiculous, if you think of it! I had to set this man on fire, and here I was wearing my cotton panties and over-machine-washed bra! Anyway, I rationalized this by thinking it didn't matter very much this first evening, and I'd take them right off anyway, and so on.

Back in those days, the format was a little different. The first date, even though it was still primarily a get-acquainted period, going out to dinner and drinks and talking, *would* end up in bed. Just a warm-up, just to touch and kiss, but nevertheless getting down to birth-day skin, naked together in bed. I was aware of this as I smiled mechanically and let him help me off with my coat and tried not to see the way his eyes went over me. What I tried to see was his nervousness, the trembling of his hands, and also his clothing. He was very well dressed —a beautifully cut gray suit and a pale blue shirt and rich, expensive-looking shoes. I remember trying to think that I was somehow going to be making love to those beautiful shoes! Clothes make the man and all that, and this man was his clothing, and so I was going to have a *loverly* time.

Pathetic! But not to belabor the point, it was the first time I'd ever gone to bed with anyone for money, the first time I'd ever gone to bed with anyone for any reason other than love or desire, the first time I'd ever gone to bed with anyone—or even dated anyone—*nearly* that old.

I suddenly heard myself saying that I was hungry; "famished" is the word I used. I wasn't, but I just had to get out and away from the prospect of bed with him. He said we'd soon have dinner. "But first let's have a drink and a little talk."

He had a habit—I noticed it then for the first time— of pulling out a little amber comb and running in through his hair. He had plenty of hair—thick, graying hair; it must have been his pride and joy. He did it twice as I repeated that it might be best to eat first; and when he couldn't convince me otherwise, he put his comb away and made a little hands-out gesture—and those hands trembled. "Well, then, that's what we'll do. I've rented a *cah,* and we'll go wherever you wish. That's what we'll do. Drive somewhere in the *cah.*"

His nervousness got through my own nervousness. Hoping my smile looked genuine, I said, "We'll have plenty of time after dinner, Glenn."

He was at the closet, and turned and looked at me. "That's so, isn't it? Plenty of time. Two weeks to get to know each other." He smiled, his spirits revived, but my own fell through the floor. Two weeks! He helped me back into the coat he'd helped me out of only a moment or two before, and got into his own, a really striking Chesterfield, and then put on a gray snap-brimmed hat. He was quite nice-looking now, and if only I could have kept him that way, fully dressed and reasonably quiet, I'd have been happy!

We went down to his car and drove to a nearby restaurant—a Tudor-type place with the big beams and fireplaces and pub-style bar. I liked it for one very special reason: it was kept darker than most St. Louis restaurants, and if you don't think I was sweating over running into someone from the hospital, a personal friend, or someone who knew my mother, you don't know little Valerie! How could I explain this "date"? And just remember that St. Louis is very much a small Midwestern town in some ways.

Neither of us ate very much. He started with a martini, and so did I. He wanted another. I cautioned him about liquor reducing his ability to *feel,* to respond. "I wouldn't want *that* to happen," he boomed. "Not *now!*"

I cringed, not daring to glance around. But I had at least one thing on my side—no particular man in my life at the moment. No fiancé or boyfriend or heavy love affair. As I mentioned earlier, one thing that helped push me into the surrogate-wife program was the recent end of my short-lived marriage.

We fiddled with our food, and he talked about Boston —it was the center of the universe for him—and his voice was every bit as powerful as Caruso's, at least to my

ears! Now I couldn't wait to leave and get back to the
privacy of the motel. Now I was ready to face whatever I
had to face, which—thank goodness—wouldn't be much
this first evening.

Again, I have to apologize for my lack of professionalism. You'll just have to remember that this was my first
case.

As we walked out of the restaurant into the darkened
parking lot, Glenn put his arm around my waist—in
flat shoes, I was just a little taller than him—and said
that he liked me very much and that he was going to
enjoy the next two weeks. I murmured, "Thanks," looking
over to where a group of people, three couples, was
coming toward us. One of the men looked at me, looked
at Glenn, and seemed amused.

Glenn drove his *cah* very quickly on the way back. He
talked very quickly too, and quite a bit, about his daughter, the tennis player. Seems she had been seeded last
year and almost reached the finals at Forest Hills. Seems
she was also very good at dancing—ballet—and had
passed up a chance with the Balanchine troupe. He talked
and talked, the proud father . . . and the nervous male, covering his nervousness. I think I began to warm to him a
bit at that point. I'd been very close with my own father. . . .

But it didn't help much once we were back in the
room. He hung up our coats again and combed his hair
again, and we both stood there. And then I reminded
myself why I was here and what I had to do—had to
treat this man; had to involve him in sexual therapy;
had to save his manhood; *and* had to earn my fee and not
disappoint the Foundation. So I said—and I wish I had a
tape of my voice, it must have been *something*—"I guess
we'd better undress now, Glenn," and turned my back
and began unbuttoning my blouse.

At about the time I had dropped the blouse on the
couch and was unzipping my skirt, he said, "Barby." I
kept undressing. He said it again: "Barby?" and I realized
that he was speaking to *me*. Cloak and dagger, and the
Mata Hari forgets her code name! I turned and said,
"Yes?" and then swallowed hard. He was down to his
shorts, and once again he was a distasteful old man to me.

"How far . . . you want us . . . stripped?" he asked.

I nodded, and turned quickly away. If I could have spoken to Gini at that moment, I'd have said two things. One: "Why did you ever assign this patient to me!" And two: "You've made a mistake; I'm as hung-up in some ways as your patients, and I just can't handle this!" But I continued to undress, right down to buff. As I slipped out of my panties, I felt his hand on my hip. I froze, and if you want to know what I was thinking, I might as well tell you and complete the picture of a heartless girl you can't possibly like or respect. I was. thinking: "Get your hand off me, you pot-bellied old bastard!"

The dedicated therapist. The girl chosen for her intelligence, her quite considerable sexual experience (from age fourteen), and her ability to converse with doctors and psychologists on most aspects of sexual dysfunction and possible methods of alleviation.

I was shaking badly.

Glenn never noticed. He had his own shakes; and besides, I was his therapist, and he would necessarily have confidence in me.

"How very beautiful you are," he whispered, and both his hands stroked me, down over my hips and across my buttocks. His palms were sweaty; and my stomach lurched and my mind screamed, *What am I doing here!* But I made myself smile, and he kept stroking, kept talking. "How big in the bottom. Bigger than you looked with clothing." And he turned me around. I kept the smile on my face. His shorts were off, and his belly bulged out so that his genitals were practically hidden. He saw my breasts for the first time, and his mouth literally fell open.

I've always been rather proud of my breasts. Girls are, you know. I'm a size thirty-eight, D cup. But at that moment, I really wished I were flat-chested.

He touched them. He leaned forward—he didn't have to bend *too* much, short as he was—and kissed them. I muttered that genitals and breasts were taboo, but I doubt he even heard me, and I didn't push it. I was aware I was not following the strict procedure, and neither was he. However, I had *some* discretionary powers to change the procedure, at least in minor matters in this first case. He kept kissing them, rubbing them, muttering how *big* they were—"Bigger than my wife's; bigger than any girl's I've ever seen. . . ." And just when I felt I couldn't stand it anymore, would have to shove him away and run, I began to feel something.

Erogenous zones, bless 'em. The mind can do you dirty just so long in such a situation . . . at least, mine can. Then comes that feeling, that warmth, in spite of everything. I've often suspected that in certain cases of rape, where the violence doesn't lead to severe injuries, much the same thing often happens. Anyway, I had stopped being turned off.

I'm not saying I was burning with desire, or anything even near it. But I lost that sharp, bitter edge of distaste; lost the disgust and panic. His lips on my nipples took it away. His hand stroking my ass, then my belly, then going between my legs, took it away. And perhaps *that's* why I hadn't stuck to the no-genitals-no-breasts stricture —for *myself!* To get into this thing as I *had* to!

But now both his hands were below my waist—one squeezing my ass, the other trying to enter my cunt. . . .

Should I say "buttocks" and "vagina"? I did, earlier. That's when I was remembering being cold, turned-off, and when I'm cold it's "penis" and "vagina" and "buttocks" and "mammaries," if you want. But when the warmth starts coming . . . Not that I would speak that way to everyone. I'd have to use my instincts as to who would or would not be offended.

Funny about words. Later on I began using words to help me get through some bad cases: clinical, technical words. I would find myself thinking of everything that happened in cold, analytical terms—"I mounted him," and, "He entered me digitally and later engaged in male-position coitus," and, "I ejaculated him orally"—that kind of thing, to remove myself personally from impossible situations, and to forget what I was actually doing. It wasn't difficult to fall into such terminology when I wanted to—and even at times without really thinking of it—because Gini and Dr. Masters used it all the time. In fact, I never heard them deviate from the purely clinical in all the years I knew them. However, if *I'm* telling the story of my life, I can't speak that way; I have to speak more naturally.

Anyway, Glenn was pushing his hand between my legs. I stopped him from going any further. "The doctor doesn't want any genital play this time." Hearing my own voice, my own words, and seeing how quickly and obediently Glenn responded, I began to grasp hold of both myself and the situation. I took him by the hand, avoiding looking at him, and led him into the bedroom area.

That particular motel had a nice setup. There was one large room, but a curtain partitioned the bed area from the sitting-room section, and there was also a little kitchen unit. The whole place was torn down a short while later. I was sorry to see it go. In addition to the nice rooms, it had other advantages for me in my role as wife surrogate that a hotel, for example, doesn't. It was only three stories high, for one thing, and so I didn't have to use the elevators if I was coming to see a patient. I could slip up and down the stairs unnoticed. I'm afraid that my fear of being seen by someone I knew and found out in my "sideline" remained right up until my last case, though it varied according to my personal attachments and the individual patient. And, unfortunately, it wasn't based purely on my imagination, either.

Glenn and I went into the bedroom area, where a bedside lamp was on. I didn't turn it off, even though I'd have welcomed darkness. That was up to the patient. If he was willing to have a light on, that's the way it had to be. In fact, that's the way it *should* be. A man should enjoy looking at his woman.

Glenn left it on. Score one for him, but not for his uptight therapist!

I let go of his hand and lay down on my stomach, cradling my head in my arms. "Lie down beside me, Glenn. Remember what Dr. Masters said about learning to touch, to feel, all over again? That's what we're going to do—just touch each other. Arms and legs, face and back, all over . . . but not the genitals. You'll find excitement in these touches. The entire body is erogenous, if you'll give in to the feeling, allow yourself to touch and be touched. . . ."

The bed creaked beneath his weight, and I felt his side touch mine. I really should have been on my back, doing most of the touching, and guiding him in *his* touches, but I needed a little more time—just another moment or two, I kept telling myself.

He put his hand on my shoulder, then moved it slowly down my spine . . . and my skin crawled!

I had to get back into this thing! I couldn't let him, let Dr. Masters and Gini, let *myself* down! And yet, everything I'd ever been taught about sex, about love, fought my giving in. When I was with someone I cared for, someone I loved or *could* love, I could break the rules of my upbringing, but here the rules had me by the throat—almost literally; I felt I was choking! Yet here was a man whose bitch wife had castrated him. How much would that castration intensify if I allowed him to see what I felt?

He was stroking my behind again. He had to be slowed down, kept to the less sexually specific areas of the body, made to feel and enjoy the warmth of a woman's flesh. But it helped *me,* and so I gave him a moment, and breathed more easily. Then I rolled over, in control again. He kissed me, hands gripping my arms, and I returned the kiss. He went back to my bottom, pulling at it. I stopped him. I said, gently, "There's no need to press, you know. Nothing can happen tonight. You can't make love to me, so there's no need to do anything but simply touch, stroke, feel, kiss. . . ."

He kissed me again, more gently. I took his right hand in both of mine, kneading it, squeezing it. He was up on his left elbow, and slowly sank back, murmuring, "That's good." He watched me through half-closed eyes as I stroked his biceps, which were large but no longer firm, and as I touched his chest, which was covered with a thick mat of gray hair.

Finally I looked at him as I would look at a man I'd gone to bed with, as I would look at a lover.

His stomach was the part I found most distressing; I had simply never been with a man whose stomach bulged that way. His legs were surprisingly thin and muscular for a man his weight, and also veiny under much hair. His genitals were the *least* different from men of my experience; in fact, they weren't any different at all. That's one area where age isn't apparent. His penis was limp, which wasn't surprising. He was, after all, battling a problem of five years' duration.

He was reaching behind my head, drawing me down to him for a kiss. I could sense his need to get close to me, and not just sexually. Some of my reticence was obviously getting through to him; he was looking at me questioningly.

He'd paid for help, and he was going to get help!

I came down to his mouth, and kissed him. He gave me his tongue, very cautiously. I closed my eyes and ran my hand along his body—over his chest and stomach and down to his thighs, deliberately brushing his testicles and penis. And as I did, I felt the penis stir.

When I opened my eyes, the questioning look was gone. He stretched and sighed and said, "It felt so good. Can't you . . . ?"

Rules or no, I knew I had to bring him along now, continue the good feeling for him. I stroked his thighs again, brushed his genitals again, and saw the penis grow turgid. Within seconds he had a partial erection, though not the swollen, pulsing, angry-looking thing a young man without problems has. I sat all the way up and stroked his calves, rubbed his feet. I looked back at him and smiled.

"Is it . . . ?" he began, and fell silent.

I waited. I honestly didn't know what he wanted to ask. But in the years to come, I *would,* almost before the words were formed. He finally got it out, muttering so that I barely heard him.

"It's . . . sort of small, isn't it?"

Almost half my patients were convinced they were too small. I'm willing to bet that all had measured it. I guess all men everywhere measure it at some time or another. And some just won't believe that penises don't vary that much, and even when they do, it's not size that counts to a woman. It must be all those pornographic books and pictures, where they photograph near-freaks hung like mules, and the descriptions fantasize about nine and ten inches!

Anyway, I reacted to Glenn's question without thought, and luckily in the right way. I laughed and said, "Any larger, and you'd have trouble with *this* girl."

He grinned, and I stroked his belly and chest and told him to turn over. He did, experiencing some difficulty tucking his partial erection under him.

I massaged his back, not like a masseuse but with intent to *feel,* and to show him how *he* should touch and feel. The idea was to teach him—and in this first case, I must admit, to teach me too—how many areas of excitement could be found in a member of the opposite sex. I bent and kissed his neck.

He murmured and turned over. The erection was almost complete, getting to look red and ready, and it ceased being an erection and became a hard-on to me. I stroked his thighs again, and thought it wouldn't be unpleasant to grasp his shaft and massage it a little. And that's what he wanted; that's what his sighing and arching meant. And that's what this first session was all about. He had no fear, and so he had a hard-on. There was no reason for fear, because he knew he couldn't make love to me, and he was secure in my care, and all was well for him.

And it was getting better for *me.* At least, in a physical sense. Later, I had to go through all the doubts and shame and what-am-I-doing-here again, but at the moment I was doing my job and beginning to feel just a little pleased.

I had a time limit—fifteen minutes to half an hour—and after a while I checked the night-table clock and was startled to see that we'd been in bed twenty-five minutes. It made me happier than anything that had happened that night!

He was getting a little fervent, pressing his prick up against me, sighing, "Barby, Barby," and that name reminded me again of the role I was playing and that it was time to end the game for this particular night.

I sat up and told him it was over. He said, "Just another few minutes."

But now I was rapidly becoming divorced from the

action. It was penis and patient and time-to-go, and I was anxious to get home and take a bath and become myself again, Valerie the hospital employee and not Barby the wife surrogate.

I got off the bed, smiling—a legitimate smile, because I was on my way out!—and shook my head. I went through the curtain and began to dress. He joined me a moment later, and once again I wasn't looking at him. He got into a robe, went to the kitchen, and returned with a bottle of Scotch and two glasses.

I said I had to be going. He pleaded for me to have one drink. I wanted to refuse, but felt my departure might appear too abrupt, so I nodded. He sat at a distance from me on the davenport.

"Davenport." Glenn called it a "couch." I guess we both meant "sofa." But my father said "davenport," and so do I. Well, we sat and drank, and he talked. He went back to his family again, and after still another round of raves about his daughter and her tennis and her dancing, he began talking about his wife.

"You won't believe this," he said, "but you resemble her. She's not as big as you are in . . . uh, certain ways . . . but she is younger than I am by ten years, and she's young in the body anyway . . . and still good in the chest, and in the rear too. You're both just, generally, very much the same."

I murmured something cutesie about considering that a compliment, and he quickly said, "Oh, yes! I really admire . . . and besides, I'm sure this is the luckiest break. Do you see what I mean?"

I did, but stressed that once he was finished with his therapy, he would be able to make love to any woman he liked, whether she resembled his wife or not.

Five minutes later I was in my car, zipping back home, and all I could think was, "Well, Valerie, you got through night number one!"

Incidentally, this was on a Thursday, and I'd been told that my role in the treatment would probably continue until the end of the weekend after next—a Sunday—or ten nights. We always spoke to the patients in terms of two weeks, because that was the length of the *total* treatment, office sessions included. There were always days off to give the patient time to assimilate what had happened, so I could begin to think, happily, in terms of six or seven nights.

When I got home, the practical nurse left, and I checked my mother, who was asleep, and had a quick thought of what would happen if she were ever to find out what I was doing. With her code of ethics, and her delicate hold on life, it's no exaggeration to say it would probably kill her! (The divorce had come close to giving her another stroke.) That's when all the fears returned, and all the distaste. Before I knew it, I was crying, and it just seemed impossible that I would ever go back to that motel and that man and that bed again.

I phoned Gini. My eyes were still wet when I told her how things had gone, and then I admitted I didn't know how I could continue, and said that perhaps if the man were younger . . .

She heard me out, and even though I could sense her sympathy, she said nothing . . . because we both knew it was impossible to drop a patient in mid-case. It could be disastrous for him. And while my own feelings were relevant, she said, the patient came first.

She felt I should look at it as a brief "adventure," and to enjoy it as such. Why, she wanted to know, couldn't I imagine I was on a two-week cruise with a man who turned out to be something less than I'd dreamed of? I was stuck for the two weeks, so I might as well make the best of it. I'd never see him again, and that was an advantage of sorts, because I could do anything I wanted to, and so on. She was full of such good ideas in support of the project, but it didn't really convince me, didn't change my gut reactions. Neither she nor Dr. Masters was *ever* able to change my gut reactions, though I never let them know it; that's why it was such a *long* four years!

But, basically, she was pleased. My report corroborated much that they'd learned during the interviews, and she wanted me to go through the same kind of evening tomorrow. Just touching each other. No expectations of performance. No tension, and hopefully an even stronger erection and a desire to go further.

I don't remember if I said, or merely thought, that

Glenn would be disappointed, but somehow the information was given me that on the one hand he would probably expect more—at least before he was told at tomorrow morning's interview that there would be no more—but that on the other hand he would again be getting a reprieve from having to perform and possibly failing.

I took a sleeping pill to make sure I wouldn't stay awake that night, and the next day at work I was only partly efficient. All I could think about was what I was involved in and what the people I worked with would think if they knew. It was a funny feeling working during the first case, looking at everyone and trying to imagine their reactions.

The next night I came to Glenn's room, and almost immediately decided I wanted to go out for dinner, once again putting off getting into bed with him. Besides, Masters and Johnson *preferred* a specifically social evening before bed; it helped the patient relax, and being in the room and seeing the bed all during dinner might not be too good. Except that Glenn *did* seem disappointed that we were leaving, when he had bought steaks and bean salad and wine for a meal in.

We went to a very fine Italian restaurant, one of Masters and Johnson's favorites. (They recommend restaurants to their patients, so that strangers to St. Louis can have a reasonably good chance of enjoying their meals.) I heard a great deal more about Glenn's family as we ate, and this time we both managed to finish the meal. The daughter who played tennis got most of the wordage, as she had the night before.

Glenn continued to talk about his wife and children on the way back to the motel, and I nodded and murmured an occasional comment, and found myself disliking the wife intensely, though I was also aware that I was getting only one side of the story. Still, I wonder if wives in general have any idea of how much destruction they can cause when they ridicule their husbands, put them down as social or physical beings. They must have something pushing them—emotional drives of their own —but that sort of treatment can cause so much damage that it seems criminal.

In the room, we undressed rather quickly, got into bed, and repeated more or less what we'd done the night before. And I experienced, at first, more or less what I had the night before—disgust, desire to run, and then a gradual loss of tension and uptight feeling. Glenn was definitely more relaxed. His erection came more quickly and was more complete, it seemed to me, though he said it didn't feel as if it were really up there the way he remembered it from before his troubles. I said this was only the second night, and we were doing fine, which made him happy.

His erection lasted almost unchanged throughout the first ten minutes of our half-hour session, until I used the Masters-Johnson "squeeze technique" to make it go limp. Most patients dislike it intensely, and Glenn was no exception. However, when I brought him back up again, I proved a very important point. Losing an erection was not necessarily the end of any particular attempt at coitus. He *could* get it back up again. And if he remembered this, it could stop him, at some future date, from spiraling back down into total incapacity.

I experimented with him, varying my touches and my kisses. I experimented with *myself,* closing my eyes, encouraging him to touch me, stroke me, caress me; blanking my mind to the individual and giving in to the general sensation. And after a while I again realized, more strongly this time, that it was possible not to want a particular man and yet to respond to erogenous touching, to petting . . . and eventually to intercourse itself. I know one thing for certain; I *did* respond at some point—perhaps halfway through—to the sensation of having my body caressed, my breasts kneaded and sucked, my ass squeezed, kissed, and though I stopped it quickly, tongued.

That second evening was a revelation to me. A man I cared absolutely nothing about, a man I was actually appalled to be with, could make me respond to him! It's not something many American girls get a chance to learn. Perhaps in the days of arranged marriages, when a girl was forced to marry a man she found repellent—perhaps then in her bed of anguish, she learned that there was nevertheless one compensation, one area of

pleasure: the purely physical response, the glandular reaction, to a male's touch and thrust.

I don't know how women's lib would look at this;
probably with horror. I'm not sure I approve of it myself! But approval or disapproval has nothing to do with
nature, and Masters and Johnson were counting heavily
on nature to reassert itself in their patients, and probably
counting on it to assert itself in me!

On the way home, I backslid again. I could sympa-
thize with Glenn and understand what *he* was doing
here, but I couldn't justify my own actions and was
ripped by guilt. And tomorrow, if all went well, I was
to get on top of him and perform coitus.

The sleeping pill wasn't quite as effective this night. I
got through the next day at the hospital, doing my work,
lunching at the desk of a friend and chatting and smiling.
But don't ask me to remember anything or anyone in
particular!

By the way, when I say "hospital," I mean the Washington Medical School Complex, about ten minutes' walk
from where Masters and Johnson have their Foundation.

When I called for Glenn at his motel, he seemed different. He had dressed in a new suit, another fine one,
but that wasn't it. He was very quiet at first, very quick
to open doors for me when we went out to dinner, very
solicitous of my comfort and, at the restaurant, of my
getting exactly what I wanted. He kept combing his hair
with his little amber comb, kept adjusting his tie. Also,
he wanted to drink more than was allowed.

Now that I think of it, at the beginning Masters preferred that the patient have no more than *one* drink, not
two, as in all my other cases.

I realized a little later what was different about Glenn
tonight. He wasn't talking about his family. He was
hardly talking at all. *I* was doing most of the talking.
During the course of what was really an excellent meal
at a fine French restaurant, I finally asked him if anything was wrong, because if, for example, he was worried or upset by news from home, it could really mess
up what was going to happen at the motel.

He shook his head, muttered, "Not at all," and kept
eating.

And then it hit me. Of course! Masters had told him that tonight he would have intercourse with me. Glenn was either anxious or fearful.

I began to think of ways to ease his obvious tension. So I did quite a bit of talking about Dr. Masters, about Boston, which I'd visited, about St. Louis, about baseball and football and whatever else I thought might interest him. And I ended with what little I knew about tennis, speaking of a boy from my college who had been in the Davis Cup matches.

That did it. He talked about tennis in general for five minutes, and then about his daughter the rest of the time. One sentence struck me then, and sticks in my mind now. "She used to think I was God Almighty when she was younger, and even as a teen-ager. . . ." He smiled self-consciously and went back to tennis.

Again I felt sorry for this father who wanted so badly to be the big man for his children; well, I guess all fathers want that. Mine did. But mine didn't have to face a reduction in pride every time his wife opened her mouth.

Back at his room, we began to undress, and this time I was wearing my black lace undies. I moved around a bit in them, bending, posing as I arranged my dress on a chair, feeling his eyes on me; and then I stripped. When I turned, he was nude . . . and limp. I held out my hand; he took it; I led him to the bed, this time for genital play.

First we went through the stroking, the touching, and during this he stayed passive, and down. Then I began brushing his testicles, his penis, and he began to respond. He lengthened a bit, and breathed more heavily, and his hands went to my breasts and then my behind . . . and finally he reached between my legs. At that point I felt my body stiffening, felt myself ready to reject him as I would any man I didn't want.

The panic swept over me, and I closed my eyes and trembled, and he thought it was passion and murmured, "Barby, Barby," and that name was like everything else with this man: false, an act, an abomination, a *sin*. . . .

Stop it! I screamed to myself.

I closed my eyes. His hands worked on my body, though I kept my thighs clamped tightly together so he couldn't get there; not there; not yet, just a little while longer so I could think. . . .

But thinking was what had brought me to this panic. Thinking, in fact, was what had brought my patient—and all my patients to come—to *their* panic, their troubles. I had to *stop* thinking!

I kept my eyes closed. He played with me. And little by little, first having to force myself, and then doing it naturally, I played with him. I felt my way down his body, eyes still clamped shut, and caressed his testicles and took his penis in my hand. He was partially stiff and he sighed and I squeezed and he groaned and I stroked and his body writhed.

And I felt the heat, the dampness between my legs, and without being aware of any decision, my thighs parted and his hand moved in. He simply stroked the outside at first, squeezed and stroked, and *I* began to sigh, began to groan. His prick felt good and hard now; his prick pulsed in my hand. His prick, not his penis, because I was *feeling* now, and it had changed for me, and the medical-technical jargon was gone. But I was careful not to *speak* any of this. I could shock him, turn him off.

His fingers worked their way into me. We kissed, and for the first time he became truly passionate. He crushed me to him, and those muscles were no longer flabby but tensed *hard*. He kept working those fingers inside of me —first one, then two, and finally three, and my thighs were wide-spread, and I wanted that tool in me, deep up in me. . . .

He was rolling over onto me, just as I wanted. I felt my breath mounting, felt my heart pounding. My eyes remained closed, and it was a body, a human body, a *man's* body with that hot thing still in my hand and soon to be guided into me. I wanted it then. Not Glenn but IT. And I began to adjust under him, began to ready myself.

But we couldn't do it that way! My instructions in this area were definite—*I* had to remain in control.

I told him *I* would get on top; and quite suddenly he

grew still and began to lose passion, his prick wilting in my hand.

I asked if he disliked the woman-on-top position, and before he could answer, said it could be most satisfying. He said no, he didn't mind it at all . . . but . . . he struggled for words, and finally got it out. His wife would allow only one position—male-on-top—called the Missionary position by some and the Mamma-Papa position by others. She had always stopped him from experimenting, saying everything else was "dirty" and "degenerate." He had, at various times, tried to go down on her, asked her to go down on him, wanted to enter from the rear, and also to have her sit on him—all this at the beginning of their married life. She had rejected each such suggestion with disgust, claiming it was a result of his "lower-class" background. Even with his mistress he had found it difficult to break the habits developed at home . . . and except for her sucking him, they had done very little in the way of different positions.

I listened, still holding his organ, still running my other hand over him, and said something like, "Well, let's try it." And because I'd lost myself in *his* problems, and because that purely physical response was still with me, I climbed on top of him, straddled him with my thighs, worked his now partially hard prick into me. He stiffened, and came, almost in the same instant. It was over before it had begun, and if he had been a boyfriend, I'd have been damned disappointed!

He was a little upset, and I was very surprised, because no mention had been made of his having that kind of problem—premature ejaculation. But I quickly recovered and said it had gone very well and that it was *expected* that he would react that way, and so he began to feel better about it. After all, it was the first orgasm he'd had beyond his rare masturbations in almost three years.

Let me explain why we prefer that at least the first and often further copulations with a patient be done with me on top. Americans copulate most of the time in the Mamma-Papa, man-on-top position, and so most male failure takes place that way. In therapy, it's good to get away from the position of failure. Also, when the therapist is on top, she can control the situation, and so relieve the male of at least part of his performance anxieties. He has a better chance of succeeding on *two* counts; and once he does, the transfer to the more common male-dominant position can be made with less chance of failure. He's proven he can function with me on top, and so we reverse positions, and it works—we hope.

I went to the bathroom and washed. When I came out, Glenn was very quiet again, almost shy I'd have said, and asked me to have a drink with him. I felt I had to say yes. Ten minutes later he kissed me good-bye at the door, looking as if he wanted to believe things were going well, and that was just what I said as I left. "It's going *beautifully,* Glenn."

I drove home and found my mother awake. I had to spend almost an hour with her, make her some tea and toast, chat with her—and of course, all the guilt and all the confusion were back, in spades. Because we'd done it; not just petted and played, but done it. Brief as it was, I'd had sexual intercourse with Glenn, an old man and a stranger!

My mother finally went to bed, and I was able to go to my room. It was Saturday night; big date night. I was sure I'd have Sunday off, and so I called Gini, feeling almost gay. When I mentioned the quick ejaculation, she said it was extremely common in such situations. After all, he'd had two nights of physical play and was all worked up. Besides, when a lone male patient comes to the Foundation, he often is excited by the idea of a wife surrogate. Glenn had been building excitement for six full days.

Gini was generally pleased.

By the way, Glenn had come through his physical exam with no area of disability. Like many men, he'd probably built a little myth about falling apart in a physical sense at his age. So the relief of learning that he was in good shape probably helped steam him up a bit.

Just thought of something. While some results of the physical examination might be slow in coming, the blood

tests for venereal disease are in before I have anything
to do with a patient. Conversely, Dr. Masters insists that
the wives surrogate undergo periodic examinations by
him or by their own gynecologists.

I talked with Gini a while longer, and then she pulled
the rug out from under my plans to relax the next day,
Sunday. Gini said Dr. Masters felt I should go ahead
with Glenn tomorrow night, that it would be dangerous
to break the continuity at this point. I could've cried.

But after a complaint or two, I shut up and learned
that it was going to be an afternoon session, not involving
dinner or anything else. That, at least, was a blessing.
Masters and Johnson just didn't want Glenn to have time
to think too much about the premature ejaculation because then he might start worrying in still another area.
I had to agree with that line of reasoning, and so I put
as good a face on it as I could.

And I went to bed with a sleeping pill. I don't think
I'd ever taken more than half a dozen of those pills in
my life previous to becoming a wife surrogate, but I can
assure you I've taken quite a few since.

At about three the next afternoon I drove to the motel
in slacks and sweater, used the stairs, scurried to the
door, and knocked. It opened so quickly I had the feeling he'd been waiting with his hand on the knob. But
it didn't open all the way. He peeked out first, then
opened it, and I saw the reason for his caution. He was
wearing nothing but his shorts and a big smile.

Now, I have to say that this bothered me terribly.
Even a lover, at least at the beginning of an affair,
respects a *few* of the proprieties. And here was this
man, this stranger—all right, my patient—treating me
like . . .

I walked in, not looking at him. He wanted to kiss me
right away; I wanted to tell him what a boor he was.
What happened was that he kissed a very tight-lipped
girl. He looked at me, surprised. I took a deep breath
and said, "Had a hectic morning. I'll take one of your
drinks, thank you."

He came back with two Scotches and water, and I
remembered to ask if he'd had any liquor before I'd
arrived. By his guilty expression, I knew he had.

I learned later that Glenn really liked his booze. He was far from an alcoholic, but he admitted to me that under stress he could put away eight to ten drinks. He never did it at home, and only rarely with his mistress, so it wasn't a part of his sexual problem, which it can be. A man who drinks heavily performs poorly. One or two drinks might reduce social tensions to the point where inhibited men and women think they're performing better, but they're merely thinking looser. The *body* performs best on total abstinence.

I used my drink to relax, and I also had half the drink he'd brought for himself. Then I stood up and undressed quickly—very quickly, because I wanted it to be over very quickly. I didn't look at Glenn; I kept my mind professional and clinical; I concentrated on certain things Gini and I had discussed. When I walked into the bedroom and lay down (allowing him to follow on his own), I was prepared to carry out the plan we'd devised to make sure there would be no repeat of the premature ejaculation, no loss of confidence, and a good strong "mating." My personal feelings were rejected. At least that's what I told myself as I struggled to be the perfect Masters and Johnson wife surrogate, the involved therapist.

But how can a person eliminate everything she's lived by—her tastes and beliefs and, yes, morals, when it comes to strangers—at the snap of a finger? It would take a whore to be that cold-blooded about it, and even whores must have likes and dislikes!

It's in this area that I believe the surrogate program is at its weakest. I don't know about the other surrogates, but speaking for myself, I *never* succeeded in being purely objective. And I was, from what Bill and Gini said to me, one of their most successful therapists. When I enjoyed my work with a patient, it was because I would have enjoyed him as a friend, a date, a lover. And the reverse is also true, as it was with Glenn.

Still, I entered into the stroking, the kissing, the petting, and he was quite strong in his approach to me, and with my eyes closed the loss of tension began to take place. And again, as before, I was amazed at the turn-on, the flow of juices, the growth of my physical response.

We began to touch éach other's genitals. I began to heat up in that purely glandular way, and felt him stiffening in my hand.

I reached a point in my own excitement, and saw that he had reached a point in his, that made it right for me to climb on him as I had the night before. No male-dominant position yet. Dr. Masters and Gini felt that, because of his long history of failure and last night's premature ejaculation, I should be in firm control of the act.

I lowered myself onto his prick, and it went in without softening. After a moment he softened a bit, and I moaned, "Glenn-baby!" and moved more strongly, and he hardened again. I moved faster, more erotically, and repeated his name—and it began to feel good.

His face began to change, began to twist in the way that indicates rising passion. As Dr. Masters has stated, no one smiles when in the grip of passion. The expressions are more like those caused by pain.

I slowed my movement, watching for signs of approaching orgasm. We wanted him to have a reasonably long go today. When I felt that his excitement had dipped a bit and that he was going to hold out, I began moving quickly again, plunging up and down. He reached up with both hands and grabbed my breasts. Now I was definitely beginning to awaken, definitely beginning to enjoy myself. I ground my ass against his thighs, feeling him working inside me, and it felt better and better.

When about five minutes had passed, I really began to go. I mean, I was fucking, thoughtlessly, instinctively, and with mounting need for release.

I was no longer trying to watch him. My eyes were closed, and I concentrated on *me,* the feeling of that prick up my insides. It was very much like masturbating, since I had shut out the individual who was providing the means of pleasure.

I felt that if I could go just a little longer, lose myself just a little more—and then I did and then I was gasping and then I came. I remember thinking it was about the mildest orgasm I'd ever had, but still, it *was* an orgasm. And I played it up with cries and clutches and facial contortions, so he would be sure to

know he had satisfied his partner. After a brief pause, I began to swivel and grind and give his prick every bit of friction I could. His face twisted, and he gasped, "Barby!" and
I felt him shudder.

"God," he said. "God, it happened!"

I said yes, and very nicely too. He had lasted for
close to ten minutes, a respectable figure for any man.

When I returned from the bathroom, he was sitting
on the davenport in his robe. He'd had time to think,
and he said that his erection hadn't been quite as big and
hard as before he'd begun having problems. I replied
that it had been good enough to do the job for me,
and that it would improve with time. After all, this was
only the beginning. And when he left here, he would go
on with women of his own choice. It would get better
and better.

It brought a smile to his face. He then said he wanted
to go somewhere and have a drink. I said he had better
use his bottle of Scotch, because Sunday in St. Louis is
dry, dry, dry. His face fell. "Well, uh, I finished that
bottle."

That's when I first suspected he was drinking more
than he should have, probably after I left.

"Isn't there *any* place we can get a drink?"

I should have said no, but without thinking I mentioned that he could buy a bottle in East St. Louis,
which was across the Illinois state line. He said fine,
that's where we'd go, and jumped up and began to dress.

It was the last thing in the world I wanted to do.
First of all, East St. Louis is a depressing place for
anyone with an ounce of sensitivity about the suffering
of others: a grim, shabby black ghetto, and by all police
statistics, dangerous too. Also, by this time I was entering my guilty, shamed, what-are-you-doing stage. So the
place I wanted to be was home. But then again, it was
only four-ten, and my mother would be awake, and since
I hadn't made any plans for the remainder of the day,
we would spend the hours until her bedtime together.

I loved my mother, and I spent quite a bit of time
with her, but by no means could I classify it as fun! She
wasn't a cheerful person, nor had she any reason to be.
Her illness was constant, the threat of death continuous;

as soon as I'd walk in, she would say, "What did you do today, Val?" Today she'd be sure to add, "We haven't had a good talk in almost a week. Tell me who you dated and what you did."

What had I done today? What had I done this week? The truth was impossible! So when Glenn said he would never find East St. Louis on his own, and he dreaded being alone the rest of the afternoon, I drove him there in my car. Now, the only time I've ever been to East St. Louis is to pass through it on a mad dash to Route 66 to Chicago. But this time we went up and down those sad streets, trying to find a liquor store, and he left me alone in the car twice to ask directions, and then left me alone again while buying the whiskey; and let me tell you that no young white girl spends any time alone in that place. It's not a judgment I'm making; it's a *fact*. There are just too many incidents on police blotters for anyone in her right mind to risk it.

My luck was bad. While he was in the liquor store, a group of three young hoods came along and looked in the car, and before I could lock the door, one opened it. They never did *do* anything, but they scared me half to death. I played it cool, simply answering their half-joking, half-menacing questions—"What are you doing here, chick?"—and trying to keep my face and voice relaxed. When one said it would be nice "if we all took a little ride over to my place," I must have reacted, because they all laughed. They rocked the car a little and then just ambled away. I saw why when the patrol car came slowly down the street past me.

A moment later Glenn came out with his bottle, looking pleased, and never did notice my pallor. I didn't say anything; I just wanted to get him and his damned bottle of booze back to the motel and *leave*. At that moment I wouldn't have cared if his penis fell off!

I didn't go up to the room with Glenn, though he pleaded for me to have just one drink. I didn't go home either. I drove to a movie theater on Lindell. About ten minutes after the start of the feature, I ran to the ladies' room and locked myself in a booth and broke down. I cried so hard my chest ached. And do you know what caused it—at least in an immediate sense? A man and woman had sat down in the row in front of me and snuggled up to each other and kissed and looked so happy, so much in love. And what was *I* doing? Where was *my* man and *my* happiness and *my* love? I was between men, between loves. I was alone and I was a wife surrogate.

Wife surrogate. It was a dirty phrase that grim Sunday. . . .

I called Gini from a phone in the theater lobby. She'd been wondering what was keeping me. I gave her the good part of the day: Glenn's success in getting an erection, regaining it, and going on to orgasm after about ten minutes of coitus. I also described our trip to East St. Louis, and blamed my calling in so late on that. My voice must have given away more than I thought, and under her skillful questioning I let loose with some of my pain. Not nearly all of it, mind you, but enough for her to see that I needed a day off. She and Dr. Masters were furious at Glenn for having involved me in a non-therapeutic situation, and at me for allowing myself to be involved.

I wouldn't be seeing Glenn tomorrow, Monday. Tuesday would be the next session. The logical thing for me to do was go out Monday evening and relax with friends.

Driving home, I thought that I really didn't have any friends—not close ones, anyway. I'd never been too good at friendships with women. I'd always had a man, one man at a time, to fill the role of best friend. He was also lover and all the world to me. From the age of fourteen on, always some one man.

I worked Monday and had lunch with a doctor who was interested in me. But he was married, and while I'd had an affair with a married man and didn't automatically reject anyone on that basis—he might be on his way *out* of the marriage—he revealed more than he should have and I was able to define his interest as too specifically sexual. So I said no, I would *not* see him that evening.

I went home that night, to find that the mail had brought the end-of-month bills, including a whopping four hundred dollars for mother's medical expenses. Still, I managed to create a happy story in answer to her questions about my day. Before I took my sleeping pill, I looked at myself in the mirror and again wondered what was wrong, what was happening to me?

My instructions for Tuesday, after my *loverly* evening off, was to get back in the sack with Glenn, work for that all-important erection. . . .

I know, Herb. I'm showing my claws. But I still felt that way Tuesday; and you said we were going to tell this thing the way it was.

All right. I was to go through the touch-and-feel process, the genital-stimulation process, and if he attained a good erection, to engage in coitus with him. Only this time he would be on me. If, however, he seemed shaky or didn't maintain a strong erection, I was to again get on him.

Tuesday was much like the other times. We went to dinner; he talked about his family; we returned to his room and went to bed . . . and he said his erection was *not* secure and *he* was not secure, and so I again climbed on top. And I brought him, and myself, to orgasm.

By this time I knew that about the only way I was going to get Glenn to achieve a good enough erection for him to get on top of me and thereby bring this thing to a successful conclusion was to go down on him. Using medical-technical jargon such as "oral-genital stimulation" and "fellatio" didn't help much. I put it out of my mind . . . until Wednesday evening.

We ate in the room, then undressed and played. He still felt he wasn't getting the proper erection. Also, he seemed dispirited; and guilt attacked me once again. I wasn't doing my job. He was picking up vibrations, bad ones; he sensed how much I disliked him. I couldn't allow him to remain at this plateau; I just couldn't!

How and when I started doing it, I honestly don't know. I don't remember moving my head down to his genitals, but suddenly I was there, eyes closed, his penis in my hand. And then I had it in my mouth, semisoft, and began sucking it. There was a second when I felt myself beginning to gag. It was the flaccidity, and my mind's-eye picture of his bulging gut. I played the great American-marrieds' game—substitution—thinking of someone else, someone who had brought me to such violent parox-

ysms of delight that I despaired of ever achieving anything like it again. And I felt Glenn stiffening in my
mouth, growing harder than he had during any of our
other meetings. The feeling that I·was committing the
ultimate sin—the ultimate intimacy for reasons other than
love—attacked me much as the nausea had, and my throat
constricted, and I couldn't breathe.

I was about to lift my head when I heard Glenn's
moans, heard him gasp, "Barby! Barby!" and his pleasure, his enormous pleasure, came through to me. And
—in that way that doesn't bear repeating and yet re-
mains a marvel and a wonder to me even today—I began
to enjoy it too . . . via the substitution at first, but then
simply because it was a prick in my mouth, pulsing with
desire; simply because a male was writhing in ecstasy
because of what I was doing; simply because it was a
very erotic thing, sucking a cock.

He began to hump upward into my mouth, and I withdrew immediately, feeling he was close to orgasm. I
looked at his face. He was, for the first time, *completely*
involved, taken out of himself, freed of any thoughts but
that of getting at me, of being male to my female, of
feeding his cock into my cunt.

He begged me to get on my hands and knees and put
my bottom up. "Let me!" he gasped. "Just a little . . .
your big . . . behind!" I felt he'd wanted to use other
words, stronger words, and hadn't dared.

I did as he asked, and he got into me nicely and
began working. Then, somehow, I sensed that he was
cooling, that he was at the critical point of *just* beginning to fear failure. Besides, it was time to end this
phase; it was the Mamma-Papa position we had to use; it
was with him on top, male-dominant, that held the
memories of failure, and that had to hold a memory of
recent success.

I rolled onto my back, drawing him over me. I took
his cock, and it was considerably softer than it had
been. I stroked it, felt it stiffen a bit, and quickly put it
in me. He humped a few times without enthusiasm. He
looked at me. I saw the cooling, the fear, the failure
approaching. And for the very first time, I *truly* felt for
this man; ached for him, for his pain, his wanting, his

love for a bitch-wife; truly wanted, *personally,* to make him well again. Wanted it so badly I grasped his face with both hands and said, "Glenn, fuck me, baby, fuck me!" He changed, and I had a moment of horror, thinking I'd done it now, turned him off with obscenities. Then I saw that the change was back toward heat, back toward passion.

"She would never say that," he muttered. He began to move in me again. "Never say anything . . . exciting, except at the end, when she was coming, when it was too late for me." He was driving on me now, in and out, and his hands reached down to my ass and gripped me and he said, "Barby, tell me, what am I doing to you?"

It was a game I had played before. It was a game of lust. "You're fucking me," I said, and I moved on him.

"How, honey? How?"

"With your cock. Your big hard cock."

"Where is it?"

"Deep in my cunt. Pounding my cunt."

And it was. And I meant what I was saying. And he was totally male now, in command, pulling my ass apart and pounding me, in and out of me, and he did it with skill and he did it for at least ten minutes. I came, twice I believe, before he did. I gripped him with my legs and spoke the words his wife would never speak, and toward the end he spoke them back at me, gasping, "Fuck you big-titted red bitch, fuck!" and I did, and felt him shudder as he came.

When I walked out of the bathroom, he kissed me very tenderly and thanked me and then was silent. No talk about tennis. No insistence that I have a drink with him. No need for talk or drink at all. He sat quietly on the davenport and watched me dress, and escorted me to the door. Then he said, "Until the next time."

I was touched. But I was also reasonably sure there would be no next time. And when I reported to Gini by phone, I said as much. She very quickly and firmly told me I was wrong. Because of his age and his physician-induced fears of being sexually over the hill, because of his five years of partial failure and three years of total failure, and because of things he'd said to Dr. Masters which indicated he felt he'd been "lucky" with me up to now—because of all this, we had to go on, had to nail it down with at least *two* more successful matings. But we both needed another night off. That meant I'd be seeing him Friday and Saturday.

(Like all men who fail sexually, Glenn had seen many doctors, and among these doctors were those who spouted what Masters and Johnson have proven is utter rubbish —that a man of sixty or sixty-five or seventy who begins to fail at sex has simply run out of steam, that it's "natural," "normal," and he should accept it as he accepts his gray hair. In their laboratory experiments with human couples, as anyone who has read their books knows, Masters and Johnson have shown that men can function sexually well up into their eighties, just as long as their general health is good.)

Those Friday and Saturday sessions can be summed up in three words: just like Wednesday.

On second thought, that's not really so. It was just like Wednesday in terms of Glenn's carrying out successful sex both times in the male-dominant position, and of our both letting loose with sex words, but there *were* differences, important and positive differences. He was more in control during the petting, and even during the actual intercourse, inserting himself into me himself both times, softening only a little on Friday and not at all on Saturday. So he was more in control on Friday than he'd been on Wednesday, and more in control on Saturday than on Friday. He made love with imagination, doing much that had been denied him by his wife. He went down on me, briefly, Friday, and stayed down on me long enough Saturday to have me close to orgasm. On Saturday I came hard and slowed a little, unconsciously, afterward. He grabbed my bottom, pulling the cheeks apart until I cried out, and he gasped, "Fuck, damnit, *fuck,* or I'll rip your ass off!" I fucked as hard and as long as he needed me. But once it was over, I was back to the old rush to get out. This time with exultation, because I was getting out for good.

Incredible, isn't it? I had made love to this man for a week, had orgasms with him, and he not only meant nothing to me but I felt *revulsion*—not to say self-disgust and hatred—once it was over! And yet—talk about see-saw emotions, talk about ambivalence—I was touched as he held my hand and thanked me over and over. "I wish," he said, "there was some way I could see you again. I'd like to buy you something—be with you without your being my therapist. . . ."

I smiled weakly and said I wished so too, but it was impossible. He kissed me, holding me tightly, then let go. He was turning away as he spoke, but I'm sure I saw tears in his eyes.

"I'm a man again," he said, voice thick. "A man, because of you."

Then he went to the kitchen, and I left.

In the car, I began to feel pretty good. I'd done it! I'd completed a case, and successfully! A patient had thanked me for making him a man again—no small thing, you'll admit!

Of course, I swore up and down that I'd never—no, never—let myself in for another case. And when I made my final report to Dr. Masters and Mrs. Johnson, I thought I indicated as much . . . without, of course, allowing them to see just how much of a shock the work had been.

I was mistaken. They didn't pick up any indications of my rejecting wife-surrogate work; and when it was offered to me, I *would* let myself in for it again, some of it better than my experiences with Glenn, and some of it much worse.

My reasons? They will become clear as you read my biography, my past history.

2

I wasn't born in St. Louis, though the Midwest has been my home for ten years. San Francisco was where I came into the world, but we didn't stay there for long. By the time I started grammar school, we were living clear across the country in New York. Not New York City; White Plains, in Westchester County. My father worked for IBM, and they shipped him around a bit, the way they do many of their executives.

"Executive" has a nice ring to it, and Dad was happy enough in his work, but he didn't make all that much money, certainly not enough to accrue any real savings. He was a big, pleasant man with lots of reddish-brown hair and soft brown eyes and a crisp, decisive manner —which hid a really indecisive nature. I don't know how he was on the job, but at home he was always willing to let Mother make the decisions. Maybe that's why I later became susceptible to takeover types, men who made strong moves. Maybe I didn't really respect Dad. All I know is, I never could go for the weak, indecisive type of man in my own life.

Most children have a memory or two of hearing their parents in bed, or even of seeing them copulating. The most I ever saw or heard was a chaste kiss . . . and on the cheek, at that. If it wasn't for my being here, I'd suspect they'd *never* screwed!

Don't get the idea they had a bad marriage. They never quarreled, and they respected each other, and I

rarely felt any tension between them. She was proud of
Dad, and he was proud of her—of her looks: her tall,
slim, cool looks. They were an easygoing, placid couple,
and I was their only child. Mother told me she'd had
a very bad delivery and decided that once was enough.

Anyway, being an only child has certain advantages,
if you're not smothered by your parents. I wasn't. Mother
and Dad had a healthy interest in the world around
them, and they didn't let me get in the way. They were
cool, unemotional people, and that's the way I was
brought up. Sex was a complete and absolute mystery to
me—no, not a mystery, because I didn't even know it
existed! I didn't wonder about it, because it was never
discussed, and so far as I can remember, I didn't come
into contact with it through other children. But I *did,*
finally, run headlong into it when I was about seven or
eight.

As I said, my parents had a healthy interest in the
world. There was Manhattan, and the theater and concerts and galleries and friends who gave parties. That
meant I spent considerable time with baby-sitters.

The girls who sat for me would sometimes have boyfriends over. I was put to bed, and they would conduct
their little courtships—you know; it's the same all over
the country. All I seem able to remember of the appearance of this girl is blond hair and a jutting ass (I called
it a "moonie" as a child). She was plump, and that ass
stuck out in truly extraordinary fashion.

It was a Saturday night. I awoke and wanted a drink.
We'd had root beer with dinner, and I decided to go
to the refrigerator and see if there was any left. The
way our house was set up, when I came down from the
second-floor bedroom I had to go through the living
room to get to the kitchen. The living-room lights were
out, but there was light from the dining area—a floor
lamp. I was in my bare feet, and there was carpeting
on the stairs, and besides, the two people on the davenport weren't paying attention to anything but each other.

At first all I saw was what seemed like one figure—
just the girl's blond head. But I heard a voice that
frightened me, and I froze at the foot of the stairs, just
a short distance from the davenport. The voice was male,

and it sounded like someone in pain, someone sick. "Oh!" it gasped. "Oh, please, *please*, Mary." Over and over it gasped.

Then I made out movement, and realized that a boy was sitting with her, slouched low, his head on her shoulder and his legs straight out. He turned his head and kissed her. "Please," he begged. "Mary, baby, faster. . . ."

I came closer, tiptoeing up behind them, and then I had a view of something that made no sense to me.

The boy's trousers were open at the fly. Something big was sticking straight up out of that opening, and Mary was pulling on it. "Oh!" the boy moaned, and he seemed in *bad* pain now, his head tossing back and forth. "Oh, God! *God!*"

I began to cry.

Mary jumped up. "What're you doing out of bed, you little . . ." She stopped herself and glanced at the boy. He was twisting away, stuffing himself back in his pants, and I sobbed that I didn't want the boy to "feel so sick." Mary took her cue from this, saying yes he *was* sick and she'd been helping him. By this time he was all zippered up, and nodded and said he felt better.

Mary took me to the kitchen and poured a glass of root beer and asked me if I would do her a favor and not mention her "sick friend" to my parents, because she wasn't supposed to have him here. I was enjoying my drink—I remember she gave me several forbidden ice cubes; my mother was among those who felt that ice could do a child no good—and I nodded and drank my root beer and said I'd keep her secret.

When Mary was asked to sit for me again, she realized I *had* kept the secret, and so she grew confident and had her boyfriend over again. This time, when putting me to bed, she filled a glass with ice and root beer and placed it on my night table in case I woke up.

I drank the soda *before* going to bed, and then didn't sleep. I was curious about that sick boyfriend. Something, some feminine instinct, was awakening, and I was strangely excited about his being in the house. I'd liked the way he looked, once he was well again. He was big, and he had a nice face. And what was that thing that had stuck straight up out of his pants? So I sat up in bed, trying to hear them downstairs.

After a while I slipped out of my room. Now I was deliberately trying to go unseen and unheard, and I did all right. Except that they weren't on the davenport. They were nowhere in sight.

I became frightened. Had they left me alone in the house?

I was about to start crying, when I heard the boy's voice. He was obviously sick again, only this time he was being sick in the kitchen. I went to the kitchen doorway and scrunched up on the floor to the side and peeked around and inside. The boy was leaning back against the wall near the sink. Mary was right up against him, so I couldn't see if that big thing was sticking out of his pants, but her hand was busy in front, and he was moving his head that same way and making those sick sounds, and so I reasoned that she was pulling on it. Only I was more interested in what he was doing to *her*. One hand had Mary's dress up around her waist; her panties were down around her ankles; his other hand was squeezing her big moonie.

For a moment it made me laugh. I covered my mouth and scrunched further back and smothered my laughter. I doubt they'd have heard it anyway. They were both really flying. What I didn't know as a child, but realized later, was that with her dress up and her pants on the floor and his thing out, her hand may not have been *pulling* it but putting it in. Mary may have been getting hers, right up against the wall.

I'll never know if that was the case, or whether she was masturbating him, but after a while he said, "God, I'm . . . I'm . . ." and she twisted aside. That's when I saw the thing sticking out of his pants, and Mary's hand squeezing it. Just like last time, only this time white stuff spurted out of it, and he made the sickest sounds I'd ever heard.

I ran back to my room. Somehow, I wasn't frightened as I'd been the time before. I was, however, excited, though I didn't know why. My own "middle" seemed to bother me, to itch and burn a little. I remember rubbing it when I was back in bed, and that it felt nice. It must have given me definite pleasure, because I continued rubbing it every so often—until about three weeks later, when I did it in front of my parents.

We were finishing dinner. I'd already asked to be excused from the table—we observed all the niceties in our home—and was standing, saying something to my mother. And then she said, "What *are* you doing!" Her tone of voice and hard stare made me glance down to see that I was rubbing myself between my legs. I said, "Scratching." My mother said that nice girls didn't do such things. "Even when it itches?" I asked. She said yes, even when it itched, and told me to go right upstairs and take a bath. I did, but continued rubbing myself there for the "nice feeling." Eventually, I did it again in front of my parents. This time (and I have something approaching total recall about the scene), my father made a sound of disgust and left the room, and my mother slapped my face twice, hard. While I was crying, she told me I had a "filthy habit" and that it must end right here and now. I was *never* to rub myself "in that place again, because it is the worst thing a girl can do! It's a *sin*, Valerie! You can burn in hell for it!"

I was sent to my room, crying, and that was the end of my childhood experiment with masturbation. In fact, I was hung-up about self-stimulation for quite a while, until reintroduced to it by a man during the course of an affair.

Mary and her boyfriend were in my home twice more. I got to like the boy quite a bit when I spoke to him before going to bed. He touched my hair the last time and said, "You're a pretty girl," and suddenly I was acting in a way I'd never acted before, smiling and pushing at him and wanting to stay up long after my bedtime.

From then on, whenever any of my sitters had a boyfriend over, I would act up, flirt, resist going to bed. I spied a few more times, but never saw anything so specifically sexual as I had with Mary. Still, the boys interested me, and—get this—I remember thinking sometime later that the boys were really coming to see *me!* They'd heard about the "pretty girl" in this house and so they wanted to talk to me and touch my long red hair.

No lack of ego in me those days, or in the days that followed when I entered junior high. When I was twelve, I seemed to go from being flat-chested to wearing a 32-C bra. I know that can't be, but they grew *quickly*, that's for sure. Anyway, at thirteen my breasts were much in evidence, and, accordingly, I was much in demand at the little social events in Westchester County. But I found the boys my age or a year older dull, puerile, not nearly as interesting as, say, several of my male teachers.

We moved still again, and this move was rough on me. I'd made friends in Westchester, though still no very close girl friends. I had one boy who considered himself my "steady," even at that early stage, and I managed to see several others at parties, school affairs, and church socials.

I haven't mentioned my religious background. Mother and Dad were far from fanatics, but they did attend church regularly. I won't get too specific, in order to maintain my anonymity, but we were Protestants and I had a reasonable belief in God and his works. By "reasonable" I mean that it didn't dominate my mind or thoughts, and in fact in my early teens I managed to excuse myself from attending services most Sundays. Christmas, however, was a very big thing in our home. There were sunrise services and the tree and presents and a heightened awareness of God in our lives. After New Year's, we, and especially I, slipped back to a more secular approach to living. Still in all, Christmas was my favorite time of year, and mainly because Dad made it that way. He was the one who really built it up for me. It had been a delight for him as a child, and so he implanted Santa Claus and all the rest of it in my mind at an early age, and it stuck. When he died, something happened that he couldn't possibly have foreseen. I began to *dread* Christmas. And what with the need for presents and all the added expenses, and Mother's sickness and the enormous bills . . . well, I simply came to wish it over and done with even before it arrived.

Anyway, in midterm, two months before my fourteenth birthday, we moved to New Jersey. Teaneck is a beautiful area, a high-cost area, since it is within half an hour

of Manhattan. I was registered in a private high school
and began attending classes immediately . . . and I was
miserable. I had no way of getting from Teaneck to
White Plains, so I'd lost my friends, even though I cor-
responded with my "steady" for a few months. I was the
new girl in school once again, and this is when I really
became a loner. I couldn't explain it to anyone, but
nothing worked right for me then. My grades, which had
always been very high, dipped, though not so low that
anyone called me on them. I was in trouble, without being fully aware of it.

There was only one bright spot in my life: French
class. And it wasn't the language that made me hurry
there.

My French teacher's name was Paul (not his real name,
of course). He was an American, but had been born of
French Canadian parents in Quebec, and he had a marvelous accent. He had wanted to be a professional
hockey player, but had been forbidden to by a very stern
and conservative father. That same father pushed him
into marriage at age twenty-two with a friend's daughter.
The marriage was fruitful, in a Catholic sense: Paul had
four sons, the oldest nine and the youngest three. It was
totally arid in a personal sense; Paul had wanted to end
it before the first child was born, but at that time had
still been under the influence of his father. He had
taught French in Toronto, and then finally broken away
from the father and immigrated to the States. Because
of the children, he had stopped thinking of divorce. He
was thirty-seven, not too tall, with curly black hair and
white teeth flashing in a dark face. When he said, "And
now, Vale*reee*," my heart would almost stop!

And how did I know so much about one of my high-
school teachers? He told it to me, all of it, one very
rainy day in his car, toward the end of the term. And
how did I happen to be in his car? I knew what time he
left the school, and I waited in a doorway near the
parking area, my raincoat and umbrella safely tucked
away in my gym locker, looking properly forlorn. When
he stopped to ask if anyone was picking me up, I said,
"I *thought* so . . ." He of course offered to drive me

home. I had to fight for self-control, I was that excited!

Now, you have to understand that while Teaneck is near Manhattan, it is not Manhattan (whether for good or ill, I have never lived in Manhattan or any other part of New York City). Teaneck is sophisticated, yet because of its small-town nature it is also conservative. And when it comes to anything like a sexual and romantic association between teacher and pupil, *any* town, big or small, is conservative! So even that ride home in the rain was dangerously close to infringing on taboos.

I was only fourteen, and he wasn't very experienced himself. He had never had an affair, had never had any woman besides his wife, was still inhibited by a rigid upbringing.

But we were both loners, and both *lonely*. And perhaps there was still another reason for what happened; a reason hard to believe for a fourteen-year-old girl—but then again, Juliet was *thirteen,* wasn't she? Maybe we were in love.

At least I was, from the beginning. And if you ask me to define love, I can only tell you what it was for me: a desire to be with this man, to the exclusion of all other men, women, and children. A need for his presence that started on the first day I saw him and grew and grew until I was in agony when away from him. A deep respect, amounting almost to worship, of his intelligence, his manner of doing just about anything (and this, I now know, I would not have felt had I been an adult; I would not feel it *today*). A jealousy of any woman, including his wife, who had the good fortune to share his life. And a physical hunger for him that rejected all caution and led us into the wildest situations.

But back to the car on that rainy day. He did *not* take me right home. We started to go there, with me giving directions, but then he took a wrong turn, and we were on a street that borders on a bird sanctuary—a very country spot in the middle of Teaneck. He parked to look at something or other, and suddenly we were talking. I mean talking out all sorts of personal things at each other. I remember his asking one question that started me off. "Do you like to read, Vale*reee?*" I said yes, very much, and hesitated and then said I also liked movies very much and hoped he didn't think that "unintellectual." I admitted I liked romantic movies, romantic books, and that I always saw myself as the heroine. I went through all the crises and all the love scenes; felt I was being kissed and loved and abandoned and so on.

He laughed a little, and then looked away and said it wasn't so unusual. He too fantasized with books and movies. And some TV shows. "Everyone wants to be a hero, a heroine," he murmured. "Everyone wants to be . . . happy. And not all of us are."

I asked, "Are *you* happy?" and quickly added, "I'm not."

He asked why not. I said, "I don't know. Maybe . . . I'm lonely."

His hand moved in his lap. For a moment I thought he might reach out and touch me, and my heart seemed about to burst. But he didn't. He said I was too pretty to be lonely. He said there must be a hundred boys wanting to date me.

"But I don't like boys."

His eyebrows went up.

I felt my face growing red. "I mean . . . I don't like the young ones. A *man* . . ."

I was floundering, and he saved me. Still speaking in that quiet manner, he told me about Canada and his father and the arranged marriage and his unhappiness with his wife. Just like that, he put his life out in front of me, and just like that I, Valerie, was *part* of it.

After he'd told me all this, there was a rather uncomfortable silence, and in order to fill it, I began to open up more myself and to dig up memories—and not only memories, but *interpretations* that surprised me, since I'd never before analyzed myself. For example, I talked about how I felt while on dates. I described how casual my parents were in terms of my having to attend church, but how strict they were in terms of teaching me what I was *not* supposed to do with boys.

We talked, and talked, and talked . . . and he never did touch me. Finally he looked at his watch, and actually paled. We'd been there almost three hours! My parents would be worried, and I'm sure his wife would be having fits.

He drove back as if Teaneck were Le Mans, and he got me out of the car and drove away so quickly that I was certain he thought me a stupid little girl, and that, once again, all I'd been doing was fantasizing.

What had started out so . . . *lovely,* ended with my feeling an absolute idiot! I spent half that night crying.

That was on a Friday. It was a terribly long weekend for me, and yet I dreaded Monday and French class. And it seemed my worst fears were realized when Paul ignored me: he never called on me to recite, avoided even looking my way. When the bell rang, I began to rush out. A friend stopped me, tried to talk to me, but my eyes were full of tears, and I shook my head and got to the door. Where I ran full tilt into Paul.

"May I speak to you a moment, Vale*reee?*"

Numbed, I said of course. The rest of the class left. I stood at his desk, and he sat down and shuffled through some papers. Had I flunked last Friday's quiz?

"I'd like you to baby-sit for us."

I blinked. I was so unprepared for *that,* it just didn't register! Either bad school work or perhaps a lecture on my lack of attention in class—or even something in the line of a scolding about last Friday's talk. But baby-sitting for his children?

I said I'd be glad to, and he said they would pay fifty cents an hour, and that was it. I went home, told my mother the teacher would be picking me up at seven and returning me at twelve, and quieted her complaints about the lateness of the return by saying I would study until then.

We drove to his home in near silence. I think he said something about the weather being terrible, and I think I said, "Yes, it is."

His wife was a small, plump, pleasant-looking woman about his own age (actually, two years older), very matronly. The children were well behaved when Paul and Doris were around, but as soon as they left, all hell broke loose. I got them under control through a combination of flattery, bribery, and a few good losses of temper. I wanted them in bed so I could concentrate on being in the house where Paul lived.

When they were asleep, I began fighting against doing something most baby-sitters do. I lost the fight, and began a systematic examination of the place, room by room, going through closets and drawers, thrilling to every item that belonged to Paul.

There was nothing much downstairs, so I tiptoed upstairs, past the one room where all three children slept, to the master bedroom. In a nightstand I found a large box of rubber contraceptives. I'd heard of them, but I really had no clear picture of how they were used; *that's* how innocent I was! Still, I held them, thinking of him, nude, taking one out and somehow using it on himself, or on his wife. The thought of his wife, of the fact that he used it with *her,* made me put the box away.

I lingered over his underwear drawer, and laughed when I found a pair of shorts with a hole in the seat. I went to the bathroom and took a little of his after-shave lotion and inhaled the odor, fantasizing that his face was pressed to mine. Then I entered a tiny little room, no larger than a good-sized storage closet, with a desk and two metal files: Paul's study; all his teacher's salary could give him. It made me feel sad, until I found a folder of school papers in a drawer, among them an old quiz of mine. I couldn't understand why he'd kept it; none of the other papers related to it—they were all departmental notices and the like. I looked it over—I'd made a very ordinary 75 on it—and then put it back, but *face down.* That's when I saw the scribbles, doodles, written ramblings.

For the most part, it was my name in blue ink, scattered all over the page: written normally, printed, blocked out so heavily it looked like a billboard. And there were a few other words and phrases scribbled around, some of which made no sense to me, and two which did: "sweet breast" and "eyes always there." I began to tremble. I turned the paper over again, to the quiz side, and only then noticed a phrase circled in pencil. We'd been given English sentences to translate into French. One was, *"Je t'adore,"* and I had added, "Paul," without even knowing it!

On the way home that night, I sat stiffly, nodding as he spoke about a play they'd seen in Manhattan. I was waiting. I knew something had to happen. I might have to wait a long time, but something simply *had* to happen!

Then he mentioned summer school—he was going to teach this summer—and I heard myself say I was planning on attending. He turned from the road; our eyes met; he said, "It is not usual. Mainly those who have failed . . . for makeup classes."

I said I wanted to get into college as soon as possible. He nodded. He drove. The electricity was so strong, I felt lightning would begin to crackle between us!

He didn't park directly in front of our house this time. It was a quarter to one in the morning, dark and silent, and he cut his lights and ignition and turned to me. I kept my eyes forward, afraid to look at him, though I desperately wanted to.

"Valereee . . ."

I turned, and his hand was moving, finally moving, and it took mine.

I can't tell you what that touch meant to me. Nothing *ever*—and that includes the wildest sex you can imagine —matched the tremendous thrill the touch of that hand gave me. I can feel it *now!*

It might have stopped right there. He held my hand a moment, then withdrew. I wanted to squeeze it, to hold on, but I simply didn't have the power to move. He said, "Well . . ." and I said, "Good night," and reached for the door. I was holding two or three school books in my lap—I had finals the very next day—and being in a state of absolute confusion, I dropped them.

I began to bend, and he said, "Let me," and we bumped heads. I laughed . . . and suddenly our lips were pressing. It lasted only a second. I drew back. We looked at each other, and that look was a falling into each other's eyes. It ended only when my eyes closed as he drew me to him. He said my name once or twice, softly, and we kissed again, and the kiss went on and on, and his hands stroked my head, my neck, and it was gentle, undemanding, the softest, most tender thing I'd ever experienced.

Everything with Paul was the most, because everything with Paul was the *first*. I know it all can be seen
in another way: teacher seducing innocent but hot-pants
little student. I've read things like that myself. And who
knows, maybe that's the way it was, for Paul. But not
for me. For me it was *love*, and it was the most important thing in my life.

Not that it wasn't hot too! The passion took hold very
quickly during that second kiss . . . because his hands
left my head and neck, went to my legs, my breasts. One
hand worked inside my blouse, and then under my brassiere, and it was the first time I'd ever had anyone feel
my *bare* breast. Almost immediately, I grew wet between
the legs.

He didn't touch me there until we'd kissed and petted
for about ten minutes. And then his hand was suddenly
pressing my crotch, not entering but *enfolding* it; holding
and squeezing it. I gasped. I said, "Paul . . . no . . ."
and what I meant was no, I couldn't stand it.

He let go. He did something that was so erotic it made
me run from him. He brought that hand up to his nose
and mouth and sniffed and licked. . . .

Mother and Father were both waiting up when I entered the house, and both were upset at the lateness of
the hour. I said I'd studied, would have had to stay up
late and cram for my exams tomorrow anyway, and that
way managed to get to my room with a minimum of
discussion. But Dad gave me a rather strange look.

I don't think I slept at all that night. I was so in love,
so terribly involved in all ways, and yet, by morning, I
was in *hell!* The *social* significance of what had happened
began to overwhelm me. I kept thinking: *How can I
ever face that man again!* By the time I'd washed and
dressed, I was sure he must think me an absolute idiot,
and a little tramp to boot.

As I said, I had finals that day. I have absolutely no
recollection of taking them, though I must have, because
I didn't flunk any subjects. The system in that school was
that the teachers did *not* give finals to their own classes,
so I didn't think I would see Paul. But when I came out
into the hall after the French test, he was waiting,
and he beckoned to me quite peremptorily.

We walked down the hall, and then he whispered, "Little Val*ereee*, little love," and I felt my heart leap. Still whispering, he told me where to meet him, and was gone.

At three-thirty, after my last exam, I managed to shake my friends and walked two blocks in a direction opposite to that of my home . . . and there was picked up by Paul. We drove out of Teaneck, into a country area, and parked and entered some woods. When we stopped, he leaned back against a tree and cupped my chin in his hand and kissed me. I came up against him and felt his manhood pressing hard into my body. Again we kissed, and kissed, and kissed! Again his hands moved to my hair, my neck, and then my breasts and legs. He raised my skirt, caressing my bottom. He slid his hand inside my panties, stroking my cheeks.

He took my pants down, kneeling in the earth to slide them over my shoes. And while kneeling, he pressed his mouth to my cunt, cupping my bottom in his hands. He had big hands; big, soft-skinned hands. They stroked and fondled, and his tongue began to probe, entering me. I felt I would faint! The tongue probed further, and found the right spot. I wanted to scream, the feeling was so strong. I ran my fingers through his thick, dark hair. I pressed him to me, unconsciously asking for more.

He gave me more. He gave me my first orgasm.

My thighs were wide-parted, my knees were trembling, I was half-sobbing; he supported me with his hands under my bottom . . . and then his tongue seemed to strike flame from me and I gasped his name and it happened. I sagged. He caught me around the waist. He held me, tenderly, saying my name, until I had quieted. Then he opened his pants and, finally, I understood what it was that had stuck out of Mary's boyfriend's fly.

Paul took my hand and put it on him. The flesh was hard, hot, pulsing. I squeezed, and he leaned against the tree, groaning. I *loved* seeing him that way! I loved knowing I was controlling his passion, giving him pleasure!

He directed me in stroking as well as squeezing. Then, when he was moving his head from side to side, I bent and took him in my mouth, trying to duplicate what he

had done to me. He cried out, tried to jerk away, and
suddenly hot sticky wetness was on my lips and face.

When he'd recovered, he said, "I'm sorry, honey!" and
wiped my face with his handkerchief. He seemed to think
I was upset.

That was the beginning. My mother was pleased that
I'd decided to go to summer school, but my father
wondered aloud whether it was healthy for a growing
girl to give up her vacation, her days of play in the sun.

I played, all right, but not in the sun! Paul and I met
once before school began, but only briefly, driving to a
deserted spot and parking and kissing. He said he *needed*
me because his life was devoid of true love. I said I
needed him because he *was* true love. He then said he
had to go, and started up the car, but I said, "Just one
more kiss," and we came together and I pressed my
hand to his crotch and he opened his pants and I took
out his cock. Once again, I was drawn to kiss it, to
suck it, and this time I didn't stop until he came in my
mouth, even though he tried to draw away at the last
moment.

Driving back, he was silent—downcast, I would have
said. I asked if anything was wrong, if I hadn't made
him happy. He said, "Of course . . . but . . . didn't
it bother you . . . in your mouth, I mean . . . ?"

It hadn't. Not at all. And I was surprised that he
would think it might. It was part of Paul, wasn't it? Part
of our feeling, our excitement, our love? If *that* was
bad, was disgusting, then everything else was too, right?

Only later did I find out how many women are re-
volted by the thought of semen in their mouths, and how
few actually swallow it.

Our first meeting after the start of summer school was
in a department head's office. (You have to remember
that the school was more than two-thirds empty, that
classes ended at noon, and that this gave us all the opportunity we needed.) The door was locked, the shades
drawn, and Paul and I were alone, indoors, in reasonably
comfortable circumstances for the first time.

He removed my clothes slowly, one piece at a time,
pausing to kiss each part of me as he uncovered it—my
arms, shoulders, breasts, belly, ass, thighs, and finally,

putting it off to the end, my cunt. He then had me undress him—please remember that we were in a school,
in an office, and that there were at least a few teachers
and pupils around after the noon hour! He expected, and
received, the same treatment as he gave me—I kissed
every part of his body, ending with his rigid cock. Then
he placed me on my back on the desk, spread my thighs,
and went down on me. He masturbated himself as he
ate me, but not to a conclusion. It took a while to
make me come; I was so aware of where I was. But
come I did, and so hard that I burst into tears!

Then we stood together, and he kissed my tears away,
and I held his cock and stroked it, and before I could
go down on him, as I'd planned, he came in my hand.
It was a tremendous feeling, that thing pulsing and his
mouth gasping my name, and knowing it was I who had
this beautiful man so enthralled, so captured.

We made love just about every place you can think of
in that school. And always the slow undressing. And always the kissing, the constant kissing, the touching and
caressing. Sometimes we met only for a moment, to kiss
and touch, and other times we stayed for an hour or
more, and did everything—everything but have intercourse. He wouldn't do that. He said it was for my
protection, my future . . . and I believed it at the time,
even though I would plead for him to put it in and
forget my welfare, forget my future.

I'm not so sure I believe his reasons anymore. Perhaps he was still fighting his father's moral influence.
Perhaps he was still hooked by church dogma and felt
that as long as he didn't actually fornicate, there would
be no real sin. Perhaps he was simply afraid—but how
could it be fear of pregnancy, since he could use a rubber? Or, and this I think comes closest, it was a combination of all these, with one thing added: He had coitus
with his wife, but little else, he told me; little experi-
mentation. With me he could do whatever he wished—
my desires matched his—and for him coitus was simply
less attractive than all the rest!

It was in one of our favorite spots, the art room, that
we came closest to being discovered. This was toward
the end of the summer session. He'd put two tables to-

gether, lowered the large green shades, and locked the door. Oh, yes, he always put a large piece of cardboard, kept hidden in a closet, over the glass top of that door! We undressed and played on those tables as if it were a king-sized bed. By this time I was so sexy with him that I would come twice, if the session could go half an hour or more. I had already come once, and we were in sixty-nine position, and his prick was beginning to swell in that special way . . . *when the door rattled!*

I'd never had Paul go soft on me, except after orgasm, but this time he wilted instantly. We scrambled off the tables, and somehow he kicked something. The door rattled louder; a voice said, "Open up, please! This is Mr. Gershem," or some such name—he was the principal for the summer session.

We froze, both stark naked, afraid to move, and the door thundered under a series of blows! "If you don't open up, I'll get the key . . ." Someone interrupted him then, and there were several voices in the hall. When I looked at Paul, I think he was praying. His eyes were closed, his hands clenched together, his lips moving.

The voices went away. We dressed frantically, and he went to the door and listened intently. Then he used his key and motioned me out. I just couldn't move, I was that frightened! He actually had to shove me out the door, and then I ran as hard as I could, down the hall and outside and halfway home!

I worried about him all night, and couldn't wait for our scheduled meeting near my geometry class. We went to the gym teacher's office, where he locked the door, lowered the shades, and said, "We've got to stop . . ." It was he who stopped—speaking that is. I was beginning to cry, shaking my head, the fear of losing him overriding any other fear I might have. I remember I was wearing a snug yellow sweater, and his eyes slipped to my breasts, and when I saw that, I rushed to him, desperate to hold him with my body, with anything he wanted of me. He tried to speak again, but I sealed his mouth with mine. When he pulled back, looking a little angry, I pressed my hand to his crotch. He said, "Val, it's terribly dangerous after yesterday."

I opened his fly and took him out and dropped to my

knees and sucked him and sucked him until he was gasping; then I stopped and looked up, and he said, "Go on, go on, please . . ." and I went on and drained him. And there was no more talk of not seeing each other.

Summer school was coming to an end. I was fifteen now, and more in love than I've ever been, before or since. I didn't think there was anything more Paul could teach me, except actual intercourse, but he managed to surprise me. Once again we were in the art room; the summer session had actually ended, and we were almost alone in the building. The tables were pushed together, the blinds down, the cardboard on the door, and I was about to lie back, legs apart, when he asked me to turn around and "assume the position," my behind stuck out. I liked that. I liked when he rubbed his cock between my legs and between my cheeks until he came. But that wasn't the game today. I was bending over when I felt him kissing my ass. Yes, that we'd done—but then his tongue began to probe.

He licked my anus, and at first I was turned off. My first turn-off with Paul. I wanted to ask him to stop. I wanted to say that he couldn't expect me to do that to *him!* The anus . . . I mean, who could find the asshole sexual?

Well, I could, within ten minutes. The sensations became so pleasant, and then so exciting, that I returned the compliment. We finished with him between my legs, as if to make love in Mamma-Papa position, but merely rubbing on the outside until he came all over my belly.

He did something before we left the art room for the last time that touched me, and made me laugh. We had put the tables back in place, and I could see the damp spots where my behind had rested on one of them, and I also saw two little pubic hairs, lighter by far than Paul's black ones. I was going to brush them away when he stopped me. He picked them up and very carefully put them inside a folded sheet of paper and then folded it again and again, and put it in his wallet.

I wonder if he still has them? We could never exchange pictures or gifts, so that was all he had of me, and I had nothing of him.

That's not right, because I have these memories. With

all the sex, all the erotic meetings, there was always the kissing, the touching, the words of love. Always the words of love, to make things beautiful. He never, not once, touched me without saying he loved me, needed me, couldn't think of living without me. I never, not once, was with him that I didn't tell him I loved him and wouldn't be able to survive a day without him. Maybe it was a game . . . I don't know. But it filled me with joy, with tenderness; and without it, sex is so much less to me.

It was Paul who awakened me to the pleasures of the body. I know that my sensitivity to touch, which stood me in such good stead as a surrogate wife, was developed at this time, during the many furtive meetings, the constant petting, the touching and stroking and bringing to orgasm by finger and hand and mouth. He made me aware of every little sensitive inch, every little nook and cranny and hair of my body.

We were remarkably lucky escaping detection. No more rattling of doors, and no one ever coming upon us. But what we didn't know was that some of our comings and goings had created talk among my friends, and the talk had reached several of my friends' parents. All discounted it, or were unwilling to pass it on. *All but one.*

Paul and I went on this way until I graduated—four full years, because I managed to load my program with nonessentials and so stayed with my class despite the summer sessions. I was the happiest girl in the world, and the most miserable.

Why the most miserable? Because changes had taken place in my feelings. Not my feelings for Paul, but . . .

I was seventeen, in my senior year. I'd been growing, and was almost as mature as I am now. I was a woman in love, and I wanted to tell everyone how marvelous my lover was. I wanted to dine with him in public, dance with him in public, go out with him and show him off to everyone. I wanted him at my dinner table, speaking to my parents, smiling and laughing with me in front of them. Other girls talked about their boyfriends, their lovers, their fiancés; talked about plans for the future; talked about marriage. I couldn't say a word. I couldn't be seen with him. And I couldn't even *dream* of a future with him.

I had to go out on dates with boys I cared nothing about, boys who annoyed and upset me with their attempts at sex. (If I didn't go out, my parents would wonder and worry.) Even the nicest of them—and there was one, a fine student and basketball player, whom I think I could have liked, and who was crazy about me— never had a chance. They were all second-best to Paul, and a poor second at that. I've always been a one-man woman, starting then and going on until now. One love; one man; no one else can make a mark.

I guess Paul did me a lot of harm that way. I never did develop a real relationship with a boy. And I never could take males in my own age category very seriously. A ten-year difference, roughly, has been mandatory for my really feeling anything. And yet, at the same time, I'm hung up about age—I mean, *old* men.

Hey, maybe Masters and Johnson ought to treat *me!*

Those four years were, in retrospect, a time of constant turmoil, of being one thing on the outside and something very different on the inside. And then, to cap it all, just two months before my graduation, my father died of a massive coronary. I had lied to my father, and, it seemed to me, he had suspected something. Now he was dead, and the lie was for all eternity.

And yet, once the funeral was over and the relatives gone back to wherever they came from, I turned even more strongly to Paul; turned to him as father and lover both.

When I received my diploma, Paul was on the stage with the faculty. I left the stage, walking down the aisle, diploma in hand, seeing my mother in front of me, feeling Paul's eyes in back of me. I sat through a final speech, and then I was in my mother's arms, and we were both weeping, she for my father, me for my father but also for Paul, thinking that the days of our love affair were numbered. I felt my life was ending instead of, as the valedictorian had said, "now first beginning."

I had applied for admittance to Fairleigh Dickinson University right there in Teaneck, which was about as far as I wanted to go from Paul. But after graduation, Mother sat down with me and said she didn't know how long we could continue to live in Teaneck. We didn't need the

house anymore, small as it was. We could make do with
an inexpensive apartment in an inexpensive section of the
country. Dad carried considerable insurance, but
Mother felt that it would have to last a long time, and
also that she should get a job. Living was expensive in
the East . . . and so on.

I was panic-stricken, but kept outwardly cool and
discussed *both* of us working . . . in Manhattan. We could
then keep the house . . . or we could move closer to
where we worked—Fort Lee, for example (which was
only ten or fifteen minutes by car from Teaneck and
Paul). Mother wasn't impressed by my reasoning. She
said she would see about selling the house, but no major
changes would be made "for two or three months while
I try working and we adjust to our new circumstances." I
muttered a thank-God under my breath.

Paul was teaching summer school as usual. Mother
didn't urge me to take a vacation, not even for a week
or two, because for the first time in her life she had to
consider a tight budget. And what did I do? I applied for
a job in the school, and got it! I worked in the cafeteria,
behind the hot-plate counter, and Paul and I went right
back to our sessions in various offices.

But not for long. It was about three weeks later that
the talk among my friends and their parents finally caught
up with us. One of the parents ran into my mother at a
church bazaar. My mother offered her a ride home, and
during the course of the drive the woman blurted out
what she felt was her "duty, long deferred."

"Your daughter has been seeing far too much
of that French teacher . . . the children say there have
been meetings on the street, and perhaps even in school offices. . . ." So in the end we were caught by an accumula-
tion of small incidents, gossip, and guesswork.

Paul and I were coming out of school, after two beautiful hours in the art room. As we got into his car, my
mother walked from her car, parked a distance away,
and came right up to my window. She was pale, as pale
as on the day Dad died, and she said, her voice very quiet:
"Please go to our car, Valerie."

I must have gone white myself, and I glanced at Paul.
He was trying to put a good face on it, and he said, "You

must be Valerie's mother. I've been wanting to meet you for some time. Valerie was one of my best pupils."

Her eyes were as cold as ice as she looked at him. Again she said, "Valerie, go to our car."

But having heard Paul speak so calmly, I too gained courage. After all, what could she know? "What's the matter, Mother? I simply accepted a ride home after work. . . ."

"Two hours and fifteen minutes after work," she interrupted. "And I've been all over the school, asking for either one of you . . . and one young lady said you often disappear together."

"What do you mean by *that?*" Paul said, and though he tried to sound indignant, his face was reddening.

"I don't want to have to say what I mean by that. I don't want to have to go to the principal and discuss what I've heard, what has become common knowledge."

I jumped out of the car and said she was *insane* to say such things . . . and she slapped me; slapped me as hard as I've ever been slapped. *"Go to the car!"*

I looked at Paul. If he had said to get back in beside him, I would have. If he had said damn the consequences, I'd have accepted anything that might have come. But his face was flaming, and all the fight had gone out of him, even though he continued to mutter about not understanding.

I ran to the car. Mother stood with Paul another moment; then we drove home in absolute silence. In the house, she said, "I've told that person that if he ever so much as *looks* your way again, I'll go not only to the school authorities, but to his wife."

I was crying, and tried to tell her nothing had happened, just a ride or two and some conversation, that we were simply *friends*.

"Perhaps," she said. "I certainly hope so, for your sake. But I'm going to assume the worst, still for your sake. Just don't make the mistake of thinking I won't do as I said."

Again I tried to speak. This time she held up her hand. "You're not to work at the school anymore. And we will never refer to this matter again. *Never!*"

And we never did.

I was accepted at Fairleigh, and Mother took a job in Manhattan. It was hard for her—the traveling by bus to and from the city, and working as a secretary after so many years as a rather pampered housewife. While she worked, I went right back to seeing Paul. That's right, I was waiting in a corner of the parking lot the very day Mother began work! He was upset, and motioned me away, but I came to the car and got in. I said I would meet him on the street from now on, but we had to make our arrangements. He stared at me, and we drove off.

We parked in a wooded area. He talked to me as he never had before. He told me how fed up he was with being a teacher—with the deadly repetition of teaching high-school French, and the low salary. He told me how he despised his department head . . . and for the first time I realized that this man, a god in my eyes, was pushed around by quite a few people, including, he added, his wife. He told me how Doris dominated their household; how she had money of her own; how his children didn't give him the proper respect . . . and then he turned to me, to our kisses and touches, and when I went down on him, sucking his cock, worshiping him with my mouth, he cried out his love for me.

I didn't quite absorb it at the time. Later, of course, I understood. He *needed* me, and not only for love, for sex, but for the respect, the awe, the *homage* I paid him. Of course, it made him less the big man, but it never changed my love. Big man, little man, beggar man, thief —whatever he was, it was too late for me to stop loving him.

Still, it all came to an end a week later—except for one more meeting, deferred almost a year. I was at home, preparing supper. Mother was a good hour late, and just when I'd decided to call her office, the phone rang. It was her employer. Mother was at Flower Fifth Avenue Hospital. She'd had a stroke.

That was the end of my childhood, the *true* end. I had to grow up, *fast*. Mother was totally paralyzed on her right side, and a helpless invalid. A sister arrived from St. Louis—Aunt Berta. She was eight years older than Mother, but healthy . . . or so she seemed. She too was a widow, and she asked us to come and live with her. She had a house in Ladue and could take care of Mother. I could combine work and school, and probably get a partial scholarship.

It all happened so fast, I never had time to see Paul. All I could do was risk a phone call to his home. I was lucky; he answered. I whispered my eternal love, gave him my St. Louis address, and told him he was to write, he was never to forget me.

He wrote, three times in seven months. I couldn't answer, of course. His wife might get the mail. I felt I was losing him, and I wanted to die. But I had little time to consider dying. I was attending college, working part-time to help pay the tuition, keeping my grades high to gain a partial scholarship, and helping to take care of Mother in the evenings.

That summer, I took a terrible chance. I phoned long distance, not person-to-person, simply dialing Paul's home. Had his wife answered, I'd have hung up. A son answered. I asked for Paul. The child didn't ask who was calling, thank goodness! Then Paul was on, and my voice shook as I said, "It's Valerie. I want to see you. You have two weeks free between semesters. Please come to St. Louis. I can't live without seeing you."

He answered as if I were a local student calling for private tutoring, and said he wouldn't be available for a while; he had a convention to attend in Atlantic City. He would be there for five days. Then his wife must have left the room, and he whispered, "Next Thursday, in the morning, meet me at the airport, American Airlines," and hung up.

I wasn't sure I'd heard him correctly. I wasn't sure he would actually be there. But that Thursday I was at the airport at seven A.M., and met every American Airlines flight from anywhere east of St. Louis. At about eleven A.M., Paul came striding toward me, and my heart leaped as it hadn't since the last time we'd met. We merely touched hands; then, half-blinded by tears, I led him to the valet parking section, where we waited a lifetime—actually about ten minutes—for the little Rambler American that was Aunt Berta's car.

I had cleared myself for the day, and was prepared to

be free for the night too by making one quick trip home. I tried not to look at him too often as I drove, wanting us both to get there alive and well! But I kept touching his hand.

I'd made reservations at a motel for Mr. and Mrs. Someone-or-other—the name escapes me. I had the key in my purse, and we went directly to the room. He put down his valise and looked around and said, "Very nice." I said, "Yes." He went into the bathroom, leaving the door open, and washed his hands and face. I stood there watching the longed-for, the beloved, and I said, "Do you realize this is the first time we've ever been together in a room with a *bed?* In a room where no one can disturb us? Safe, at last?"

He finished drying hands and face, and turned to me. He nodded. And then, finally, his eyes moved over me, over my body, and he said, voice weak, "How very beautiful you are, my Valer*eee.* I'd almost forgotten." At that, I literally *threw* myself at him. In a moment, we were straining together, and all the words that had been bottled up inside me came pouring out—that I loved him still, that I loved *only* him, that he was the one man in all the world for me, and it would always be so, would never change. And his words came too, as his hands began moving over me, over my breasts and bottom. He had never stopped loving me, he said. Life had simply torn him away from me. After this, he would write far more often, at least once a week.

As we talked, we stumbled toward the bed. The bed, at last! And complete lovemaking, at last! Because I hadn't taken any chances this time. I'd bought rubber contraceptives myself. And he had some too. And we undressed each other, those rubbers on the nightstand, both of us knowing the time had come.

But during the petting and touching and kissing and tonguing, something changed for me. I was so intense, so determined to have it all, that my body began to rebel, to tighten. It was something like being so hungry that you can't eat, or so tired you can't sleep. I was so in love, I couldn't fuck!

The same must have been true, in part at least, for him. Because the classic situation developed: he couldn't get in! He was reasonably large, but that wasn't it. I was a virgin, but that was only part of the story. I was tensed up as tight as a steel spring. My muscles, all of them down there, were pulling *inward* instead of relaxing *outward*. (*Vaginismus,* the closing of the vaginal entry, is the technical name for it.) And I wasn't wet enough, and that rubber needed lubricant—Vaseline or something like it—and we didn't have any, and no matter how much saliva he put on his hand and then on his cock, he could *not* get in.

He tried once. He tried again. And then, as I lay there turning to stone, he went soft on the third try.

As a wife surrogate, I'd have known what to do. First, I'd have tried to relax us both with a drink and some music and some talk. And I'd have thrown that damned rubber away and taken a chance at having him go in bare and pulling out. I'd certainly have made him lie down with me after he went soft.

I wasn't a wife surrogate. I had no experience at all in fucking. All I could do was burst into tears.

He got up, muttering something about being sorry and having to make a plane, and dressed in record time. I continued to cry, hands over my face. Before I knew it, the longed-for, the beloved, the one-and-only-love had gone. After all those years, those intense years, he'd simply . . . gone!

I ran to the door, calling for him to come back. But I didn't open it. I just stood there weeping, and then, somehow, *laughing!* I was miserable; I'd lost everything I valued; and yet, it was also funny. Four years of building up to the real thing . . . and now this!

I tried calling him again a few times, but even when I got him, he was cool, remote. Little Vale*reee* had put him down, but good. End of Paul. Beginning of further hard knocks. Aunt Berta died of cancer after an abdominal exploratory while I was in my junior year. Her insurance covered her burial and a bequest to a church charity, and that was it. But she left us the house. We sold it, and moved to the apartment in West County, St. Louis, where I was living at the time of my first wife-surrogate case.

Mother's expenses had really begun to climb. She had

two additional minor strokes, and needed a practical nurse when I wasn't home, and the money really ran through my checking account. Dad's insurance was long gone, and the money from Berta's house wouldn't last too long, so that's when I, personally, began to know what it was to sweat financially. I was determined to finish college, but I could see where life was going to be one hell of a struggle.

I went to school and I worked and I dated. I dated *heavily*—to forget Paul, I suppose. I dated college boys mainly, but also men from the medical-school complex where I worked. The boys all tried to seduce me, and the men all tried to seduce me, and I resisted all of them, until Mother suffered still another stroke and really became depressing to come home to.

I don't know . . . I thought myself reasonably intelligent, and also reasonably hip in a sexual sense, but what I'm about to tell you makes me look like a fool; a naïve fool. Perhaps some women never get over their sense of surprise, their naïveté, at what they do with their bodies. Perhaps I'm one of these women.

I met this boy, Ross. We dated and liked each other, and soon I found I was dating *only* him. We petted rather heavily, and one night he asked me to wear his pin. Anyone who's gone to college knows that being pinned is equal to being engaged, and that many pinned couples go on to marriage; so this was a big step for me, right?

Wrong. I didn't consider marriage. I simply liked Ross, liked his dark good looks, liked his calm, quiet manner, liked his undemanding ways in sex. What I didn't consider was that *he* might not feel quite as casual about pinning.

The night we were pinned was the night I finally lost my virginity. It was a shock, yes, but only emotionally. That first screwing worked rather well, despite a little blood and a little pain. I had an orgasm, nothing spectacular, nothing to match those I'd had via hand and mouth with Paul, but my body accepted it all with pleasure. My mind, however, was something else again. After it was over, I went to the bathroom to clean up, and with the water running to cover the sound, I wept, thinking this first time should have been with Paul, thinking there was a dullness, a deadness inside where once there'd been the wildest desire, the deepest tenderness. Then I came out, and we had another go at it, and it was better. Ross's words of love, of adoration, were just what I needed at the time—and, of course, helped make what I was doing *right*.

The second time we slept together was still more successful, and the third and the fourth and the fifth and the sixth. After our seventh bedding, this in a quite luxurious motel suite on Lindbergh Boulevard, not far from my home, with Ross having provided champagne and candlelight and music via a portable radio, he asked me when I'd gone on the pill.

I said I wasn't on the pill.

"I didn't see you use a diaphragm."

"That's because I don't own one."

He blanched. "Then what . . . ?"

I stared blankly. I had always relied on Paul. Paul took care of everything. My father figure was always so considerate of my well-being, my safety.

I was pregnant. Ross immediately offered to marry me. Pinned or not, I immediately realized I didn't love him. He was a nice boy, period. I didn't tell him that. I said, instead, I couldn't consider a marriage forced on me by pregnancy. I said nothing more, but I knew that he hoped things would work out for us later.

At that time, abortions were illegal throughout the United States, and girls were dying, and being physically ruined in terms of their sexuality, by nonprofessional butchers. Ross, however, had an uncle in Kansas City who had something to do with the rug business and something more to do with the rackets. We went to see him, and he was a wrinkled, dried-out little man who looked at me with cold, cold eyes. Then he said, "So I send you to my friend, the doctor, who do like I say . . . *just this once.*" The cold eyes turned to Ross. "Don' you be a fool no more, you hear me?" Ross nodded hurriedly, as if this ungrammatical old man could strike him dead; and I guess, from what I later read about the old man's funeral and the racketeers who attended, he could!

The uncle sent us to a very respectable gynecologist, who looked very unhappy, but who performed an abortion in his office and kept me in an adjoining room for a full day and provided a nurse for a full day, and who said to Ross as we were leaving, "Don't forget to give your uncle my *kindest* regards."

I'll say this for Ross, he looked ashamed.

In the car on the way home, he again asked me to marry him. I said I couldn't think too well at the moment; I was groggy; I wanted to sleep. He nodded, but watching him from the corners of my eyes, I could see a grayness moving into his face. I think then, for the first time, I realized he truly loved me.

We stopped at a motel that night. He did everything he could to make me comfortable. I'd slept so much in the car I couldn't sleep in bed, so we watched television. An old movie was on—a very romantic old movie that ended in happily-ever-after fashion with a big wedding. I think Ross knew what my answer was going to be, but for the third time he asked me to marry him. This time I had to answer, but I still couldn't say I had never loved him. Instead, I said that the abortion had killed something inside me, that I couldn't help associating him with it, that I wanted only to forget, and being with him wouldn't allow that. He shocked me. He got up very quickly and rushed toward the hall door. But before he got there, the sobs tore out of him.

I wept too. I fell asleep crying, and in the morning Ross was beside me, acting cheerful and normal and saying it was time to go.

I returned home and to school from (for Mother) a quick vacation and (for school and schoolmates) an emergency visit to a dying relative. Mother at that time was no problem. She was, to be brutally frank about it, concerned only with her next breath. School and job were a little more difficult. The abortion was a success, but I bled rather heavily for six days.

Still, a month later I was back to normal, with a little practical education in the necessity for birth control. And, of course, I was no longer a virgin.

As I think back to my final year, it seems I had no more than three or four sexual experiences, all with college boys. Why I held back with the *men* I'm not sure, but I guess it was because of Paul, because I knew that I was susceptible to an *adult* male, a mature male.

It wasn't a very interesting part of my life. I'd decided I didn't want to teach, and a major in English with a minor in psychology doesn't prepare you too well for anything else. I was happy enough working in the medical complex; the pay wasn't bad, and it would go up when I began working full-time. Anyway, for whatever the reasons, I wasn't prepared, wasn't *able*, to move myself toward any sort of professional career.

I saw Ross around the school, and while we were always friendly, we didn't date. After graduation, he left for his home in Chicago, but said he would be back— "to see you, honey, to try once again." I had one evening of blues, thinking about what might have been had I been able to love him.

After graduation I met the man who taught me just about everything there is to know about erotic love. I was almost twenty-one, and no longer a student, which seems to me the time you really become an adult in America.

I was going out with half a dozen men who worked in the medical complex. The youngest was twenty-eight and the oldest forty-seven. All were nice enough, and all wanted me to unlock my legs, and there were times I wanted to do just that, but still I waited. Not for romantic love. I was in a different bag at that time. I wanted . . . roaring chemistry! I wanted to experience total satisfaction of the senses, and to hell with getting hooked emotionally. And I felt I would need a very special man, a very strong and knowing and physical man, to help me to this.

I didn't know I'd met him when a rather short, heavy-set salesman stopped at my office to leave his card for one of the hospital administrators. Abner—his real name wasn't much more exciting than that—worked for a major New York pharmaceutical house. He asked if I could suggest a decent place to have lunch—he was new in St. Louis. I asked if he had a car. He nodded. I then suggested a place on the other side of Forest Park. He rubbed his chin after I gave the directions, and said he navigated like a blind homing pigeon away from home. I laughed;

he smiled; his eyes went to my breasts. He asked me to take him there. I looked him over again—a round, rather pale face; small, close-set eyes; not too much' hair; in his mid-forties. Definitely not the man of my dreams.

But that smile, those hard eyes . . .

He waited outside for twenty minutes, and then it was noon, and I joined him. His car was a dusty Chevy sedan, about as exciting as warm milk. His conversation wasn't much better, what little there was of it; about the latest in "legitimate drugs." But his eyes were very, very busy, flashing to me time and again.

In the restaurant, he ate seriously and silently, but his leg touched mine at least five times. He was finished long before I was, and leaned back and said, "I'm a gourmand, not a gourmet . . . but still, I'd like to take you to a few Manhattan restaurants, just to show you what food *can* be."

I said I'd lived in New York State and New Jersey and had been to Manhattan a number of times.

"With a *man?*"

It made me hesitate. With a *date,* yes . . . but a man? I finally shook my head. At that, his evil little smile returned. "You're honest enough. I wonder how good you are?"

"How *good* I am?"

"In bed."

I laughed.

He called for the check. Driving back through the park, he kept his eyes on the road and his mouth clamped shut; then he pulled over into a deserted parking area near the art museum. (Deserted because it was Monday and the museum is closed on Mondays.) I began to say I was late as it was, but I never finished the sentence.

There were no preliminaries. He simply put one arm around my shoulders and his lips on my lips and his other hand under my dress and directly onto my crotch. He didn't do it roughly, and he didn't do it gently; he just *did* it. And I was wet immediately, desirous immediately, on fire immediately, and shocked that I wasn't shocked! He squeezed my pubic bulge, stroked me through the cloth of my panties, kissed me with open-mouthed appetite. He said, "You're the most beautiful thing ever to come out of St. Louis, and that includes Stan Musial."

I laughed briefly and said, "Well . . . it's late."

He let me go as abruptly as he'd grabbed me. In a moment we were driving again. He said, "The question I asked before, how good are you in bed. I'd like to know the answer. And I don't mean your *telling* me."

When I didn't reply, he said, "Can we get together some evening?"

"How long are you going to be in St. Louis?"

"This trip, five days. I leave Saturday morning. But I'll be living here as soon as I arrange to have my furniture shipped from New York. I've taken over as assistant manager of this territory."

My heart still pounding from the excitement of our sex play, I said, "Congratulations."

"Again, when can I see you?"

I shrugged.

"Tonight," he said. "I'll pick you up at the complex."

I never said yes. I simply didn't say no. At five-thirty he was waiting for me, and I went to his car, and we drove to his hotel. We had one drink; then he went into the bathroom . . . and came out nude and with a throbbing erection. I shook my head, began to say something, and was in his arms. My own clothing was scattered over the floor, piece by piece, as he undressed me on the way to the bed. He put me on my back and went down on me and ate me, all without a word. When I began to writhe and cry out, he stopped. And got on top of me, not on hands and knees as my thoughtful Ross had done, but lying full *on* me, crushing me with his weight, his not-inconsiderable weight, *churning* inside me rather than going in and out, his arms locked around me, his face pressed against mine, his everything crushed to my everything.

I couldn't breathe! I couldn't think! I could only feel, and all feeling was concentrated in my cunt, and when I came I had to fight back a scream. He never even paused. He said nothing. But he changed his lovemaking. He came up off me, onto his elbows, and he began to plunge in and out. Then he removed one elbow and came down on my left side—not his full weight as before—driving into me from the right. That free hand went under my body, grabbed my ass, probed between the cheeks. By the time I felt myself approaching a second orgasm, his finger was up my anus and his mouth was sucking my breath away and he was plunging wildly. This time I did scream, directly into his mouth.

He went on. He moved and changed me around, and my legs were over his shoulders, and he was kneeling and plunging back and forth. I saw his orgasm coming, but he didn't let himself go. He was a man who knew control. A hand went to my breasts and kneaded and pulled and *squeezed* them just short of pain. His face twisted, and his movements slowed, and then he had control again, and went on about five more minutes.

He came, ramming me back against the headboard, face intense and cruel. He hurt me with his hands. He hurt me with his body, slamming it so hard up against me. But I loved his orgasm almost as much as my own. Watching it, feeling it, was *joy!*

Later, we showered together. He said I "wasn't bad" but would get better. He asked if I could stay the night. When I said no, he wrote my phone number and address on a slip of paper and drove me back to the hospital parking lot. I went home to Mother. I chatted with her. I read a little to her. We watched some television. I emptied her bedpan. I made sure she was asleep, and I too went to sleep. And I mean *sleep*—beautiful, dreamless, uninterrupted, solid, deep sleep!

Don't let anyone ever tell you that fucking isn't the best nerve treatment yet devised! (*Good* fucking, that is.)

As I said before, I was dating other men, and I continued to date them. There was one, a young doctor, whom I liked better than any other man I knew, and we had heavy petting sessions and played with the concept of love and marriage. And we eventually had sex together, which made him very happy and made me . . . what? I'm not sure. I liked it. Fine. Every month or so I'd give in to him. Fine. But it was nothing that could change my life.

Abner was changing my life. Abner was going on to

bigger and better sex. And I was going along, for the ride at first, and then, as emotions took over, for him, for love.

Love. That's the name of the game. Women searching for love. And the strange thing is just how many times we *can* love, and in so many different ways. Abner became my second love, and yet so different from Paul, my first.

At about this time, Dr. Masters was finishing up certain experiments in human sexual behavior in the medical school of Washington University. Everyone connected with the scholastic world in St. Louis, and especially in the medical complex (which is about six blocks from the Foundation), was aware that a most unusual and exciting type of research was taking place. Stories circulated. We knew students and outsiders had been recruited to have sex under laboratory conditions—in front of scientific observers and cameras—and that a mechanical penis had been invented that could stimulate a woman to orgasm and, at the same time, photograph, measure, and record her responses; that all sorts of recording devices were being used, and developed. As I mentioned earlier, during the course of my work I had met Dr. Masters several times in the hospital, and I had also met his assistant, Mrs. Johnson. I heartily approved of what they were doing.

I said that Dr. Masters was "finishing up" his work at the university, because for one reason or another he wasn't getting the facilities and the support he required, and felt he had to move into a setup of his own. That too was becoming common knowledge; but as yet, I wasn't involved in any of it. Oh, Gini had chatted with me about certain aspects of their work, but I wasn't asked to join in, and I didn't volunteer. First of all, I wasn't quite that emancipated yet, and then too, I was involved in my own love life and in my struggle to keep things going financially. The money we'd gotten from the sale of the house was slipping away. My salary, despite two raises, wasn't adequate, and I wasn't eligible for any sort of aid or welfare because I wasn't destitute. But the pressure hadn't really hit yet, the *crunch* hadn't begun.

I saw Abner for about two years, two or three times a

week. I became more and more involved with him. The involvement can't be generalized; it has to be described. If it sounds like something out of De Sade, I can only say I enjoyed almost all of it.

I forgot to mention something about the formation of my new code of ethics, or morals, or the lack of them. Working around a medical complex, a medical school, or a hospital is a broadening experience. Doctors and nurses and interns and students . . . well, dealing with the human body as they do, nothing is sacred, at least in terms of human sexuality. I remember the time a doctor approached me (this was when I was still a student and working part-time) and said, "Your breasts seem even larger than usual, Valerie. You on the pill, or is it your period?" It shocked me into a silly laugh. (What it should have done was to make me remember birth control.)

All sorts of things were said. If I was grouchy, someone was likely to ask if I was sweating out my period. And there were occasional pats or touches, casual enough, but had I responded, the casual nature could have changed, and later did, as I've indicated. Anyway, by the time Abner came into my life, I was not quite the little innocent I'd been in Teaneck. A few times a week, after work, doctors and nurses and students and technicians would get together for drinks in a local bar, and there'd be arms-around-each-other and little feels, and I was rapidly developing a healthy appetite—and so, again, I was ready for Abner.

Oh, another thing. By this time, many of the students and hospital workers involved in Dr. Masters' research had begun talking, and Dr. Masters had published an article or two in medical journals, and so the word was getting around about what he was doing. We chatted a few times, and he was much involved in his work, his original research, just as he is now. It was the driving interest, the obsession you could say, of his life—but it would have to be, wouldn't it, for him to have accomplished as much as he has? He would talk about his work, and I got the feeling that he believed sex was, overwhelmingly, the single most important factor in the relationship between men and women—the most destructive thing if it went wrong, and the greatest if it went right. Now, by definition, male-female relationships depend upon sex, but not, in my opinion, to the virtual exclusion of everything else. I remember disagreeing with him, though mildly, since he was such an authority. I remember thinking that he couldn't really *mean* it, not to the degree I assumed he meant it. That tremendous emotional high with Paul . . .

Of course, it all started with sex. And in my experiences since then, the serious relationships were always the good sexual relationships. But why, if it's overwhelmingly sexual, did other relationships of mine, which held the possibility of good sex, mean nothing to me?

I keep thinking of this. Maybe some of those dying marriages are dying for lack of *love* as much as for lack of sex. Or the sex dies as love and the hope of love dies. A surrogate can only create an aura of *sex*, not love—though in one case, perhaps my most disturbing in some ways and most successful in others, I think I *did* create love.

Remember when you and I discussed this, Herb? You felt it was a matter of definition of terms, that Dr. Masters, involved as he is in isolating *facts*, must necessarily stay away from the nonfactual. A copulation is a fact. An orgasm is a fact. But the word "love" can be defined in so many ways that it fails utterly to register as fact. So what Bill probably meant was that given the proper sexual union, the proper frequency of satisfactory sex, and given no great differences in social and other personality factors, what we term love, the emotional hook-up, will take place. And I probably proved his point (if it *is* his point) with Abner.

Abner didn't ask to see me again, nor did I hear anything at all from him during the next four days; but on Friday night, candy and flowers were delivered to my home. The card was laconic: "For Valerie, Abner." I was surprised, and I was terribly pleased. He hadn't said any of the things I was accustomed to hearing during lovemaking, certainly not anything relating to *love*. So gifts—the accouterments of courting—were what I wanted, what I needed to justify what had happened.

The following Friday, I again received flowers and

candy, telegraphed this time from New York, the note reading, "See you soon, Abner."

And the Friday after that, the same thing, with the same note as the week before.

My other dates grew increasingly wearisome. I was waiting to see that stout little man—though with his clothes off he was not so much stout as *thick;* there was plenty of muscle; he was strong; even his stomach, which was far from small, was *hard*. With his clothes off, he was altogether larger.

Only my young doctor managed to make his company pleasant to me. He was beginning, however, to press me for a more permanent relationship. He had previously skirted around the question of marriage. Since I was clearly not willing to discuss it, he had never quite come out and *asked* me. But now, perhaps feeling me slipping away, he began to talk of a "friendship ring, or if you prefer, an engagement ring." I didn't love him, and I was waiting for Abner to move to St. Louis, and yet I thought of marrying Chris and having a home and children and getting from under the increasing financial burdens imposed by Mother's illness. Chris knew about Mother and said she would "of course live with us" and I could work or not, as I saw fit. You can't know what a temptation this was. But the dream of finding perfect love was still strong in me. And even though I had no thought of marrying Abner (not at the beginning), he *was* the male interest in my life just then, and he made it impossible for me with Chris.

In my office the following Wednesday, I looked up to see Abner. He said, "Lunch?" and I said, "Yes," even though I had a date . . . I think it may have been with Chris. I broke my date, and Abner was waiting outside and drove me to an apartment house on Westminster, about fifteen minutes' brisk walk from the medical complex. He had a nice two-bedroom place, rather disorganized since his furniture had been delivered only the day before. But the bed was up, was neatly made, flowers were in a vase on the nightstand, and there was a large cheval glass on casters.

I said it was nice. He said, "Let's have some lunch." He'd prepared sandwiches, salad, and beer. He finished quickly, and I said I wasn't really hungry and left half of mine.

He took me around the shoulders and led me into the bedroom. The dresser mirror wasn't up, but as I said, there was a cheval glass, a full-length mirror on a swivel and rollers, something like the ones they have in small clothing stores or tailor shops. He walked me in front of the glass and said, "Look." I looked, and he undressed me.

When I was nude, he stood behind me, my breasts cupped in his thick hands. He said, "Keep looking," and one hand went down across my belly into the thatch of hair, and the fingers entered me, and his mouth worked over my neck. I tried to turn around, to embrace him, but he stopped me. He said, "Look at Valerie. She's the important one." He held me there, made me watch while he masturbated me. I came, looking into my own face, at my own body, and it was fantastic, explosive!

He asked me to undress him, still in front of the mirror. And when he was nude, he pushed me down, firmly enough, until I was kneeling sucking on him. And always he moved me and himself and the glass so I could see what I was doing.

In bed, finally, we had a long, long go. I wanted him on me, as he had been the first time, but he said no, not this time, and took me doggy fashion, crouching behind me and entering from the rear and plowing me, jolting me, gasping and grunting and, toward the end, exhorting me to: "Shake your ass, baby! Shake . . . shake . . ." And I shook, ground, swiveled, bumped, and exulted as I came . . . and went on and exulted in *his* orgasm, *felt* his orgasm.

He collapsed beside me. I curled into his body, into his arms. He held me, and fell asleep. I thought nothing more exciting could happen. I was wrong. I was *always* wrong when I thought this with Abner.

The next time, as he would do every so often, we made love in Mamma-Papa fashion, except that the way Abner did it made me think of Mamma-and-Papa Greek gods!

After that I no longer remember specific nights, or dates, or meetings. We made love two and three times a week, and we almost never went out. I went out with Chris, mostly on Saturday nights now, because Abner didn't care to "fight the crowds," as he put it. In fact, I rarely saw him on weekends, and the times he called to say he wanted to "bust out" were always on the shortest possible notice. I broke several Saturday and Sunday dates for him; for his lovemaking. But I began to suspect the obvious—that he wasn't just lying around reading or watching TV all those weekends. That his sudden calls on Saturday or Sunday afternoons were due to broken dates rather than simply wanting to "bust out."

At first I told myself it didn't matter; I was just using him for sexual excitement and release. But then I began to burn at the thought that the other girl had the coveted Saturday-night dates, the weekend dates. I spent several weekends visualizing him with another girl in his arms, heard him telling her he *loved* her, as he never told me, and it finally led me to phone him on a Saturday night. There was no answer. I phoned again Sunday afternoon, and he answered, and I said it was a great day to go to the park, drive around, have lunch in a nice restaurant. He sounded different—as if there were someone with him, listening. I asked point blank if he had another woman there. He laughed. He said, "I've got paperwork to do," and hung up. I called right back. Voice trembling with hurt and anger, I asked him where he'd been Saturday night. This time he was silent for a while, a long while, and then said, "I don't ask you if you see other men. I don't demand that you see only me. I expect the same courtesy from you." Again he hung up.

I told myself I would never see him again. But when Abner phoned me at the hospital Monday, I couldn't hold to my resolution. And I continued to see him, even though my suspicion of another woman in his life grew to a conviction.

While I was careful not to again humiliate myself by questioning him about other women, I tried to get him to talk about himself in general, in order to learn more about him, to grow closer to him; but getting him to talk *at all* was almost impossible. Still, over a period of time, I did learn a few things. He was a widower. His five-year-old daughter was living with a married sister back in New York. His wife had been a "drag" in bed, and he had always had women friends to satisfy his erotic appetites. And yet, he continued to carry her picture in his wallet—a cool, composed, aristocratic face with dark hair back in a bun—and I became jealous of that dead woman, as well as of the unknown other girl, or girls.

Abner hadn't been particularly ambitious when his wife was alive, but after her death he had begun striving to rise in the drug company. I asked if he had loved her very much, and his answer was a shrug and a muttered, "What's love?" I tried to comfort myself with this—he didn't believe in love. The most tender statement I ever got from him was after a particularly violent sex scene when he said, "You're the greatest piece of ass I've ever had." And yet, don't think that he was a crude, uneducated man. He'd graduated from New · York University, *magna cum laude,* as a chemist, and had begun graduate school when the money ran out. He had taught, been offered an instructorship with a grant to continue his studies, and had turned it down because his temporary job with the drug company had triggered his competitive nature. He felt he would soon be manager of the entire Western division. He wasn't currently considering bringing his daughter to live with him, "but someday, yes, of course."

I had two years of Abner, missing only those times when he went home to visit his daughter, which was about five days out of every three months. And I successfully resisted calling him again on weekends, and also resisted a growing impulse to spy on him those weekends.

One night, we undressed and I stroked his penis and wanted to put it in me, and he said, "No, pull it, pull it. . . ." I used a little Vaseline and masturbated him to orgasm. Then he reached under the pillow and took out a candle, long and thick, and set up the cheval glass, tilting it so that I could see between my legs. He kissed me, and inserted the candle, deeper, deeper, until I could actually feel him "touch bottom." Hunching over me, he worked it in and out. Crouching like some squat beast, some marvelous animal, he worked me, played me, strung it out until I was trembling, gasping, and then, looking down into my face, he whispered: "It's someone else in you, not me, someone else, and I'm watching; someone nameless and faceless who grabbed you; someone raping you, and you can't help liking it, and you can't help begging for it. Beg for it, Valerie. Beg!"

He'd stopped moving, and I began to beg. First I merely said, "Please," and then, when he shook his head, I said, "Move it, please," and when he moved it, but so slowly, so mildly, I said, "Ram me, for God's sake shove it into me!" And he increased the movement, but still not what I needed, and he made me keep begging, pleading, until the words were pure sex—"Fuck me with that thing, my cunt, my ass, *please* . . ." His fingers went to my rectum, and he put one in and two in, and even though it was killing me, he made me come, come so hard, so long, I felt I was fainting.

Afterward, he made love to me Mamma-Papa, and fell asleep without a word. And drove me home, listening to the news on the radio and hushing me when I wanted to talk, to say how much I'd felt . . . and was beginning to feel in other ways.

I'd never thought I could experience pleasure in pain. I'd heard of flagellation and masochism and De Sade and whips and boots and ropes and beatings and all the rest of it, of course . . . but *me* to get *pleasure* from such sick horrors? Nonsense!

He had me on my hands and knees one night, but instead of entering my cunt, he began pressing at my anus with his penis. Fingers, yes . . . but I looked back and said it was too big, he could never get in, and even if he did, it would hurt. He said, "Relax, press a little, as if you're moving your bowels." I laughed, but he was using Vaseline, and he was pressing again, and suddenly he was in me. It hurt like hell! I *begged* him to withdraw! He did, but he repeated that I should relax, press outward as if on the toilet, stop worrying about pain; and his hand came around one thigh and fingered my cunt, and I began to grow hot, and when he again pressed into my anus, it didn't hurt quite as much, or if it did, I didn't feel it quite as much, because his fingers had me going now. Also, the *idea* of his cock in me that way was exciting, and I began looking into the cheval glass, began watching the way he was hunching into me, that big, thick animal, and I melted away; I moved and groaned and felt pleasure; pain yes, but more and more pleasure. He held back a long time, looking into the mirror and meeting my gaze there, and then he began forming words with his lips, all the erotic words, mouthing them at me and moving in and out, almost all the way out, so that I felt I was finally ridding myself of that stiff thing up my ass. My orgasm hurt, because he rammed home very hard, to the hilt, when he saw I was coming. He came almost immediately afterward himself, which proved his skill, because this time I wouldn't have enjoyed waiting for his orgasm; this time pain swelled the instant my own violent stimulation was gone.

It hurt to sit the next day; and yet, it was a constant excitation, a constant reminder of Abner.

He broke me in quite thoroughly to rectal intercourse over a period of three weeks, and the time would come when I would *ask* for it, with my posture if not my words, even though the element of pain never left the act. (I didn't know about the dangers of E. Coli, an infection, then.) It was as if pain made it even more exciting; and when I mentioned that to him, he smiled and nodded. Our next few meetings were relatively normal—Mamma-Papa and doggy fashion and some masturbation.

We masturbated *ourselves* as well as each other. He wanted to see me masturbate, and while I'd done very little of it, I found I wanted to in front of him. And as I masturbated, he stroked his shaft, worked on himself, and we looked into each other's eyes and did it until we came, almost always me first, sometimes me twice before he did. Several times he would get to his knees and come on my body—my belly or my breasts. One time I was in such a frenzy that I pulled him over my face, and he came there, all over, and into my hair, and I watched him spurting and I wanted it to continue, like a fountain. . . .

Shortly after I admitted that the pain of anal intercourse was somehow adding to my pleasure, he spanked me. He had slapped my bottom a few times during play, but this was something else. He didn't undress me. He simply took the drink I had in my hand away from me and stopped me from going to the bedroom and right there in the kitchen hauled me over his knee and pulled up my dress and pulled down my pants. I looked back at him. "Have I been a bad girl?" He nodded. "Very bad. So you have to be punished."

It was straight out of those nineteenth-century erotic girls'-school books. I laughed. Okay, a cute game to lead up to bed. A little stimulation.

And at first, that's all it was. He spanked my bottom rather gently, and I wriggled about, feeling a definite warmth in my cunt, waiting for him to put his fingers and then his penis there. But the slaps grew harder, more stinging, until I let out a yelp and said, "Enough!" No, he said, not enough. Not nearly enough. And he really went at me. He hurt me so that I was crying and fighting to get away from the continuing blows. But he held me like a baby, helpless, and I grew furious with him, hated him, shouted I would never see him again, all this through sobs and tears. He never paused. And after a while I seemed to grow numb—everywhere but between my legs. There all my anger and hurt and fury concentrated into a raging heat. I'd stopped crying. I was panting, gasping, unable to get a full breath.

Finally he stopped and carried me to the bed and threw me down, and without undressing me further, dropped his pants and shorts and attacked me. That's the only way to put it—attacked me. Shut me up with a slap in the face when I tried to say he'd gone too far, and held me down when I reacted with new anger and didn't ask me to put it in as he usually did (if I wasn't already shoving him up me), but reached down and found the spot and slammed in. I came so fast I doubt he moved more than once or twice. He came too, but stayed in, and we went again—a long, furious bout.

I really think I hated him for a day or two. I know I refused to speak to him on the way home, except to say, "There are limits, you know!"

He nodded. He said, "We haven't reached them."

I actually turned him down when he called two nights later. He said, "Well, if you're busy . . ." and hung up. And didn't call the rest of the week.

I called *him,* to say I'd acted like a baby. I was bruised and aching, and every ache reminded me of how much I wanted him.

He beat me, attacked me, four more times that way, after which we entered another relatively normal period. Then he took me shopping one evening—for tall black boots. I knew what was coming, but I still laughed and said, "You must be kidding," when I saw the whip and the neatly cut lengths of rope he'd laid out on the bed.

He wasn't kidding. He *asked* this time, though. He said, "I promise you'll like it, but once I start, I won't stop. If you don't want any more after this evening, there won't be any more."

He'd never failed me, and I nodded.

He didn't fail me then, either. But how to explain it —the pleasure, I mean? He tied me, nude, to the bed, face down. I wasn't too uncomfortable, but I *was* helpless. Then he proceeded to walk around me, touching me here and there. He stuck a finger between my legs, and when I laughed, he slapped my rump hard. That ended the laughter, and I wondered if I shouldn't try to get out of it.

He walked around me again, slapped my bottom even harder. At that point I asked him to take it easy.

His answer was to pick up the whip, a homemade affair—half a dozen long leather shoelaces tied to a piece of wood. He drew back his arm, and I looked over my shoulder. I said, "Now, wait a minute . . ." He cut me across the buttocks so viciously I shrieked.

He said, "I'm sorry," and went to the kitchen. He returned with a dish towel and tied it firmly around my mouth. The next time he whipped my ass, my scream was effectively muffled. I was whipped about twelve times, and the same sense of numbness set in all over my body . . . except for the important part. And then he cut me across the back and thighs, and I continued to scream behind my towel and wept and wanted out of this game, this insane game . . . and then he grabbed my breasts and kissed me and reached under me and grabbed my crotch, grabbed and squeezed and said, "Scream all you want, bitch!" And I came.

I'm glad I don't have to tell this to you in person, Herb. I even had trouble recording this part; my voice was so low the first time, I couldn't make it out myself. It's not something I remember with pride . . . but with *passion*, yes! Because he whipped me three more times in the next year and a half, and each time I came with just a touch or a little fingering. And each time, we ended with such furious, such satisfying love that words just won't do.

I never actually asked for it, but I only refused it twice, and then because I was beginning to resent Abner's silences, the blank wall I ran into whenever I tried to discuss his emotions, how he felt about me . . . after I told him how I was beginning to feel about him.

I wanted this man. I wanted to marry him! I wanted his wild sex, yes . . . but I also wanted more. I could go just so long without the words of love. We'd been seeing each other twenty-one or twenty-two months by then. His silences were beginning to depress me, to *offend* me, and also beginning to remind me of what I'd managed to put out of my mind; my certainty that there had to be another woman in his life. What I hoped was that it wasn't *one*, but *several*.

I hate to think about those last two months with Abner. Even now.

Did I mention the ants and honey? That was the last great kick. It was also the least successful kick, but that may have been because of my suspicions.

We went out that night; one of our rare restaurant meals. I drank a bit more than is usual for me; and I talked a bit more than I should have, given his lack of response. I said that love could grow from passion; didn't he agree?

He shrugged.

I said that when two people shared *magnificent* sex, they could share other things, given half a chance; didn't he agree?

He called the waiter.

In the car, I said that I couldn't help it . . . I was beginning to care for him; didn't he have anything to say to me?

He said, "Let it pass."

Let it pass!

Pride took over then. I shut up. But I couldn't make myself say, "Take me home."

In the apartment, he took me in his arms and kissed me and ran his hands over my body, and said no woman had ever excited him more in all his life. He said it with intensity, with passion, and I believed him and I made myself believe that this was, in effect, a declaration of love. That was when he brought out the jar of ants and the jar of honey.

Very simply (if you can say that about something like this!), he tied me down to the bed, spread-eagled, smeared my breasts and belly and thighs with honey, and dumped the ants on me. When I began to scream, he covered my mouth with his hand and said, *"Feel!* It's just another sexual sensation. Think of those ants as males; little males running over your body, trying to find a place to stick their things. Soon they'll begin fucking your pores! Feel, and enjoy!"

I felt . . . but what I felt was fear and revulsion. I was beginning to panic when he finally brushed the ants off me, methodically killing every one of them, washed me with a soapy towel, and tried to get on me. But this was the one time it didn't work. It was at least two hours before I was able to accept his lovemaking.

When I asked him where he'd gotten the ants, he said on a picnic in the country the previous Sunday. When I asked *who* he'd been with, he shrugged and left the room. I jumped up and followed him to the bathroom. He tried to close the door in my face, but I pushed it open. He shrugged again, and sat down on the toilet. I insisted on an answer. He proceeded to defecate . . . and I ran out, raging.

I rarely had less than two orgasms with Abner in any one sex act, and sometimes three. I never, not once in the two years, failed to come to orgasm with him. He would sometimes finger me as we drove in the car, fantasizing about all sorts of things, and I would come.

I forgot to mention his fantasizing. It was the only time he spoke at any length. But, of course, he wasn't really speaking to *me*. I guess I forgot a few other games too; we did just about everything you can think of.

The fantasies took various forms. He would be an animal, a dog or wolf or even a bull, and barking or howling or bellowing, would attack and ravish me, from behind of course.

He would be the host at an orgy, and I would be subjected to various men of various races and nationalities . . . and *afflictions!*

And I had to respond in kind, play my part; and it *was* fun, and it *did* keep the juices flowing.

Once he pinched me all over until I screamed into the pillow, and that was like the whippings.

Several times he covered us both with cold cream, or mineral oil, and we made love slipping and sliding and gasping in laughter. I really didn't like that very much, though it was harmless enough. It offended my sense of cleanliness, neatness, and I hated looking at the sheets when it was over. But never doubt, it *worked!* Everything worked with that man.

He tied me to the bed once, legs wide apart, and tickled me with a feather, and brought me to orgasm without using anything *but* that feather. It took almost half an hour, starting at my neck and working down along my body and my sides and my thighs and down to my ankles and my feet, and then back up to finish by tickling my clitoris until I came, weak with laughter.

There were all sorts of crazy positions—on chairs, on the table, in the tub, standing, crouching, sitting, held upright on my hands—*everything*.

It all worked, despite my growing need for sentiment, emotion, *love*. It all worked, until just a week or two past our second year together, he went on one of his visits to New York. I drove him to the airport; he kissed me; he boarded the plane. A week later I received a letter. His promotion had come through, though not quite as he'd expected. He'd been made manager of the Eastern division, and he'd already arranged for his things to be shipped back to New York. "Good-bye, Valerie, and best of luck." And that was supposed to be the end!

I cried, raged, consigned him to hell . . . and wrote him the next day that I expected to spend my two-week

vacation with him, just as soon as I could. I mailed it to
him in care of his company, since that was the only
return address I had.

His answer was quick in coming—four days—and
was as terse as the way he spoke. I threw it away immediately, but I couldn't throw away the words.

Dear Valerie:
I was married this week to a woman I met in St.
Louis. I used to see her on weekends. I'd hoped I
wouldn't have to tell you.

                              Abner

I was sick. I didn't go to work for three days. I drove
around, since it was no good staying at home with
Mother. I took tranquilizers, and drank quite a bit. At
night I tossed, longing, raging, crying, wanting him . . .
and wanting to kill him. I'd never experienced such *wild*
emotions, and for the first time in my life I understood
how the terrible things men and women do to each other
that we read about in the newspapers come to take
place. I wanted to die . . . and I wanted *him* to die.

The next week, I took up my life, but I was still
suffering, and people at the hospital kept asking if I was
ill. I felt *debased;* he had used me as a rag, to wipe up
his passion, his semen! His dead wife hadn't allowed him
fun and games, so he'd had outside women. Maybe his
new wife, his weekend love, hadn't allowed him much
either, so he'd had *me*. I became hung up. I wouldn't
let anyone touch me, though I went out as much as I
could—to stop from thinking.

In addition to everything else, money was getting very
short; the crunch was beginning in earnest. I had to pay
an additional hospital bill when Mother had a relapse.
Christmas presents had come from various relatives, and
so, of course, we had to reciprocate. I was putting in as
much overtime as I could, but half of what I made
that way went in overtime to Mother's nurse. There
was about one thousand dollars left from the sale of the
house, and that would certainly be gone in six months.
Then what?

I was now twenty-five years old. I met a man. I guess

I always do. It was during one of those let's-have-a-drink sessions after work. He was an X-ray technician, and while I'd seen him around, I'd never really noticed him before. He was good-looking, very well-read, and very openhanded. I needed someone to spend a little money on me. He spent a lot, and he asked for nothing in return, except my company. He was cheerful, and he loved dining and dancing and movies and sports and theater. He spent at least two weeks a year in New York, taking in all the theater, ballet, and opera he could. He painted. He played the guitar. He wrote poetry. And he drank.

He drank quite a lot, but it didn't seem to be a problem. Anyway, I did a bit of serious drinking myself for a while.

We went out for about three months before he tried, gently, to make love to me. I accepted, and it was good. Not wild and not fantastic and not incredible, but definitely good. When it was over, he said, "Val, honey, I've watched you for two years. I think I loved you before we ever said hello. I want to marry you."

God, it was good to hear that! I wanted to say yes, let's do it now! There was only one thing stopping me. I didn't love him.

The way I put it to myself was, I didn't know him well enough to love him, yet.

I *tried* to love him. I tried for almost a year. I almost made it, until the night he came to my home, absolutely plastered, bombed, stoned. I'd never seen a man that way, except perhaps a skid-row bum stumbling along the street. He knocked on the door, and when I answered he said, "You don' love me, honey . . . why?" And he cried, rocking there with his mouth sagging open and his face all different; cried and said I was his last hope because he was slipping down a long, long tunnel . . . or something like that.

I brought him in. I gave him coffee, though that's a myth, and only the passage of time and the assimilation of alcohol by the body sobers a man up. I wanted him to sleep on the couch, since my mother was already asleep and he could be out by morning. But he wouldn't stay.

He left, and I worried about his driving home.

When he came to my office the next morning, hung-over and hangdog and mumbling apologies, I took his hand and said I was the one who should apologize. He didn't understand. How could he? I was apologizing for keeping him on the string so long when what he wanted was marriage. I was guilty.

But that was nothing compared to the guilt I felt a month later. He asked me to come to New York with him for a week of theater and general fun. I said I didn't think I could, but he pressed me, said he knew I'd lose a week's pay and would have to pay a nurse for seven full days, but he would cover all expenses.

I let him talk me into it. We went to New York and had five marvelous days, though he was drinking an awful lot, then drove up to Boston in a rented car to visit his folks. They were nice people. They liked me. But I couldn't wait to get out of there, because he had told them I was his fiancée.

I was cold to him on the flight back to St. Louis. I didn't say anything, but he knew the reason. He drank his limit on the plane, and bought a bottle near the airport, and after dropping me off at home, he drove away.

Want to guess the ending? The lousy soap-opera ending?

Correct. He killed himself and an innocent young couple in a head-on auto collision.

It was at this time that Gini and I began speaking about the wife-surrogate program. I'd lunched with her before, spoken with her before, but she knew that something was wrong, had heard about the accident, and might have heard gossip about Abner; and since she's a professional psychologist and a very sharp observer generally, she could see I was down, way down, and guessed I was close to cracking. I was invited to her home. I met Dr. Masters there, and we all spoke, and I was able to open up a little . . . and it helped. Not much at first, but little by little.

I went to the Foundation a few times and saw the setup—Dr. Masters' and Mrs. Johnson's offices, the conference room, the examination rooms, the lab—and we kept talking. They didn't rush me, and I didn't rush myself. The talk was an education—into their motives and methods; and I found I liked everything I heard. Still, I waited.

And I began dating in an entirely different way. I knew now, consciously, that I needed someone I could love both physically and emotionally, someone who turned me on but who also made me want to live with him, marry him . . . and I wanted the man to feel no less. In Abner's case, I alone had felt that way. He had been able to give passion, sex, and no more. In the cases of Ross, Chris, and my poor dead technician, they alone had felt the right way. In Paul's case, I had been a child, and he had been married. So as yet, I had not experienced a total love affair. Once I did, I was sure I would marry, and the search, the loneliness, the troubles would be over.

A woman can wait a lifetime for that kind of love, and not find it. I think most women, and men, settle for something less, something available and comfortable, but definitely less. I didn't seem to be able to.

A postscript. Abner called me. He was in St. Louis to set up a new regional organization. He wanted to see me. I was in my office at the medical complex, and I took a deep breath, preparatory to giving him the coldest possible rejection. But what I said was, "Where are you?" my voice shaking. He said the Forest Park Hotel, and that's where I went at five o'clock.

He let me in, took me in his arms, kissed me, kept kissing me as he undressed me and led me to the bed and made love to me. It was almost an hour before I was able to say a word. And then I said: "She doesn't seem to be taking much out of you."

He smiled thinly, and began to get up. I pulled him back down. "Show me her picture."

He said he didn't have one.

I got up and went to the chair on which he'd hung his trousers. When he began to come after me, I took the pants and ran to the bathroom and locked myself inside. He knocked on the door, said, "Valerie!" and knocked again.

"I won't sully the dear lady," I said, and found the picture in his wallet. She looked something like his dead wife—dark hair, cool and aristocratic features. There was also a full-length shot of her standing with a little child—his daughter, I assumed—and she was tall and lean and somehow sexless-looking. It was signed "Affectionately, Norma." *Affectionately,* to her husband; or at that time, perhaps, her husband-to-be!

When I came out, Abner was dressed and sitting on the davenport. I brought him his wallet and said, "Affectionately, Norma. Affectionate in bed too, I presume?" He took the wallet and put it in his pocket without answering. I turned away. I was still nude, and I got a stinging slap on the rump. I whirled and returned the slap, to his face, as hard as I could. His head rocked. He leaped up, and I prepared to use my fists to defend myself. Fists and tongue, because I said, "Like your first wife, isn't she? *Just* like her. A drag in bed, as you once admitted. That's the kind of woman you want in your home, as mother for your child. That's the kind of woman you think *right* for cook, maid, and bottle-washer. But what do you do when you need a lover? What do *all* men like you do when they want to *fuck?*"

He said, "Let's drop it, please, Valerie."

It was the first time he'd ever said *please* to me! And his voice begged along with the words. And so I knew I'd hit a nerve; knew I was close to the truth. And I wasn't about to stop!

"Undersexed women, that's the kind you and men like you have to marry. Because you probably believe—deep in your heart of hearts, your lousy psyche—that sex is *dirty,* that making love is *low,* that it's what your Mother and Father said it was—a bad thing, a naughty thing, little Abner, and don't ever let us catch you at it, you dirty-minded boy!"

He slapped me then. His face was white, and he looked as if he wanted to kill me; and it gave me the greatest satisfaction!

I didn't hit back this time. I stood there, stark naked, and spat my words into his face. "Look at me, Abner. I'm the girl you want to fuck, the girl you'd like to fuck every night for the rest of your life, the girl you *could* have fucked every night for the rest of your life if your mind wasn't so sick!" I ran my hands over my breasts and hips and grabbed my crotch. "Look, Abner. *This* is what you want, and you know it! This, not the woman you married, the one you're cheating on with me, and the one you'll cheat on with anyone you can get who makes you hot. I'm so sorry for you, Abner. You'll be masturbating too when she won't . . ."

He came at me, murder in his eyes, and I ran back to the bathroom. He began breaking down the door. He was saying, "Bitch, I'll kill you! Bitch, I'll kill you . . ." Just when I was beginning to believe him and panic, he stopped. I waited about ten minutes. When I finally peeped out, he was back on the davenport. I went quickly to the bedroom and my clothing. He said, "Valerie, don't go yet."

I turned. He got up and came to me. He took me in his arms.

"I'm right," I said. "Admit it."

He tried to kiss me. I turned my head away, tore free of his arms.

"Val, honey . . ."

"Admit it."

He went back to the couch.

I dressed and left.

He called me at home about an hour later. He began to ask to see me. I interrupted with: "Admit it."

There was silence; then, "All right, yes . . . but can I see you tomorrow?"

I said, "I'll be at your room at five-thirty," fully intending to cap my revenge by letting him wait there and wait there and never seeing him again.

But the next day I began longing for him. My revenge was fine, but it didn't change the fact that I still wanted this man, still loved him. So I went to him. And we made love until three in the morning. And I went to him the next night too, when he told me he was leaving in the morning.

That was the last time. He did call twice more over a period of a year, but I'd gotten off the hook by then . . . though, truth to tell, I *was* tempted.

Thinking back, I'm far more sorry for him than I am for myself. He married the kind of woman he felt he *had* to marry, and then was driven to find love with others. It's a miserable way to live, isn't it? And so many men live that way.

Now for a part of my life hard to explain . . . so I'll simply tell it, short and not-so-sweet.

Ross came back to St. Louis, as he'd said he would, to see me, to "try again," as he'd put it. And he kept telling me he loved me, needed me, wanted me. And God, how I hungered for just that kind of talk. And when I finally let him take me to bed again, he was so sweet, so tender, trembling with his need and pouring out his love.

Three weeks later, he asked me to marry him. It was a night of love, and of loneliness hovering just outside the periphery of love. If I said no, I knew he would go away, forever. And he wanted to take care of Mother. And he kept talking and touching and kissing, and I let myself *dream* it could work, and I spoke aloud in my dream. And what I said was, "Yes."

We eloped, and in two months I couldn't stand it, and had made *him* so miserable he was glad to fly to Mexico for a quick divorce. The only one *not* glad to get out of that marriage was Mother. We'd all lived together in the apartment, and she'd liked Ross and simply liked a man around the house. After Ross left, she could hardly believe it.

I could hardly believe he'd ever been there, it was all so ephemeral, all so unreal!

This brings me up to the time when I decided I was going into the wife-surrogate program. I discussed my life, my sex experiences, and my marriage with Gini and Dr. Masters. They felt that not only could I handle in-bed therapy, but that it would help me in my own life.

And so I accepted Glenn as my first patient.

After that first case, I went on with my life, and there *was* a change for the better. Maybe it was as simple a thing as appreciating the young, normal men I dated. But the money problems accelerated. The first surrogate fee quickly went for Mother's medical expenses. And with Christmas approaching, I began to get desperate. I needed gift money. I needed extra money for a nurse, because the one we used was taking a full month off, and the replacement we were able to find wanted about a third more for her short-term job.

That was the situation about two weeks before Christmas, when the Foundation called. They had a case for me. Not a young man, but younger than Glenn. In his fifties, and a member of a good St. Louis family. And, I was told, truly cultured, exceptionally good-looking, and a perfect dear. Nor was his problem too serious.

I didn't hesitate very long. I needed the money. And the description of the man I'll call Wallace comforted me. I said yes, and was told to come to the Foundation for my briefing.

3

The second briefing was much like the first. It consisted of a description of the overall program of treating those with sexual dysfunctions: taped interviews with Masters and Johnson, bringing out the salient psychological problems (as in most forms of analysis), and a transfer from words to action (for the single male via the wife surrogate) in a series of bedroom encounters. Again, the basic premise of our in-bed therapy was: remove all pressure, all need to prove sexual ability, so that responses become unstrained and natural. Make the patient understand that he has been an observer at his own matings, watching and fearing and therefore failing. Give *nature* a chance to take over. Then, when a good response is attained, repeat it, prove to the patient in the only way possible—by having him make love—that his dysfunction was temporary, and that he is now able to handle his own woman or women. And while this is going on, Masters and Johnson are interviewing the patient each day, listening, talking, engaging in what Dr. Masters calls "directive therapy"—the direction being sexual self-understanding, and later sexual ease and functioning, instead of broad-spectrum psychoanalysis. The combination of directive therapy and in-bed therapy (a simple process, actually; but then again, aren't all truly great and creative ideas simple?) has worked wondrously well in a large majority of their cases.

At my first briefing, there had been another element;

educating *me*, making *me* feel at ease and competent to handle the job. This Masters and Johnson had done easily and well. They knew, via our earlier conversations, a great deal about my sex life, and from this had felt I was able to understand and handle almost anything. They also had questioned me about my physical responses, and learned I was able to respond easily and well: I had no particular problems, such as needing a certain amount of foreplay in order to perform. I had no particular hangups—though, of course, they were not privy to *all* my mental stress and emotional needs; and, I guess, neither was I! What I mean to say is, so much that's coming out on these tapes is a revelation to *me*. Hearing myself say these things is often the first time I've been aware of them!

Well, between the first case, in October, and the second case, in December, was the Thanksgiving holiday. All holiday seasons are traumatic for me, associated as they are with my father, and with expenses. And then, Christmas—the worst of them all, emotionally and in terms of my finances. I know I'm repeating myself, but I have to stress this, because despite my accepting the second case without much resistance, there was *inner* conflict. I still hadn't reconciled what I was doing—screwing strange men—with what I'd been taught, with what I believe sex should be. I wasn't then, and am not now, a swinger in terms of enjoying any and all sex that comes my way—this despite Abner. I'm not suited to play the whore bit.

But back to case two. Wallace was, as I said, of a wealthy St. Louis family, well known locally. He was an attorney, prominent in several civil-rights organizations, donating his services in various cases, and had appeared before both state and federal courts in important cases in recent years. Altogether a man of considerable success, as are so many Masters and Johnson patients—since until very recently only the well educated and the well heeled have known and been able to afford their services. But in Wallace's case, since St. Louis was both his home and his base of operations, the problem was that of keeping everything secret. A hotel or motel was out, since he, at least, felt there was too much risk of being recognized.

About his home life. He was married, happily by all accounts, and had two sons and a daughter. He had begun to have failures a few years ago—just a few at first, but now increasing—and had spoken to his wife about using Dr. Masters. She had refused, feeling it was *his* problem, not hers, since she regularly achieved orgasm when he was functional. But it was more than that; she was a very shy woman, a very private person, and exposing herself to sexual analysis and therapy was unthinkable for her. But she *did* want Wallace to be helped, and agreed to his using a wife surrogate. Since she didn't want to be in St. Louis at the time, she had left for a week's skiing in the Rockies with two of the children. Wallace spent the usual three days in talk sessions and physical exams, and so he had four or five days until his wife returned. She hadn't said he would have to be finished with his treatment by the time she came back, but he had told Masters that's the way he wanted it. He couldn't, he felt, do anything with another woman knowing his wife was at home. It was something he could *not* be talked out of, and so we had only these four or five days.

Dr. Masters was of the opinion that this would be sufficient, taking into account the fact that Wallace *did* function at least half the time and that he had never tried other women. I was, however, to accelerate the process, getting into bed and proceeding to genital play on the first evening.

Wallace had been given my true first name, as I had decided that "Barby" or any other pseudonym stood between me and the patient. I had been given an address, an apartment number, a key, and considerable information on my patient. And despite the need to accelerate his treatment, I was also to use my own judgment on just *how* quickly to proceed toward the bedroom—this because Wallace was the result of money, private schools, a very starchy and moral upbringing, a dedication to career and worthy causes. He had slept with one girl before marriage, and none since. A paragon of virtue, who was beginning to fall apart.

He had made it absolutely clear he would not go out on any social evenings, would not dine out, would not be seen with me anywhere, would not meet me anywhere but the place Dr. Masters had rented (and was considering keeping for other such cases). It was all to be kept strictly undercover.

It was exactly one week before Christmas—seven days until Christmas Eve—and the weather was beautiful: crisp, cold, a feel of snow in the air.

I rode over to the apartment ahead of time to familiarize myself with the setup. It was nicely decorated; a living-room/dining-room combination, small kitchenette, bedroom, and bath. The closet held about a dozen robes, various sizes and colors—this in expectation that the apartment would be used for other patients. A liquor cabinet was fully stocked, and there was a hi-fi and television. There were both blinds and draperies over the windows, all drawn; lamps cast a soft yellow light; the entire place had a warm, snug look.

But Wallace wasn't there, and didn't show up for about half an hour; and in that time I was left to my thoughts. Once again I became prey to self-hate, shame, the what-am-I-doing-here feeling. Once again I thought of the men who, because of what they were and what I was, had led me to this apartment. Paul and Ross and Abner . . . and the others; the less-important others.

Finally I put on the hi-fi and danced along with some rock music, watching myself in a mirror. I was wearing a short skirt and matching jacket over a yellow ruffled blouse. I'd begun letting my hair grow, and it was getting long again and looked thick and shiny. My figure had always been good. My face was rather tired, I felt; there were shadows under the eyes.

The doorbell rang. I froze momentarily, then took a deep breath and hurried to let my patient in.

The man who stood in the hall made me feel better immediately. Gini hadn't exaggerated in the slightest. Wallace was, if anything, better-looking than her description. Six-feet-two, athletically trim, with a warm, appealing face topped by crisp, medium-long, graying black hair. And his voice was soft without trace of Midwestern accent. "Hello, Valerie, I'm Wallace."

I smiled and nodded, but he remained outside, holding on to a large brown-paper bag with both hands—until I realized he was waiting to be *asked* inside. I then said, "Won't you come in?" feeling a little foolish, wanting to giggle at this display of formal manners when before the evening was over . . .

He came in and went directly to the kitchen, showing that someone had taken him through the apartment before he'd agree to use it. He put his bag down on the table, saying it was dinner.

I began to unpack the meal, but he suggested a drink before dinner. He mixed two martinis, rather large ones, and served them over ice. His own was half gone an instant after we'd touched glasses, though during my briefing I'd been told that he rarely drank. He was terribly, terribly nervous, talking constantly in his quiet, well-bred way, but not saying much. And barely looking at me, either. He walked around the apartment, commenting on this and that, opened the closet, and closed it instantly on seeing the robes! I felt myself smiling, and hid it.

I finally managed to get him beside me on the davenport, where he finished his drink and sat rather stiffly. He was quiet for only a moment, then began speaking again. I'm sure that we spent a good fifteen minutes on the weather. I moved a little closer, sipping my drink, and put my hand on his thigh just above the knee. I moved it back and forth while speaking, a soft, seemingly preoccupied gesture. It must have had some effect, because he turned to me and smiled in a natural and charming manner.

A few minutes of that, and he said, "We really shouldn't wait too much longer."

I must have registered surprise, because he flushed and mumbled, "To have dinner, that is. It'll get cold."

I laughed, taking the chance that he would too. He did, though still red in the face, and we went into the kitchen, where I dished out our meal. Incidentally, it was a *great* take-out meal. Prime ribs of beef, medium rare, baked potato, salad, and a half-bottle of good red wine. I was hungry, and everything tasted perfect; but the conversation remained difficult and stilted.

He ate, and he had two glasses of wine—which I felt had brought us to the alcoholic limit set by Dr. Masters —and he tried, he really did, to carry on an easy conversation. But for most of the meal, he didn't succeed. It was after I'd cleared away the dishes and made some coffee that he began loosening up. Perhaps it was the martini and wine and food, warming his insides. Perhaps it was my walking back and forth, brushing past him on my way to the stove and sink . . . and when I served him, bending over and touching his shoulder with my breasts. Perhaps it was the questions about his family, because he began to talk about them, the things they did, the hopes he had for his children in terms of social work. He was very committed to social work.

By the time he'd finished speaking, we were done with our coffee, the table was cleared, and we were back on the couch, where I again put my hand on his thigh, a little higher, and stroked him as I admitted I was rather conservative, that in my family "good works" had been church charities and donating money for missionary projects. I added that I was beginning to feel differently, both personally and politically. This too seemed to have an effect, and he said something, his voice *very* low, that indicated we were making headway: "You'll have to forgive me . . . my being so . . . cold, but I've never dealt this way with a stranger . . . and now, I don't feel quite so . . . . strange. . . ." He was looking down at my hand, which continued to stroke his thigh. I waited to see if he would make a move toward me. When he didn't, I asked if he had much time to himself, to spend with his family, with his wife.

His answer indicated he didn't. The demands on his life in terms of business were sufficient to fill the time most men devoted to all nonleisure activities. And then there were the various social causes, and heavy work for those political candidates he felt worthy of support.

Despite all this, he always found time to stay in shape, to work out and swim at an indoor pool. The one thing he *didn't* seem to have time for was vacations. For a man in his high-income bracket, he had hardly vacationed at all. For example, in the last year he had joined his family for three days in the Bahama sun, then returned to St.

Louis while they stayed on for two weeks. They'd had several other vacations which he hadn't taken part in at all.

I began to want to try to help him; I mean, I the woman began to feel an involvement; not just I the surrogate wife under instructions from Masters and Johnson. When I caught him looking at my breasts, at my legs, I decided it was time to make a move. The hi-fi was still on. I went to it and found softer music. "Do you dance?"

He nodded. I waited. He rose and took me very gingerly in his arms, but I came right up against him, as if to say this is the way adults danced. We began to move, and despite his continuing nervousness and a trembling I felt throughout his body, he danced quite well. This was a man I felt could do *everything* well, and why that didn't include lovemaking was a mystery. Certainly no woman could help but find him attractive.

When the number ended and he withdrew, I asked him what his wife was like in bed. I said it just like that, "What's your wife like in bed, Wallace?" and then added, "I think it would be of help to know . . . and the only reason we're here is to help you." He hesitated so long I didn't think he was going to answer. Not that I really needed his answer. During my briefing, I'd been told what he'd said about his sex life. His wife was a good social partner, a loving and compassionate companion, but as repressed sexually as he was. They engaged in very little precoital play, and they *never* varied position —it was always male-dominant, Mamma-Papa. His one premarital experience had been the same—a quick and rather unsatisfying mating. He wanted his wife, but there was so much else to think of, and there was so little excitement in it lately.

He finally answered. He told me what he had told Masters, though briefly, mumbling part of it; but once it was out, he was obviously *looser*, and I had become far less the stranger. I was now privy to his problem, which he hadn't been able to accept, despite knowing my role here.

We were back on the davenport, and he very shakily put his arm over the top, and then allowed it to drop onto my shoulders. My hand was back on his thigh, quite high now, but still far from an aggressive sexual maneuver. I stroked him and felt his hand rub my shoulder and then my arm. I leaned into him, chatting so as to keep things natural . . . but no longer about the weather. I told him what I hoped we would do at this first session. I told him there was no reason to be uptight or nervous; nothing in the way of actual sexual intercourse could take place (though this wasn't entirely true: I was on my own, and could carry us into a female-dominant act). I thought he had relaxed sufficiently for the next step, and so I turned to him, smiling, looking directly into his eyes, definitely inviting him to kiss me. Again he hesitated, so long I felt I had failed; yet I made no further move. It was important, I felt, that he be the aggressor at *some* stage, and so I waited, not speaking, holding his eyes, until he very carefully, very gently, leaned over and gave me a soft, tender kiss. It was a most pleasant sensation, and I prolonged it as best I could, pushing up just a little with my lips when he began to withdraw, at which he came back down again, still gently, and held the kiss another moment.

It was *I* who withdrew. I took his hand and murmured, "Why don't we go into the next room and get more comfortable?" I didn't look back at him or give him time to answer; I simply rose and led him to the bed. He answered me just as we reached the bed. "Good idea," he said, and despite the tremor in his voice, I think he meant it.

I didn't undress myself. I began to undress *him*. I unbuttoned his shirt, and as it came off, I kissed his shoulder, his arm. Then I paused, and he got the idea and removed my jacket and then my blouse . . . and kissed me on the cheek. I let it pass this time, helping him off with his undershirt, kissing his chest. I then turned my back, and after fumbling a, moment—his hands were trembling very badly now—he unhooked my brassiere, and I faced him again and he took it off. His eyes went to my breasts, and his lips parted, but again he bent to my face for his kiss. This time I caressed his head, and while so doing pressed down gently. He got the message, and soon his lips were at my nipples.

I don't recall, but I must have made a sound, because he pulled away and asked if he'd hurt me. "No, not hurt . . . no . . ." and I brought him back to me. I was acting then, but not too much, because that first contact had really given me a thrill, reached me as a boyfriend's lips at my breasts would have. He stayed there quite a while this time, and I finally disengaged myself and unbuckled his belt and lowered his trousers. He raised first one leg and then the other, his entire body rigid . . . except for his penis. There was no sign of life under his trim boxer shorts. But that was no surprise; that was why he was here!

Still, I must admit I was slightly disappointed. I was reading my own growing pleasure and excitement into him; and that reminded me that I had to get more objective, pull back a little and work at this professionally.

He took off my skirt and my panties, and I waited so that he knew what I expected. He kissed my thighs and caressed my bottom, and I saw some life behind his shorts. I then bent and removed them, my face very close to his genitals, and in the course of drawing his shorts over his feet, I brushed my cheek against his prick. It lengthened perceptibly, but was still far from erect. Before rising from my knees, I stroked it, and then kissed it.

It had an effect, but not entirely as I'd hoped. He did rise about halfway, but his trembling also increased. I decided we'd better lie down, relax, get to the touching, the petting, and I told him so.

I remembered what he had told Dr. Masters about he and his wife never having this kind of sexual involvement, never really exploring each other's bodies, and so I had to lead him into it, train him to it, so that he in turn could lead *her* and train *her* and revive their sexual interest. I say "their," even though she hadn't shown signs of failure, because there is always a chance that part of a man's failure is his sensing a lack of true erotic response in his partner, no matter how well she *seems* to perform.

These two people had to learn to make love—not just to stick it in and jiggle. What had sufficed for years was no longer enough. And it was up to me, as wife surrogate, to *show* him the delights, the sensations, the sexual pleasure in touching and kissing and playing. After that, it would be simple. Yes . . . I felt, because of the briefings and because of this man, that once we broke through, he would function beautifully.

In bed, as I touched him and led *him* to touch, he became quite ardent, but still without a full erection. In fact, it had gone back down a bit. Yet he held me very tightly and pushed his genitals up against me; and I realized he was trying to perform, right then, right there.

And that was a mistake. And of course he didn't get it up and couldn't perform. I stopped him. I spoke to him. I told him it was pleasure enough simply to play now. I said he was exciting me, and I knew I was exciting him, but that I really didn't want to go any further this time. And all the time I felt his hands, his fingers, trembling violently as they moved over me. So frightened, so anxious, this successful attorney, this leader of society, this helper of the underprivileged! So desirous of simply playing the part of a man in bed, this handsome, distinguished much-more-man in so many ways than any I'd ever known! I really liked him. Had he had an erection, I'd have been happy to make love to him, knew I'd enjoy making love with him.

Oh, I forgot to mention something; rather important, I believe. When I first entered the apartment, I'd turned on several lights, among them a nightstand light in the bedroom. When we entered the bedroom, and before I could begin undressing him, he quickly stepped to the lamp and turned it off. I felt that was far from a good sign, but I refrained from commenting on it then. I would have other nights to teach him the pleasures of a clear view of a lover's body. And there was enough light from the living room so that we were able to see each other, in shadows, as it were.

We went on with the touching. He was still trembling badly, and his touch was so light, I was afraid he wasn't getting sufficient *feel* of my body. I kept maneuvering around, trying to make him grab hold of a boob, or my bottom, but he wouldn't. When I looked at his face in the shadows, he seemed full of wonderment, full of delighted surprise that he was actually doing as much as he was—touching a woman.

It wasn't good for our rate of progress, but somehow I liked it, was flattered and touched by it, responded to it so that my own touches, my own caresses, were legitimate and gave me pleasure. Once again my responses were taking over, strong ones this time, untinged by any dislike of the patient. I took his hand and placed it on my cunt and said, "Touch me . . . your fingers . . . touch me, Wallace," and at the same time I touched his prick, lightly, feeling the semihardness of it, and then grasped it, still lightly, undemanding, and fondled it.

His fingers were still fumbling for me. He truly didn't seem to know how to excite a woman digitally, this man who'd been married twenty-two years! It's almost unbelievable that a man and woman could live together so long and never explore each other's bodies. From what Masters had been able to learn, Wallace had simply come to his wife with an erection, and she had taken it and placed it in her, and in Mamma-Papa position they had gone along until orgasm, he always late enough to give her satisfaction, but all so cut and dried, so completely without sight and feel and the fun that comes from man and woman playing.

His fingers finally entered me. I was considerably excited, and I responded with wriggles and sighs, and he began saying my name. Over and over, he said, "Valerie . . . Valerie," as if he couldn't believe this was happening. We kissed, and the way he said my name brought me out of myself. I was with a lover—and yet I *had* to remember not to pull him onto me, not to maneuver him into a position where he would feel demands put upon his sexuality. So I let myself go just so far, and enjoyed his fingers churning inside me just so far, and pulled his cock just so much—and wanted him, wanted that rapidly stiffening tool inside me just so much.

He began to groan, and I felt a full-fledged hard-on in my hand. Slowly, saying we would play a little differently, I got astride him. Again I stroked his tool, again he groaned and called my name, and then his pelvis arched upward, showing me he wanted it. I was free to do it, and I *wanted* to do it, wanted to ride him to completion and satisfaction. But I waited, making sure, speaking a little, first saying perhaps we shouldn't, then saying that it was all right if we did, and even as I spoke I slipped him into me and lowered myself, burying him in me, and began to move.

He came quickly, but not as quickly as Glenn had that first time I'd mounted him. Wallace took about a minute, I'd say. It wasn't satisfactory in a normal sense, in terms of his satisfying a woman, but it wasn't too bad either. I was disappointed, but more for myself than for him! I quickly said he'd done very well, and he seemed to think so too.

I told him to lie still and went to the bathroom, washed, and came back with a warm, wet cloth and a towel. I cleaned him, dried him, and when he began to get up, said, "Let's relax a while, here in bed." He sank back, looking surprised. This too, I gathered, was not done in his marriage. I lay down beside him and took his hand. "Didn't you and your wife ever just hold hands when you finished lovemaking?"

He said no, and the way he said it showed he was becoming aware of how little *real* love he'd experienced. I felt it was time to make him talk about himself to me, and complete the process of changing me from stranger to an intimate—if only for a week.

I asked questions, and he answered, his voice low, his hand absolutely still in mine. I rubbed his fingers, and after a while his voice strengthened and I felt a corresponding growth of strength in his hand—his fingers tightening, beginning to squeeze and caress mine.

His background, as it emerged during our conversation, was one of upper-class liberalism; liberal, that is, in all areas but sex. He had been taught by both mother and father, and by a very dominant paternal grandfather, that sex was not really for enjoyment but for the procreation of the species. His private-school education hadn't weakened this very much, if at all, since he'd had nothing but contempt for those boys who didn't concentrate all their energies upon studies, sports, and accepted social activities. Screwing was *not* such an activity to Wallace! Neither was masturbation, which he considered truly degenerative. He was either fortunate or unfortunate (according to the frame of reference) to have as a prep-school roommate a boy of similar leanings, and he came into college not only a virgin but a full-fledged sexual repressive.

College had been a real shock for him, because here he met young men who considered it not only normal but absolutely necessary to try to have sex with every girl they dated, including those they both liked and respected. Wallace couldn't understand this. Still, some of these men were excellent scholars and athletes, and he was forced to accept the fact that sex outside of the marriage bed was not always criminal, low, and degenerate. But this had little effect upon his *own* activities.

He was too good-looking to escape female attention, and after making his letter in both basketball and football, he found himself invited more and more often to various sorority affairs. In his sophomore year he'd gone to a party with a particularly aggressive girl—and later learned that his football teammates had maneuvered him into the date. The girl was known for her generosity with handsome athletic men, and had already taken on about two-thirds of the varsity. (You know the type, Herb. There's one in every school, who wants to fuck the entire football team.) She got him to drink more than his usual beer or two, and in his car on the way to her home directed him to a lovers'-lane spot, where they parked and she came into his arms. He'd kissed girls, and even touched them, very tentatively, on the breasts, but this girl was out to add him to her list, and he soon found she was on his lap, her dress up and her pants and brassiere off. Animal passion fought with his background and training . . . and seemed about to win. But the girl overplayed her hand, *literally!* After much fumbling, she got his prick out of his pants, and he came before she could put him into her.

Now, this is *not* the way Wallace told it to me. He made it sound like Sunday prayers! But I got a clear picture of the scene anyway. He added that it was the first time he'd ever had an orgasm *except during sleep!* In other words, at the age of nineteen, not only hadn't he ever had sexual intercourse, but he had never masturbated or—until this girl—been masturbated by a female. Wet dreams were his total sex life!

Coming in the girl's hand had a traumatic effect upon Wallace. Once he admitted to himself that it had been delicious (his own word), he began thinking of it, and despite a continuation of his desire to remain pure until marriage, hungering for it. Yet he didn't call the girl or try to contact her in any way. When a week had passed and she realized he wasn't going to make a move, *she* did, calling his fraternity to invite him to "a little party."

It was, indeed, a *little* party—just Wallace and the girl in an apartment she shared with two other co-eds. The co-eds were out. Once again Wallace resisted. I mean, he just wouldn't move toward bed the way a normal man would. And this, rather than turning the girl off, intrigued and stimulated her. She figured he wouldn't be able to resist a brief sucking, and she was right. He couldn't. She'd no more than taken him in her mouth, with him gasping and protesting at the "incredible intimacy"—again, his words—than he came. By the time she'd brushed her teeth, he'd slipped out and gone home. And I mean *home!* He was so shook up that he drove all the way to St. Louis, where he played sick for a few days.

By the way, if my language seems rather . . . well, *stilted* on this portion of tape, it's because I'm remembering the way Wallace told me his story. The man managed to make cock-sucking sound like a meeting of the faculty of his university!

But it really wasn't funny. He was so terribly brainwashed against sex, so completely inhibited, that there was just no way for the girls he dated to bring him to an awareness of the pleasures of the flesh.

There I go again! Wallace actually referred to sex as "pleasures of the flesh"!

The aggressive girl gave up when she realized Wallace was actively avoiding her. Because she felt rejected, she didn't spread the word about his unmanly reticence, and Wallace's teammates assumed he'd made it and accorded him the grins and slaps on the shoulder and all the rest. So he was spared any further fix-ups and was free to date only nice girls—those, that is, who waited for a boy's advances. And they had a long wait with Wallace!

He finally lost his virginity in his senior year. The pressures of his sexuality had led him to several acts of masturbation. He felt immediate pleasure, he said, but long-range guilt. Still, it built up fantasies and lust, and these were concentrated on a hostess at a local restaurant. The woman—she was close to thirty, Wallace guessed—was tall and plump and big in the bottom. She always greeted him with what seemed to him an especially sweet smile when he brought a date to the restaurant, and he couldn't keep his eyes from that big bottom when she led them to a table. Once, when his date had gone to the ladies' room, she stopped at his table to say she had seen him play in that year's Thanksgiving game. He'd been in only a few minutes during the second quarter, and the fact that she'd remembered what he'd done—made a fine defensive play, tackling a pass receiver—indicated that she was perhaps interested in him. His fantasies had intensified, despite himself, and that same evening he'd gone to the bathroom and masturbated while visualizing her bending over, thrusting her bottom out at him. (An interesting point—even his fantasies were "controlled," since she was always wearing her clothing!)

About a week before graduation, his fraternity had a party, he drank a bit and found himself driving to the roadhouse restaurant. It was a weekday evening, and late, and they were just about closing when he got there. The hostess, however, said she would see he was served. He took a table, and she brought him the menu. He examined the entrées, without actually seeing them, wanting to say something to her, until she asked if she could be of help. At that, he looked at her, and something must have shown. She said perhaps he would like to skip dinner and have a drink at her place? He nodded. She smiled and went to get her coat.

He was then overwhelmed by fear, and almost left. He was actually moving toward the door when she joined him.

She lived just a few minutes from the restaurant in a small, cozy apartment, and as soon as they entered, she made him a Scotch and water. At that time he detested

Scotch, but gulped it down at once. She remarked that he must be quite a drinker and made him another. This time he nursed it awhile. They sat together, and she asked what he was going to do after graduation. He told her about his ideas of donating his legal services to various civil-rights organizations. At this, she very sweetly said that as far as she was concerned, "the niggers can all roast in hell."

It was a terrible shock to him. It went against all his deepest feelings and instincts. And you would think it would kill any chance of his making a personal approach to her. But it had just the *opposite* effect. Until this point, he had considered her sweet and kind as well as sexy. This, to his way of thinking, made it impossible for him to sully her with a sexual approach. But now, she had revealed herself, and he suddenly found himself kissing her and mauling her breasts. But what he really wanted was to get at that apex of his desires, her big bottom; what he really wanted was to make his fantasies reality.

She remained on the couch with him awhile, then stood up, murmuring the usual thing about "we shouldn't" and "it's wrong." For once, Wallace reacted as any other man, reacted as she expected he would. He too got up, and came after her. Laughing, calling him "her powerful football rapist," she struggled a little, and then melted into his arms. His hands went to her bottom; he grasped the big cheeks; he moaned, "Please, I must . . . have you." At that, her own appetite broke free. Gasping that she'd wanted him for so long, she took him to her bedroom, pulled off her pants, and threw herself onto her back, dress up around her waist. He hesitated. He wanted her, yes, but he wanted her over on her stomach, that big white ass open for his hands and his cock. He wanted—without knowing it—to go at her doggy fashion. His fantasies and his passion demanded he play with that ass, satiate himself with that ass, fulfill his long-blocked erotic needs with that ass. But he had no way of admitting this to her, and so he lay on her and fumbled awhile, and she took him in her hand and put him in her and moved a little, just getting ready for what she thought would be a good long fuck. And he came. The little boy that he was, sexually, had no skills, no frame of reference, no ability to do anything but relieve himself as he did in his wet dreams, quickly and without awareness of a partner.

That was his single experience in sexual intercourse until his marriage. And I couldn't help mourning it; couldn't help saying, "If only you had let her know what you wanted to do . . . if only you'd played with her, she might have taught you pleasure; at least begun the process of showing you sexual pleasure."

He said nothing, and I stroked his hand and promised myself that he would play with an ass, make love to an ass any and all ways he wanted to . . . once I freed that wanting, once I made him *know* what he wanted. And I thrilled a little at the thought!

He hadn't met his wife on his own. He was introduced to her during his first summer vacation from law school by his grandfather. She was of a highly placed family from Chicago, where his grandfather had business interests. She was soon to graduate from college, and had attended schools in Switzerland and France before deciding to complete her education in the States. She spoke four languages, was an expert swimmer, skier, and field-hockey player, and was pretty in a dark, generous-featured way.

They got along wonderfully from the very first meeting. They were alike in their interests, their considerable abilities, their liberal political and social opinions, their conservative sexual approaches, and their almost complete ignorance of how to make love.

It was a three-year courtship. No rash decisions for these two, or for their families! During those years, they talked much, kissed some, did a little breast and leg touching—but nothing at all in the genital area. Just once—the night he asked her to marry him—was he "carried away" and put his hand inside her panties. Under my questioning, he admitted he remembered that she was sopping wet.

So there they were, both with normal appetites, but abnormal blockage of those appetites. And despite marriage and almost nightly intercourse during the early years of the marriage, and three children, they hadn't really got rid of that blockage.

As Wallace described their sex life, before retiring, he would go to the bathroom to wash up. When he came out, in pajamas, his wife would be in bed, the lights out, the shades drawn, the covers up to her chin. He would slip in beside her, reach out for her, and if she was willing—which she usually was—she would come to him for a brief kiss or two. He would stroke her arms, her sides, occasionally touch her breasts (but she claimed sensitivity there), and then her legs would part, he would slip out of his pajama bottoms and climb onto her. By this time her eyes were firmly closed. He would put his penis into her—she was almost always wet enough so that lubrication wasn't necessary—then his own eyes would close and he would hold himself up off her body on his knees and elbows, so as "not to oppress her" with his weight, and plunge in and out. Luckily, she was a quick come, so he had no problems in satisfying her. Occasionally, when she didn't come quickly, he would hold back; this much he had learned from trial and error. She never *spoke* of it: they never discussed it, or anything else relating to sex; but her breathing was a fair indication of what was happening. She would also move quite a bit, helping him to his own orgasm, which generally followed inside of a minute. During orgasm, and at no other time, he would clutch her bottom. Afterward, she would immediately rise and go to the bathroom to wash. He would wait for her return; then *he* would go to the bathroom to wash. When he came out, she was almost always asleep. If she wasn't, they might talk, but not about their lovemaking. About his legal practice, about their children, about anything but what they had just done.

This life of theirs, with great successes financially and socially, and no change worth mentioning sexually, had gone on for over twenty years—and then Wallace failed to maintain an erection during coitus. He blamed it on an exhausting and disappointing day in court. Still, it was his first sexual failure and shook him up. He tried again the very next night, and succeeded; but, as he put it, "barely." He had a very mild orgasm, and it worried him. He failed again at the end of the week; and succeeded, but with that same mildness of sensation, the beginning of the next.

That was three years ago. The incidence of failure had remained roughly fifty percent, but, more importantly, the successes were simply ejaculations with minimum pleasure. His wife continued to have strong orgasms, and wanted him to have them too—"to be normal and happy," as she phrased it. They *both* seemed to want sex less for the true pleasure it gave than "to be normal and happy." And that, it seemed to me, was another indication of their problem.

Dr. Masters was obviously aware of this, but here I was in bed with Wallace, and my job required that I make certain insights of mine clear to him—by actions if not words.

But we had done enough for one night, and he was leaning over, trying to make out the electric clock on the bedstand.

He said one thing before he left (he left before I did). "Thank you, Valerie. You're a . . . nice girl." He looked at me, hoping I'd understand, and I nodded and smiled, because I did. He was telling me I was sexy, and yet I wasn't a tramp. He was saying he was beginning to equate sex with humanity and not with lights-out naughtiness.

I spoke to Dr. Masters that night. He was very pleased at how things had gone, and said he was looking forward to speaking to Wallace the next morning. He felt we had already made great strides in regard to Wallace's normal behavior, and that his opening up to me *verbally* was a very good sign. I almost *had* to become his friend —a "nice" girl—in order for the therapy to have any meaning. (My own thought was that if I were simply a whore, a cunt, then Wallace would continue to be repressed with his wife, who was a nice girl.)

The next day at the hospital, I received a call from Dr. Masters. Wallace had been *exuberant* about his experience the previous night, going on and on about me: my looks and my intelligence and my refinement. Bill wanted me to go ahead that night with a strong manual and digital approach, teaching Wallace to use his hands and fingers on my genitals before we attempted love-making. I remembered to ask what he thought about Wallace coming so quickly. It hadn't bothered either Bill or Gini, even less than it had bothered them with Glenn. It was simply the result of a big buildup and a great deal of tension. Tonight would be better; they were certain of it.

I must admit I was pleased at Wallace's reaction to me. I needed the compliments, even from a patient. And later that afternoon, I received a call from a man I'd met at one of the after-hours sessions in the neighborhood bar. He identified himself as Gregory. I couldn't quite place him, but he sounded nice enough, and asked if I would see him that evening. It was, of course, impossible. He asked to see me the next night . . . and I had to say I was tied up for the rest of the week. I wanted to explain, but how could I? He sighed and said, "Right," and, "See you," and hung up. Oh well, I couldn't even remember who he was.

I arrived at the apartment before Wallace and took off my coat and brushed my hair out in the bathroom. I looked in the medicine chest, and it was full of after-shave lotion, men's cologne, talcum powder, tooth-brushes, toothpaste, mouth wash, deodorant, shaving equipment—everything to make a man kissing sweet. I examined myself in the full-length mirror on the bath-room door. I was wearing a black velvet mini-skirt, a frilly long-sleeved white blouse with low-cut neck, large gold-circle earrings and a black velvet choker. My shoes were high-heeled and black. Then I raised my skirt and turned, looking over my shoulder. Wallace obviously had a thing for behinds: an ass-man, as the boys say. Well, he was going to get the full treatment tonight. I was wearing black pantyhose, and no panties. I showed through the sheer stretch nylon in a way that made me feel more than just a little wicked. Then the doorbell rang, and I dropped my skirt and went to answer it.

Wallace was there, with another big bag in his hands. He smiled at me and murmured, "How very nice you look." I smiled at him, said, "Come in," and thought, "How very nice *you* look." He wore a short coat with black fur collar, and it was open to show a gray tweed sports jacket and very lean, very fine deep-gray trousers. His hair was rumpled by the wind, and his face pink and glowing. I helped him off with the coat, hung it in the closet, followed him into the kitchen where he was unpacking our dinner.

Oh, yes, Dr. Masters had suggested that this time I get into one of the robes in the closet, and ask Wallace to do the same, and that we have our dinner that way, starting the feeling of comfort and intimacy rather sooner than we had the previous night. But the robes weren't all that good-looking, and because of the way I'd dressed, and because of how nice *he* looked, I decided that it would be better if we let the robes go for another night. Tonight, I wanted him to get down to that pantyhose and remember, perhaps, that hostess at the roadside restaurant near his college and what he had wanted to do with her.

Dinner was very good: lobster and clam chowder and mixed vegetables and wine. He ate quickly, looking up at me every so often, and while I normally take my time at dinner, I hurried too, realizing that he wanted to get to the therapy as quickly as possible—and that this was a good sign. We talked a little, and then I began clearing away the dishes, and he helped me. Soon we were on the davenport, sipping the last of our wine, and the next thing I knew he was kissing me with considerable fervor. Yet before the kiss was over, I knew that we hadn't come as far as I'd thought, because that incredible trembling was in his hands, his body: even his lips trembled. I drew back, put my hand on his thigh, and began moving it up and back. "Do you ever think of that hostess in the restaurant near your college? The one with the . . ." I tried to remember his exact words, ". . . startling rear development?"

He laughed at that, and then shrugged. "Not really. Not . . . as a person. But sometimes . . . the evening itself comes back. In fact, I thought of it at the office today, because we'd talked last night."

My hand moved a little higher, and he did something he hadn't done the night before—parted his legs slightly.

I took a chance. I moved my hand all the way up and stroked him through his trousers. And felt a hard-on. He grabbed me, crushed me against him, kissed me. I kept pressing his cock. He was definitely aroused, and his kiss was strong, but his mouth remained closed. He had never kissed me with open mouth, and I drew back and said, "Give me your tongue." He seemed startled. I moved back to his kiss, and opened my mouth, and finally his mouth opened, a little. I put my tongue forward. He remained passive. I really squeezed his cock and put my entire tongue in his mouth. His trembling, which had never left, now lessened. His mouth opened farther. His hand went under my dress, but of course there was no flesh to feel, what with the pantyhose. I felt the time had come to get to the bedroom.

This time when I rose, he was right with me. And he walked alongside instead of behind me. But again, in the bedroom, he moved toward the lamp, to turn it off. I said, "Please leave it on."

"But I feel so much more comfortable . . ."

"Please," I said, and smiled a little. "I want you to see . . . something."

He came back to me. I stood waiting for him to undress me. He hesitated a moment, the strangeness of undressing a woman in clear light still strong in him, after all the years of finding *his* woman in bed, in the dark, under covers. Then he began unbuttoning my blouse.

He got the blouse off, and the brassiere, and touched my breasts, and when I stroked his head and pressed down, bent and kissed them. He unbuttoned and then unzippered my skirt, and carefully drew it down and over my knees, and I stepped out of it. When he straightened, he was looking at my pantyhose. I began to turn, but by then he'd remembered to hang my clothing over the chair, making sure it was neat and straight.

I forgot to mention that. Wallace never took off an article of clothing, mine or his own, without hanging it somewhere, neatly. I'd hoped, this time, what with squeezing his cock on the davenport and his being obviously more excited than the night before, that he would forget neatness for once. I guess I was expecting too much. Anyway, he spent a moment making sure the skirt and blouse were just so; then he finally turned.

I'd bent to the bed, taking off the spread, drawing back

the covers. I heard his intake of breath, and glanced back at him. He was staring at my rear in its see-through black pantyhose. I said, "Honey, help me."

He moved slowly, slowly, almost as if in a dream. He couldn't seem to tear his eyes from my ass . . . and I wondered if he were seeing another ass, a lifetime ago, an ass he had lusted after and denied himself. He came to me, and then he was bending past me to help with the covers!

Unbelievable, what this man had done to himself! Unbelievable, the deep-rooted denial of pleasure!

I said, "Touch me."

He knew exactly what I meant. But once again, he was shaking like a leaf.

I deliberately turned my back on him. I bent over, slowly, jutting my ass out at him. I felt deliciously sensual doing it! I *wanted* him to do things to me there. Not for him alone, but for me.

At first I barely felt the touch. Then his hand stroked my cheeks. Then both hands were there, squeezing gently, and his breath began rushing, panting.

"Harder," I said. "Please, honey, more, harder . . ."

He pulled down the nylon. His hands stroked my flesh, squeezed me, but all on the cheeks. I reached around back and grasped one hand and shoved it into the crack. I said, my own voice full of panting breath, "Your fingers . . . *in* me . . . go *in* me, Wallace!"

And guiding him, and rotating my bottom lustfully, I got him to trace the cleft between the buttocks, to insert one finger and explore my rectum—and finally, to my delight and surprise, I felt his mouth pressing my bottom, kissing my bottom. It was too much to expect that he would tongue me—that was graduate-school technique —but his kisses were fervent and his hands grasped my thighs, on the insides, and I squirmed and moaned, "Wallace, honey, yes, yes," putting it on a bit, of course, but enjoying it nevertheless.

He stopped kissing. I looked back. He had straightened and was tentatively touching his belt, staring at my ass, and then, guiltily, jerking his eyes to mine. I said, "I want you to do it."

"What?" he whispered, voice hoarse.

"Whatever you want. I want you to play with it, make love to it. . . ."

He shook his head a little.

"It's why you're here. You're not incapable, Wallace. You're perfectly able to have erections and to have sex. *You're just bored with the dull sex you've been having!*"

"Sodomy," he whispered. "Unnatural acts . . ."

I laughed. He flushed, but I laughed again. "Say that to Dr. Masters and see what he tells you. You're a lawyer. You've heard the phrase 'consenting adults,' haven't you? Everything is legal, is natural, between consenting adults."

I would have gone on, but it wasn't necessary. He was dropping his trousers and pressing his stiff prick into my ass. At first he simply stood there, eyes almost closed, holding his breath, an expression of near-pain on his face. Then he began to move, slipping his prick into the crack, rubbing it up and down. His hands came to my hips, and he crouched for better positioning; and then, believe it or not, he looked down at his feet, at his rumpled trousers, and backed away and took them off, and the shorts too, and went to the chair to hang them up. And concentrating on the clothing—his cock rampant—took off shirt and tie and T-shirt and hung each of *them* neatly, carefully!

I waited, bent over irritated, the good turned-on feeling just about gone, but telling myself to stay still and give him his chance. When he came back to me, he had begun to soften. He stood behind me, and I backed into him and rotated my bottom, and felt him come up good and hard again.

His hands returned to my hips, his cock to the crack of my ass; his body moved, hunched into mine, and I began to remember Abner and his wild anal attack. But this was no Abner. After a few minutes his movements slowed. I glanced back at him, and he looked as if he didn't know what to do next. He'd satisfied his taboo desire to play with a woman's bottom—at least for the moment.

I bent further, and murmured, "Try coitus that way, Wallace. Go in from behind. Go on, dear. I want it so!"

He tried. He didn't know how. I reached back and

guided him, my knees beginning to ache, my back straining. But I didn't want to change position, even for a moment. I wanted to break through with this automaton! He had to flame up and ram me and make love like a man! He *wanted* to. I knew it! Why couldn't he!

And I knew why, and it didn't make any difference at that moment, and I acted as if I *had* to have his cock in me . . . and managed to get it in. I bent further. He slid deeper inside me. His hands grasped my waist the right way and began supporting me. And finally, we were fucking and he was gasping and I began to *feel* it, to *love* it, and time didn't mean anything anymore, and my aching knees and back were forgotten, and crying out his name, I came.

But *he* hadn't come—though he continued to move— and glancing back at him, I knew he was beginning to lose steam, to fear loss of his erection. The "sodomy" and "unnatural-acts" concept had been with him too long. I'd made a mistake pushing him beyond just a little play with my ass.

I straightened, unsheathing him. I turned, smiling, and hugged him and thanked him for the wonderful lovemaking, and pushed him gently backward so that he sat down on the bed. His cock was at half-mast. He looked down at himself, and suddenly got up. I asked where he was going. "To wash," he said. I wanted to tell him it wasn't necessary, that he would soon be back inside me again, but he was too fastidious for such ideas, and I let him go. Lying there, waiting for him, I wondered if the two more sessions left to us were going to be enough. What had seemed a really easy case now was beginning to shape up as one with pitfalls. I could almost hear Dr. Masters' disappointed comments. I began to feel guilty. There *had* to be a way to free this man's passions, and quickly.

He returned. We lay beside each other. I remembered what Bill had asked me to do, and we began touching, stroking, petting each other. His cock began to reassert itself. He began to breathe heavily again. I turned this way and that, and finally he grabbed hold of a breast— almost as if he'd remembered something. I smiled to myself, because of course he *had* remembered something:

Bill's instructions at this morning's interview. I'd mentioned to Bill and Gini that Wallace didn't seem to know how to grasp a breast, or a bottom. Well, he'd grasped a bottom, and now he was enjoying a breast. And breasts didn't seem to hold quite the taboo feeling for him that bottoms did.

He kissed my shoulder, my lips, and I guided his head down to my breasts. He spent quite a while there, sucking the nipples, and I turned on again. He was good to look at, and good to feel, and good to be with—when he wasn't playing the neat old lady. I felt my nipples stiffening, felt my crotch warming, and took one of his hands and moved it down over my belly to the thatch of hair. Just as last night, he fumbled around, feeling for the crack and not finding it, and again I was amused, and amazed, at how little he knew! He had *never* played with his wife's cunt, not in all the years of their marriage! The poor girl didn't know what she was missing!

I helped him again, pushing a finger inside me, and he wriggled it around, and of course I began to feel good and hot. I shifted weight, trying to get him to find the right spot, and finally said, "Did Dr. Masters mention the clitoris?" He murmured unintelligibly and fumbled a while longer, and then I said, "That's it . . . the little button . . . yes . . . there . . . *yessss,* oh!"

He really went at it, rubbing the poor little thing with far too much vigor. It became uncomfortable, and I told him to be gentle, to work *around* the area. (As Dr. Masters has pointed out, strong manipulation of the clitoris itself is *not* the stimulating process it's supposed to be. Actually, most females prefer *indirect* clitoral stimulation —a light touching, with most of the action in the general area.)

He said, "How stupid of me!" and stopped completely. I kissed him and put my hand down and moved his fingers for him. When he had the proper place and rhythm, I let go.

He only needed to be taught. Once he began to gauge my responses, he worked me beautifully. I began to writhe, and my arms went around him, and I tongued him and he returned the kiss, and before I knew it, I'd come again.

I paused for breath, and realized he was terribly excited. Unlike the rear entry, he had been able to *see* my orgasm, to read it in my face, my arching body, my gasps. His cock was not only rigid, it was wet at the tip. He was holding me, uncertain of what to do now that I'd come, and I ended the uncertainty by grasping his cock. But I was pleased at his awareness of me, pleased by his lack of sexual selfishness—though it really wasn't that good for *him*. I squeezed and stroked his cock, and we kissed, and he began to move against my body. But he still wasn't lost to passion. I wanted him *raging* hot.

I began kissing his body—shoulders, arms, belly, thighs. I got down there and licked his balls. And then I took his cock in my mouth and sucked.

He gasped. He said my name over and over. "Valerie . . . God, Valerie . . . no, don't. . . ." But he didn't try to get away, and I didn't stop. They were words from his past, associated with unnatural acts, and the past had to die tonight. I sucked until I felt that peculiar swelling, that near-to-bursting feeling in his tool; then I stopped, knowing he would soon come. Not that I'd have minded. But he had to screw. He had to get on me.

And he did, as soon as I lay down beside him. I spread wide and put him in me, thrilling to his groan as his shaft came in. He began to move strongly, violently. And I moved too, hot again and rising toward orgasm!

He didn't come quickly this time. And he squeezed my breasts and grasped my bottom and kissed my lips and said my name. He made love, and I knew it was going wonderfully, and I was able to forget being a wife surrogate and became his lover, his woman.

We made love. We went on at least five minutes. And I couldn't hold back and told him I was coming and begged him to give it to me, every last ounce of cock, sock it to me, and the words made him wild—the words he never heard from his wife, the words that proved his woman was enjoying it and not just *tolerating* it. He came immediately after I did.

As soon as his spasms were over, he tried to get off me. I held him tight. I whispered, "Stay with me. Hold me. Please, Wallace."

He kissed me. He held me. We lay there, and I was

happy. I'd been loved, and he was kind and good, and I cared for him and felt he cared for me. At that moment, we were man and woman, not patient and therapist. And that was what in-bed therapy should always have been, and rarely was.

It was snowing lightly when I drove my car from the underground garage. I put on the radio and heard Christmas carols. Snow and Christmas carols—enough to send me into a deep depression, normally. But tonight . . . tonight I felt fine. I was giving a man the greatest Christmas present he could possibly get—manhood, pleasure in his body. And he had given me a present too—a wonderful physical release, and the beginnings of a renewed belief in myself as a woman. Not to say money to help pay the holiday expenses! I had hit my low point for this lifetime, I felt. I was on my way up again. Good things would soon begin to happen.

And when I got home, it looked as if I was right. I'd had a call from Greg, whoever he might be. But at least he was persistent! And he'd left a return number. I called it; we chatted; he tried again to remind me of who he was; I failed again to remember. He asked just when *would* I be free. It was Wednesday. I said, "By Saturday, I believe."

"You *believe?* Am I playing backup to someone you . . . ?"

I quickly said no, it was business, and I didn't know if I'd be called on. "Could we make it tentatively Saturday night?"

He sighed. "If I didn't want to get to know you so badly . . ."

I asked him what he did. "Lawyer. Oh, very much the junior member of the firm."

I asked how he'd come to be with the hospital group in the bar.

He explained that one of his closest friends was a surgical assistant. Greg had seen me only once, a few weeks ago, when he'd been introduced to me by his friend. "But there were at least a dozen people around you, and everyone was drinking and talking, and I'm not sure you actually saw me as you nodded."

I *hoped* I hadn't! I remembered a few men I'd met at

the bar recently, none of whom had been anything for me. Could Greg be one of them? Could that bright, appealing voice and warm manner be attached to a nothing appearance? Well, even so, now that I'd spoken to him, looks might not be quite that important.

But I knew better. A man doesn't have to be *handsome* to appeal to me, but he has to have a certain physical presence—a *chemistry* for me. I've tried overcoming this feeling several times—I think this was partly the problem with Ross—but I never succeeded. Abner, while far from the traditional handsome man, did have obvious male charisma, even before he showed what he could do in bed.

But I had a date with a new man. That in itself was hopeful!

The next afternoon, I called Dr. Masters to find out how the interview had gone. Wallace had been delighted with me and could hardly wait for our next session. Well, I wasn't exactly dreading it myself!

The next evening, Wallace was waiting for me, and in one of the bathrobes. He said he'd gotten a cold dinner this time, "So it can wait a while, can't it?"

I nodded, smiling, and he took me to the bedroom and undressed me, and while he still hung up my clothes, he did it rather more quickly and less carefully than the night before. And the lamp had been turned on, and was left on. In bed, we played with each other, and at one point I rolled over and presented him my bottom. He dry-humped me, sighing and groaning and saying my name, and after a while he became so fervent I felt he might come there. I disengaged and rolled over, and before I knew it, he was on and in me!

We had a very good go. I came quickly and went on another two or three minutes until he came. We lay locked together, and he didn't go soft. I commented on this, saying he was very virile, and his look and his kiss showed me how much this meant to him. He called me his "lovely witch" and said I'd cast a spell of love and passion on him. He went on speaking this way, stiff inside me, my arms and legs locked around him, and little by little he began to move again.

The second go was long and wild and as complete a

sex act as I could've hoped for. We both came, almost
at the same time—which was fine, though, as Masters and
Johnson have pointed out, it isn't the *necessity* that some
marriage manuals have made it out to be. It's rare, and
it isn't of any particular importance, and Dr. Masters feels
that *striving* for it can be a deterrent to natural, unthinking sex. Just so long as *both* partners are satisfied—
have sufficient time to indulge their lovemaking as well as
their orgasmic needs—the act is successful.

We had dinner, *nude*. I simply said I was warm, and
then asked him to allow me to enjoy his handsome body
while enjoying the king-crab salad and white wine. Before the meal was over, he was reaching across the table
to touch my breasts, and even though he obviously didn't
want any more sex, we did play a little. He kissed my bottom after I'd put on my dress but before I slipped on my
pantyhose. He liked the idea of raising the dress and
getting at me.

Tomorrow was to be our last meeting, as Wallace's
wife would be back Friday morning.

I tried something the next night. It was necessary, I
felt, because I hadn't made Wallace lose his hard-on and
then regain it. I sent him to the kitchen for a drink, and
when he returned I was in bed, the covers up to my chin,
the lamp off. He got in beside me, and I spread almost
immediately. After a moment's hesitation, he obediently
got on me—and went soft.

I explained that I'd done this deliberately, to show him
that his failures had been due not to any physical disability, or even a mental hangup (as with most patients),
but simply because sex had become a bore with his wife,
and by duplicating their marital technique, I had been
able to make him fail with me. Then I threw back the
covers and put on the lamp and went down on him, sucking his cock into a fine, red, throbbing erection in no time,
and paused to say he had to teach his wife to do this. I
also put my body in such a position as to invite *his* mouth,
but while he kissed my thighs and *around* the genital area,
he just didn't get down to eating pussy. It was expecting
too much from him, after only four sessions. Besides, I
wasn't his wife, his *real* lover, and it was with *her* that he
would have to do everything. I made a point of saying this:

"You should learn cunnilingus, Wallace . . . with your wife. Sixty-nine is a good way to go about it, each serving the other. You should teach her everything we've done together."

He nodded, but he was in no mood for discussions. He wanted my ass again. He was raging hot, panting for it, and entered my cunt from the rear. Tonight, I worked like crazy, as wildly and erotically as I could, and he came in me that way. Strangely, I failed to come, though I was close to it. I guess I was beginning to feel the "withdrawals." It was our last night, and reality was setting in again; if I was to find erotic joy, it would have to be with a date, a lover, and not a married client.

We had a drink, in our bathrobes, and he opened mine and I opened his and we played—and for the second night, he had a second go. This time I sat on him, and when I wanted to get off, he begged me not to, saying he loved it, he wanted it that way. I gave it to him that way, and came long before he did. We went on and on. I began gasping, and he began to show signs of coming, and I begged him to hold out a little, just a little, and he did, and I came a second time, clutching his arms and biting his lip and moaning that he was wonderful, wonderful . . . and I meant it.

I said good-bye to him. He kissed me, and then he stepped back, holding my hand, and gave it a little shake. He said, "Thank you." I nodded and left.

That should have been that. But the next morning, I got a call at the hospital. Wallace's wife wouldn't be in until evening. Could I manage one more session—an abbreviated one? Wallace wanted it badly, and it would certainly be good for him, nail home the lesson that he'd taken a lifetime to learn.

I said yes without hesitation. I was reacting as a woman now—not in love, but definitely desirous of another chance to *make* love to a likeable, attractive man. I was to be at the apartment as soon as I could, going directly there from work. (Wallace would have to leave at about six-thirty.)

I was there at five-fifteen. We went directly to bed, hardly speaking. He kissed me and petted me, and then maneuvered his body and my head in such a way as to ask for fellatio. I sucked him. When I felt that special swelling, I tried to withdraw, but he gasped, "Valerie . . . just once . . ." and pressed my head as if trying to get his cock all the way down my throat. It turned me on, *wildly*, because he was finally free of all restraint! I sucked him and sucked him, and at the last moment he tried, weakly, to withdraw. I didn't allow him to. I sucked him dry, swallowing every last drop of semen, showing him what it was to *want!*

Afterward, we simply lay there. He finally said, "I'm sorry I can't make love to you . . . but I've never been so *satisfied!*"

We kissed. We dressed. Again he held my hand and thanked me . . . and smiled. He was too happy to allow a leave-taking to get in the way. I walked out, and again I thought, "That's the end of that."

It wasn't, but I wouldn't know that for almost two years . . . which I'll explain at the chronologically proper time.

In conclusion, I felt that Wallace was ready to teach his wife to play, to engage in *real* sex. I only wished I could be sure that the wife would be willing to learn! The fact that she had refused to accompany Wallace in treatment was certainly a poor omen for the future, and her allowing him to take such treatment with a young woman was another. Some wives, it seems, aren't jealous that way, or perhaps they don't really *care* enough for the man to be jealous. They should be, in my opinion, if they want to stay married!

It seems that Wallace's wife was just too shy, too inhibited, too much the "classic lady" to involve herself in sex therapy. But shy, inhibited, "classic ladies" make the worst lays; and that, in turn, makes neurotic, hung-up, impotent men!

Well, the case was finished. I liked Wallace, but quickly dismissed him from my mind and got back to my own life. And back to a certain degree of gloom and blues, as Christmas was only a few days away and Mother wept that Thursday night, and Friday night, and Saturday as I dressed for my date; wept to think of what our holidays had been with Father alive and she well.

Greg knocked at our door at eight o'clock. I opened it,

and we looked at each other, and he smiled and softly said, "Wow." I was wearing black leather boots and a dark suede mini-skirt and matching suede vest over a very wild, puffed-sleeve hippie blouse—not too far out, according to my tastes, for a sporting event. He'd bought tickets to the Blues game, after asking whether I liked hockey. I was wild about it, at the time. (Almost everyone in St. Louis is hipped on sports; baseball or football or basketball or hockey: we have good professional teams in all four.)

I wished I could have said "Wow" back at him. He was short, about five-seven or -eight, and lean, and his face was nothing you'd remember for long. Nondescript is perhaps too strong a word for it, but it was bland. Neat and kind and bland. Or so I thought at that first sight. He had thick black hair, cut too short for my tastes, and his clothing, while obviously good, was a little too square. The total man, I felt, was square.

I was wrong; so very wrong!

The Blues won their game, making us both happy, but it was a one-one tie right up until the last two minutes, and so we didn't have much time for conversation, unless you count cheers and anguished screams! Afterward, he took me to a little Italian place where he knew the management, and we were served a truly superb meal, and during the meal he talked. No *bon mots* or unforgettable witticisms. Just a soft, rambling description of the traveling he'd done after law school—two years of it, or until eight thousand dollars left him by his grandmother had run out. He'd felt that once he got to work, the world would be lost to him, "except on two- and three-week vacations, and that's not experiencing the world."

He described the year he had spent in Scandinavia. He'd especially loved Oslo, a city not too many tourists remember with particular enthusiasm, but he had eaten and drunk in its student cafés and met its writers and artists. He went on about driving all over the Continent in a battered little Volks; then ended by saying, "But I made a mistake with that trip. Instead of wrapping up the world for myself and then being satisfied to practice law in St. Louis or Chicago, I planted a dream, and it's grown, and I'm going to give up law one day and go back and do something, anything, to live free in Oslo, or perhaps Copenhagen."

He was thirty-two, and in dead earnest about going back to Europe. "I'm just waiting for the right girl to take along with me." His eyes fixed on mine, and I looked down at my *caffè Strega* and felt a sudden . . . well "hunch" is the closest I can get to it. Because the chemistry, which *hadn't* been there from moment-one, was definitely developing now. Greg had a very strong and very attractive personality, and he was getting better-looking by the minute to me.

He asked if I were free the next afternoon. He wanted to walk in Forest Park and go to the zoo, and if I skated, skate with me at the rink. I said yes to all three. He smiled, and my heart leaped. He took me home, kissed me on the cheek, and was gone.

The next day, Sunday, there was another light snowfall; nothing to make driving bad, but enough to powder grassy areas with white. Forest Park had never looked nicer. We walked, and he took my hand. I said, "Wait," and removed my glove. He beamed at me. I wondered how he had managed to remain single this long with such a devastating smile!

My hand was much warmer in his than it had been in its glove, and we walked and talked. And on a quiet path, alone for a moment, he took me in his arms and kissed me; and I felt the need in him, and felt an answering need in myself that shook me to my toes!

We didn't go skating. His apartment wasn't far from the medical complex, near Kingshighway Road, a street of two-story brownstones covered with ivy and occupied mainly by well-to-do students. He liked the university atmosphere, he said.

We kissed again, in his apartment. We took off our coats and came together, hard. He said, "Valerie, don't laugh, but I think I've waited all my life for you," and I said, "I won't laugh, Greg," and felt tears in my eyes. The chemistry was there, all right, all I could stand; and when his hands went over my body, I wanted to faint!

Okay. So the prose flickers faintly purple. So I'm gushing a bit. But it's still nothing compared to how I actually *felt*. I'd been waiting for love, and it was coming at me head on, and I was so ripe for it, so ready for it.

We went to bed. My God, it was Paul and Abner and every strong bit of passion I'd ever had from anyone else, all rolled into one. Nothing fancy. We simply held each other's nude bodies, touched each other's nude bodies, and then fucked four times in the next two hours. It was all Mamma-Papa, because who could bother with fancy positions when what we wanted was to *look* at each other and speak to each other while we satisfied each other? I felt it would be a long time before we bothered to experiment with positions. I felt it would be a long time before we would be able to stop looking into each other's eyes as we loved. And I understood, for the first time, the attraction of that position—not for missionaries, who said it was the least lascivious and therefore the lesser of evils (*all* sex being evil, to them), and not for weary husbands and wives who simply had no desire to do anything but come as quickly and painlessly as possible—but for people in love, who want to be as close as possible, face to face, every minute of their lovemaking.

Afterward, we drank Scotch and held hands and tried to think of what else to say, because we'd said it all in each other's arms. He'd said, "I love you, Valerie, and I want to be with you always," and I'd said, "I love you, Greg, and want to be yours forever," and then we'd gone wild with fucking and said the other things, the lovely erotic words that fade with the fire; but the I-love-yous don't fade. At least they didn't for us, because after a while he leaned over and brushed my cheek with his lips and said, "I meant every word, Val. I hope you did too, because you'll have trouble getting rid of me."

He took me home. We sat in his car and held hands and watched thin snow drift down past the street lamps. Then he said, "I hope you have no plans for Christmas and New Year's. I've never spent them with a girl I loved. I don't think I could take not spending them with you."

I said, "If I had plans, I'd break them." And I realized that I too had never spent the holidays with a man I loved. At last! God, at last the grim times, the sad times, were coming to an end! From the worst time of the year, Christmas had suddenly become the very best time!

Greg had dinner with us Christmas, canceling out his trip back home to Chicago and his family. New Year's Eve, we danced in a little supper club, then hurried to his apartment to make love while the horns and whistles sounded and the people next door yelled and played music and went through all the nonsense of partying.

Three beautiful months passed, and passed more quickly than time ever had for me before. Greg talked about Europe, for both of us. He also talked about the realities of his income, and that wasn't too good. He hadn't risen very high in his firm, and wasn't likely to because of his wanting to get back to Oslo and Copenhagen. Yet I couldn't even think of extended travel, Mother being the way she was. These realities kept us from approaching a subject which was on both our minds —marriage.

And Mother had another minor stroke and ran up another major hospital bill. Greg offered me three hundred dollars. I just couldn't accept. He dated me three and four times a week, and spent enough on dinners and entertainment. He tried to insist, but I refused. Perhaps if I hadn't cared so much for him . . .

Anyway, I'd just about wiped out the bank account, when I met Dr. Masters in the hospital one day. He mentioned that, after a long spell of getting nothing but married couples (which he preferred), the Foundation was expecting several single males.

The money situation was so tight, I thought of asking him to consider me for one of the cases. But, of course, I didn't. There was Greg. How could I involve myself with in-bed therapy when I was so deeply, so happily, in love?

Except that I *wasn't* that happy anymore. Things have a way of changing, even in the best of male-female relationships. Greg and I had climbed the heights so quickly, and now we seemed to have reached a plateau. We no longer talked about travel, because it seemed so hopeless. And for the past two weeks we'd seen each other only on Saturday nights: he had work; I was tired; Mother was ill. Well, you can see what I mean. The relationship had to start up again, take a fresh turn to maintain its intensity. He either had to give up Europe, or I had to abandon Mother. His option seemed the only logical one, but who can be logical about a dream?

Gini phoned two weeks after I'd spoken to Dr. Masters, almost four months to the day I'd finished with Wallace. I remember the circumstances well. It was the last Monday in April, chill and rainy, and I was sick. I had a terrific head cold and sore throat, and had just about lost my voice. She joked that it wasn't necessary for me to talk, except to say yes. She was offering me my third wife-surrogate case. I said I was too sick to think of it at the moment. She said Dr. Masters would treat me with antibiotics and antihistamines. Anyway, she would call back later.

I thought about my finances. I needed that extra money more than ever before. But how could I explain all those nights out to Greg . . . unless, of course, we continued seeing each other only Saturday nights, and the nurse covered for me somehow.

No, it was impossible!

Gini called back after lunch. I'd had three cups of hot tea and whiskey in the local bar, and whether my throat was actually better, or I was "feeling no pain" due to the liquor, I was able to speak a little. I asked what the man was like. She said he was thirty years old, dark, good-looking, extremely intelligent, extremely wealthy, and had a home in San Francisco.

"What's his problem?"

Did she pause, or was it the whiskey? Then she said that it was the usual thing—failure to attain and maintain erections. But they would give me the entire picture when I came in after work.

Again I said it was impossible. My personal life . . .

Gini said they would try to work the schedule around my personal life, would set up appointments earlier, later, however I wanted them. I began to be swayed. A man who seemed to have everything was falling apart for lack of what I could teach him.

I heard myself saying yes.

As soon as we hung up, a sinking feeling invaded my stomach. I'd soon be going to bed with someone besides Greg.

4

If I could've gotten out of this case after it was explained to me, I would have. But it was too late; at least, that's how it was presented to me. They were counting on me. There was no one else to handle it. And Larry, as I'll call him, had already undergone his first interview and was accepted as a patient, because of my having accepted his case. *Fait accompli.* No way out.

And *why* would I have copped out? Because Larry was homosexually inclined!

My first reaction was to stand up, shaking my head. A faggot? But how could I treat him?

Then further facts were given me. He was here not because his family wanted him here, but because he himself had a strong desire to come back into the framework of normal society, to be "straight," and the fact that he wanted this made his homosexuality medically doubtful. Furthermore, he'd had three heterosexual experiences while in college. Finally, I was told he was nothing like the stereotype gay with feminine gestures and flamboyant clothes.

In addition to this, my cold was really terrible; my voice had just about disappeared. Dr. Masters examined me and prescribed for me, and I went home to take large doses of medication and to pass out in bed, which was fortunate, I guess, as otherwise I'd have stayed awake worrying.

I didn't go to work the next day, Tuesday. I was trying

to lick the cold by Wednesday evening, when my first meeting with Larry was scheduled. It was to be purely social, and the next meeting would be minimal touching: I touching him. And the third would be an expansion of the touch and feel, with Larry returning my caresses. Only when I felt he was ready would I attempt genital touching. And only when I felt the chances of failure were just about nil would I attempt coitus. All this was discussed with Masters and Johnson, in detail. They were going to stay very much on top of this case. We were going to move very slowly, very cautiously with Larry.

Wednesday, I returned to my job at the medical complex. At ten o'clock I received a call from Greg, who wanted to know if I was well enough to go to dinner that night. Feeling like an absolute monster, I said, "No, honey, I'm sorry. I'm going right home and to bed." He said he'd speak to me tomorrow.

All right. One evening, at least, was cleared. But just how much good poor Larry would get from this wheezing, coughing therapist was anybody's guess!

I didn't wheeze or cough *that* much. Dr. Masters provided me with some effective antihistamines which kept me looking and acting reasonably healthy.

It was an exceptionally mild May night. Larry was waiting outside the Forest Park Hotel as I drove up in my Camaro, and strode quickly (and manfully) to the car to introduce himself. I must say his appearance eased what was by this time a considerable buildup of tension. He was about five-feet-eleven, a little on the thin side, rather dark, and quite handsome. His hair was black, medium long, and he had extended, narrow sideburns. When he smiled, his teeth flashed white and even. I couldn't help feeling, "What a waste of man!"

He got in the car; we drove downtown; we talked all the way. There wasn't the slightest indication of femininity, or of sexual aberration. He was charming, and he was intelligent. He wanted to know what there was to know about St. Louis, as he had never been here before.

Among other things, I told him about our professional sporting events, and only when I finished did he say, "I have to admit, I'm not really turned on for sports in general."

Old prejudice and caricatures of homos reared their ugly heads then, and I thought, "Aha! Fairies are nonphysical!"

Then he said, "But I fence and hold a brown belt in judo. Also tennis is something of a passion with me."

There went a few ugly heads!

When we got to Tony's in downtown St. Louis, which many people consider our very best restaurant, he read the menu carefully, then looked up and said, "Why don't we see if the *maître d'* will oblige us with a sampling of several main dishes?"

I'd never known anyone to try such a thing, and said I doubted whether it could be done. He called the captain and spoke to him about six entrées, and before the man could voice his objections, he ordered a Bâtard Montrachet; I forget the year, but the captain said he *hoped* they had a bottle. And then the captain was gone, so concerned with the wine that he'd forgotten to fight the unusual order of entrée samplings.

It was a lovely meal. We had six small portions of main dishes, and salad, and while they didn't have the brand and year wine Larry had ordered, they did have a fine Montrachet.

I said I'd heard he lived in San Francisco. He said, "Yes. An overpriced condominium apartment overlooking the Bay." Here he paused, and his eyes fell away. "I wanted to be near certain . . . friends of mine in the same area."

I understood. I sipped my wine and said, "I know very little about homosexuality, except what I've read. It must have its satisfactions. Close personal . . ."

"Not for me." And then he apologized for interrupting, and spoke less sharply. "I haven't been able to make any strong personal attachments. If I had, I wouldn't be here. I guess I *can't* . . . my mind won't let me. No matter what I've done in the last ten years, I haven't ever been able to feel comfortable, to feel right and secure in it. This isn't true for many of my friends. It is for me. When I think of strong personal relationships, I think of marriage and children. It takes a woman for that"—he smiled thinly—"and so I want to learn, to get back . . ." He stopped then, looking confused and upset—looking

the part of a patient instead of a perfectly normal and very sophisticated man, for the first time.

I began asking questions—about his childhood, his adolescence, his young manhood. He said he'd gone into all that with Masters and Johnson. I said, "Yes, I know." He lit a long, thin cigar and sipped wine and looked around the restaurant, and began to talk.

He was still talking when we drove back to the Forest Park Hotel. We sat parked outside for half an hour more, until he finished. And I'm sure that, while the facts might have been those he told Dr. Masters and Gini, the *viewpoint*, the angle of approach, was different with me. Because I was going to be in bed with him soon, and he knew it. I was the one who would help make this try for normalcy, and he knew it.

I took my antibiotics and antihistamines when I got home, and congratulated myself on having gotten through the evening with no more than a few brief sniffles, which he hadn't seemed to notice. And I thought about what he had told me.

He taught European civilization in the Bay area, but wasn't dependent upon the income. Far from it. You don't maintain a condominium overlooking the Bay and travel the world on an instructor's salary! His family was extremely wealthy: Latin Americans involved in a broad-spectrum import business—everything from pre-Columbian art to Chilean wines—and while he took no part in managing the business, he did get a share of the profits. His father had died suddenly three years ago, and as eldest son Larry had inherited the lion's share. He'd made a deal with his two brothers; they left him alone, and he took a fixed income instead of running the show, as he could have.

But even before his father's death, he'd lived well. The family took care of its own, at least when it came to the boys. It was a large family—three boys and four girls. There were uncles and aunts and nieces and nephews and lots of cousins—all clustered around the king figure of Larry's father, Cesar.

Cesar expected that his sons would be manly. By this he meant that they would experience women, many women; but these women (in fact *all* women, except for

relatives and wealthy Latin girls chosen for wives) were looked on as whores.

So many of the strictly reared or Old World types label any woman who'll sleep with them a whore. And pretty soon any woman they can enjoy in bed is bad and they therefore have to marry a woman who is basically asexual. And then they end up gay or impotent! The wages of sin, it seems, is a trip to Masters and Johnson!

Anyway, with brothers and sisters and relatives forming a close-knit, noisy society, Larry found that he was odd man out. To the best of his recollection, this feeling of being outside the norm started when he was about twelve. Not that he fought with his brothers; they were too strongly imbued with discipline by the father. He just "drew back" from them.

Cesar was away a good deal, traveling on company business between various points in South America and the States, as well as to other parts of the world. When he was home, he played the biblical patriarch, regaling his peers with stories of the women he'd had and the shrewd deals he'd made, while the wife and other females stayed in the huge kitchen and prepared food and drink (wealthy as they were, they had no servants; the family's women did everything).

Larry hated his home. His mother, he felt, was not a person but a thing; at least, so she was made to seem by his father and the other men. His uncles were important, but his aunts were items. Male cousins could be played with, female cousins "kicked in the ass."

He once tried to express his feelings to his mother. She slapped him for disrespect to his father. He then tried to question his father as to the differences between their home and family life as seen in the movies of middle America. His father knocked him to the ground, shouting that he should "be a man and not a silly woman's plaything." The next day Cesar left on another business trip.

Larry had no homosexual experiences during grammar school and for most of high school. In fact, he made a very close friend of an "American girl" (her parents had been born in this country), and in his junior year took her to a picnic. They'd drunk beer, and suddenly she was kissing him as they lay on a blanket in the shade of a

tree. Her hands moved inside his shirt and stroked his chest. He touched her a little—her arms, her hips—and it was "pleasant enough"; but then she began to grind her body against his and to pant and to "look unpleasant." He tried to disengage himself. She said, "I know something's wrong, Larry. You don't act like other boys. I know you need help. Let me help you." Her hand slid down to his fly.

He shoved her away and ran. She told a few of her friends about it, and he was looked at and whispered about. He found it intolerable, and played sick for a whole week. When his mother insisted he return to school, he went in an agony of shame. By then, the kids had other things to talk about—a hot football team and a scandal concerning two young teachers seen petting in a lovers'-lane spot.

But at least one student didn't forget the story about Larry. That was a small blond senior named Corey. Corey waited a few weeks, and then sat beside Larry in the lunchroom and began talking to him. Larry was reserved, diffident, but Corey had done some investigation of his prey, and talked European history, poetry, and fencing (Larry was on the team: his one high-school sport). Soon they'd become friends, and three or four weeks later, Corey invited Larry over to a friend's house for a "social gathering . . . no girls; just a few guys and some beer and some talk."

The "gathering" was four other boys, Larry and Corey. Larry said he immediately noticed that everyone seemed to pair off. Then, while talking to Corey, he realized that the blond youth's eyes were fixed on something across the room. Larry turned, and where before there had been two boys sitting on the couch, talking, there was now one boy sitting, his pants and underpants down around his knees, and one boy leaning over, handling and sucking his cock. Larry was frozen for an instant, and then Corey tapped his arm and pointed. The other two boys were leaving the living room for the bedroom. They looked at Larry and smiled, and one said, "Get with it, baby." As a boy and girl might walk holding hands, they walked holding each other's genitals.

Larry said he wanted to get up and leave, but just

couldn't. Actually, he was turning on for the very first time in his life—a long-deferred and therefore powerful rush of passion. He glanced at Corey, who smiled and stood up. Corey's trousers were distended in front. He stood directly before Larry, that distension only inches from Larry's mouth, and murmured, "Let's go over to the couch and help out." Larry shook his head. Corey shrugged and went to the couch. He knelt to the boy performing fellatio and undid his belt. The boy shifted position, stretching out to help Corey, and soon his trousers and underwear were down and Corey was playing with his testicles and penis. Corey looked at Larry again, then slowly bent and took the penis in his mouth. After a while the boy at the end of the daisy chain cried out and came. A moment later, the boy Corey was sucking also came. Then both turned their attention to Corey, one on each side, playing with his genitals and kissing him, and finally, one bent to suck him. But Corey stopped it and said, "I want Larry. Larry . . . come on."

Larry said that by this time he was fully aroused. Still, he refused to move. So all three boys came to where he was sitting, kicking away their clothing. Corey was the only one in a full state of erection, and he pushed that erection into Larry's face. Larry felt it touch his cheek, then his lips—that hot, throbbing, rigid thing. He turned his head away. The other boys laughed, and one said, "'I was the same way, remember?" then knelt and began pressing Larry's crotch. When Larry tried to stop him, the other boy grabbed his arms and said, "Guess we'll have to rape you." But it was said playfully, with full awareness of Larry's excitement and the hard-on extending his trousers.

Once they got his penis out, he was lost. He said that one boy handled his testicles and shaft and another kissed and licked the head of his penis, and Corey again pressed forward with his cock. Larry opened his mouth. He'd never even dreamed of such a thing, but within minutes he was receiving and swallowing a full discharge of semen . . . and seconds later was shooting into the kneeling boy's mouth.

The party lasted four hours. Because of their youth, the

boys were able to have four or five orgasms each. By the end of the evening, Larry was "gay."

But at home, he was horrified at what he had done. What if the family found out? What if his *father* found out? The thought was so traumatic that he had nightmares all week; and when Corey approached him, he told the boy to "flake off or prepare to eat a fist sandwich!" Corey couldn't believe this show of violent maleness, and persisted in trying to join Larry at lunch. It was a mistake. Terrified of his own sexuality, and certain that if he allowed Corey time to speak he would soon be at another gathering, Larry leaped up and struck the smaller boy with a series of punches to the head and face. Both ended up in the dean's office, and both refused to explain the incident. Since Larry was an excellent student with no previous discipline problems, he was let off with a lecture. Corey was not in the school's good graces and was given extra hours in study hall for two weeks.

Larry retained the memory of homosexual passion, and when tormented by desire he would masturbate, thinking of Corey and the other boys. But he stayed away from any actual encounter with gays. In fact, he began dating rather heavily—many different girls, to lessen the chances that any one might become "serious," either socially or sexually. He actually got the reputation of being a "skin merchant," a Don Juan, loving them and leaving them! This reached his brothers, and eventually his father, and pleased Cesar no end. When Larry went off to college in another state, Cesar told him to "work hard, but keep up with the girls like you did in high school! You're a real bull, just like your father!"

The irony of this tormented Larry. He felt he had to change, had to become what his father expected him to be. And so, soon after the start of his freshman year in college, he accompanied a friend to a house of prostitution in a nearby town. Before they entered the house, Larry had three or four whiskeys and beer chasers to bolster his courage. He was therefore pretty high, but fear and disgust still mounted in him when several girls strolled into an ornate parlor. At the same time, one of the girls vaguely appealed to him, and when he described her, I knew why. She was lean, small in the chest and rear, and wore her hair cut short. While the other girls exposed their big breasts and behinds by means of loose wrappers, she stood dispiritedly aside, her one ploy a sensual licking of the lips.

She was the one he chose—a girl as *un*feminine as he could find; a girl closest to his ideal—and his ideal was a *boy!*

When they were alone together in an upstairs room, the girl undressed him, undressed herself, drew him to the bed, lay down with him. His penis was soft. She asked if anything was the matter. He shook his head, trembling in fear and shame. She then said, "I'll get it up, honey," and bent over and began kissing and licking it. He closed his eyes, stroked her short-cropped hair, and let his mind drift to Corey and the other boys. In a moment, he was hard.

When she wanted to stop, he murmured, "No, go on." She went on, but when he was close to orgasm, she drew him quickly onto her and put him in. They fucked. It wasn't long before he came, and he said it "felt marvelous, but I wasn't sure whether I was with a woman or a boy. After all, Corey had sodomized a boy in front of me, and I'd have been doing it too, if I'd attended their next gathering." So the girl's vagina became a boy's anus, and he fantasized and had a "successful" act.

A month later, he returned to the house with his friend. When he asked for Billie, the girl he'd had the last time, he was told she'd been let go because she just wasn't popular enough with the clientele. He had to choose another, and while she looked lean in her wrapper, with her clothes off she had full breasts and good-sized buttocks. He was with a woman, and his mind couldn't fantasize that fact away, and he failed to attain an erection. When she sucked him up hard, he failed to maintain it inside her. He played drunk, but was too humiliated ever to return to that house again.

He made one more attempt at a heterosexual liaison; this with a girl who worked in the college cafeteria. Her reputation was that of a semipro—her date had to spend a considerable amount of money during the evening, and a nice gift wouldn't hurt his chances any. Larry took her to dinner, to a show, and when they drove up to the shabby apartment house in which she lived, he presented her with a pair of silver earrings. She asked him up, and they petted on the couch, and he felt a certain amount of excitement. He also felt secure enough in her semiprofessional status to direct her head downward; she was quite willing. As long as she was sucking on him, he was able to maintain his erection—and in this case, at least, to enjoy a "reasonably strong sexual feeling." But as soon as they went to the bed and she said, "C'mon, baby, give Mamma what she wants!" he was limp.

He tried to get her back to fellatio, but the girl was insulted. She'd never had a man go soft on her, being only twenty-two and dealing as she did with college boys and a few of the younger instructors. Besides, she'd had much to drink and forgot herself to the extent of throwing his earrings at him and shouting, "Get outta here, you fucking fairy!"

She'd probably used the word "fairy" simply as an epithet, but to Larry, this meant he'd been found out. Tomorrow, he reasoned, the entire college would know, and so, just as in high school, he ran home to play sick for a week. But eventually he had to return to his studies; his father demanded it. Nothing had changed at the school, though several of his acquaintances had heard the story from the girl. They thought it funny: old Larry had flopped with a chick. He then realized it happened to other men, *normal* men, and while it was embarrassing, it didn't label him anything. Still, to be on the safe side, he immediately went out for the school's fencing team, began playing tennis again, and registered at a *dojo* for judo classes, reasoning that a sportsman wouldn't be suspected of homosexuality.

He was now nineteen, an age at which most men have experienced some good sex, and many have also had serious love affairs. He was alone, and it was beginning to hurt.

It hurt more and more through his third year, and he took to doing a little secret drinking. He dated, but only to allay suspicion and, as in high school, rarely with the same girl twice. He began to fear the weekends, began to fear his need for three or four or five brandies after dinner—most of those dinners eaten alone, and followed by a movie or a long drive, also alone.

Two weeks before his twentieth birthday, and about to enter his senior year, he decided not to go on at the dormitories with their constant reminders of other men's sexual and social lives. He took an apartment just off the campus, and for a while enjoyed the privacy. But then, of course, his loneliness intensified. With no other men to monitor his private life, he stopped the empty business of dating girls. Except for classes, he was now totally divorced from his fellows. And within a month he was in serious mental trouble, unable to sleep well, unable to study, drinking more and more. It was at this time that he met Ted, a math instructor at the university.

Larry feels that he was susceptible to Ted's homosexual approach not only because he *wanted* male sex (after all, he'd wanted it since the experience with Corey), but because of the near-psychotic state he was in. "It was *loneliness* I escaped with Ted—and it was a hope of true friendship, true love, that led me to invite him to room with me after that first night. . . ."

That first night had begun with a chat in the library, where Ted and Larry shared a table and discovered, by both having volumes of his poetry, an interest in Hart Crane. Ted asked if Larry knew anything about Crane's life. Larry admitted he didn't, and Ted suggested they talk about it over a beer.

Larry knew, almost immediately, Ted was gay. Not that he was swish when in the library, but he was definitely *not* manly. And after their beer, in Larry's apartment, Ted allowed the mask he wore in normal society to fall away, and a certain delicacy became a certain femininity, and the swish effect began to emerge.

Ted then spoke of how he knew his time at the college was limited; how he planned soon to join friends living in San Francisco's gay community; how he wanted to "become the person I really am." And he became that person for Larry—a small, soft, pretty near-woman. And that person kissed Larry and petted Larry and undressed Larry and served Larry with his mouth. And that person undressed himself and presented himself to Larry for fellatio. And later, that person presented his plump backside to Larry and initiated him into the pleasures of sodomy.

It was a Friday night. Ted stayed until early Monday morning, and moved in with Larry the following Monday. Larry's loneliness was gone. Larry's insomnia was gone. Larry's appetite returned, and his grades went back to their natural high level. But Larry's guilt also went back to its natural high level. As for Ted, he began speaking of love, and began pleading for a "marriage"—a permanent relationship in which both would forswear other men. He wanted to move to the city with Larry right after graduation.

Larry said no to everything. He was going home. He was going to decide whether or not to go into the family business. And, finally, he admitted that except for sexual release and someone to talk and be with, he had no feelings for Ted.

Ted reacted as anyone in love would; he was stricken, and he left. Larry went home.

Within a month he knew he couldn't live in the big old house with the family. He also knew he needed the society of homosexuals. (He never used the expression "*other* homosexuals"; he hadn't given in to the concept of his *own* homosexuality.)

He looked up Ted, and through Ted met a community of homosexuals. Having made the necessary contacts, he found the condominium overlooking the Bay, and furnished it in luxury and style. He registered in a nearby graduate school of arts and sciences. He continued to receive considerable money from his family. He began to conduct a series of affairs with various men. His life settled into a routine of study, artistic pleasure, continuation of judo, fencing, and tennis . . . and sexual release. Guilt decreased, and once he realized his family had decided to ignore his strange manner of life, once he realized that whether they suspected what he was or not they weren't going to make an issue of it, he thought he'd solved everything. (Later, he learned that his brothers were reasonably certain he was gay, but had kept it from the father and mother.)

He took his master's degree, and then his Ph.D. He applied for teaching jobs around the Bay area, and one of the smaller schools accepted him. He traveled half an hour each way to work, and his life went on as before. He enjoyed all the forms of homosexual love, though after he began teaching he found he had less time for it —or was it less *need* for it? Every so often, he had to discard a lover because the man wanted "marriage." Larry never did get to feel that close to any one partner. It didn't seem important, for quite a while.

Then his father died, and he came into considerable money, which he translated (via the deal with his brothers) into about fifty thousand a year. He was free to travel, to live abroad, to do anything he wished. He took a year's sabbatical from his teaching and went to Europe. He enjoyed the Italian Riviera and several homosexual affairs there. He returned to the States in nine months, feeling rather bored. Behind the boredom were the beginnings of anxiety. He was anxious about being bored.

Of course, it wasn't boredom; it was an emptiness of purpose. He was bothered by dreams in which he stroked a child's face, kissed it, and then watched it fade away and disappear. He found that he was attracted to baby carriages and very young children. Occasionally, he would give in to the impulse to smile at a child, or chuck it under the chin. In his own apartment house, a woman had reacted with fear and indignation when he patted her little boy's head. He was obviously known to her as a homosexual, and he was touching *her* child. This shocked and depressed him. Living as he had in a wide-open society of artists, hippies, and liberal professionals, he'd almost forgotten that the world looked upon the homosexual with disgust and, when concerning its children, with hatred.

He had two months before going back to teaching. They were bad months. He had his first failure in homosexual sex—he went soft while being sucked by his latest lover. It didn't bother him particularly; he just felt he didn't really *want* the man. He got a new lover, a boy of eighteen, and went great guns with him—for two weeks. Then, while mounting the boy anally, he again went soft.

After this, he had failures on the average of once every four times. And it still didn't bother him. He began to feel that if he couldn't love a partner emotionally, there was no great loss in not being able to love him physically. And he could love *no* partner emotionally.

He returned to teaching. The dreams of children persisted. He visited his brothers more often, both of them married, and enjoyed their children enormously. He became a doting uncle, and had to be cautioned not to spoil the children with gifts. One evening he spoke to a girl behind the counter of a local bookstore. She was bright and pretty, and he suddenly wanted to know her better. He returned to the shop many times but couldn't make himself ask her out. What was the point?

He went to Italy for his two winter vacations, and traveled widely the following summer. He had fewer homosexual affairs. He began feeling the loneliness return, the terrible loneliness he'd experienced during his senior year in college. He began suffering from insomnia, and drank heavily to overcome it. And this time there was no reasonable solution in sight, such as accepting homosexual love. This time the solution seemed impossible: he had to become part of normal society, find a woman, love her physically and emotionally, marry, and have children. That and *only* that would do.

He'd heard of Masters and Johnson; who, connected with a university or college, hasn't? But he couldn't make himself do anything. It was just too hopeless. He was a homosexual, had been for ten years.

Then one night, about a month before coming to St. Louis, he'd gone to the bookstore. The girl he'd liked had disappeared almost a year before, and he'd completely forgotten her. But when he brought his book to the cash register, she was there. His "Hello!" and warm smile brought a flush to her cheeks. He asked where she'd been. She said she'd saved and traveled. She was a would-be writer. She had lived in Mexico.

It was almost closing time, and he suggested they continue their discussion in a nearby coffee house. Three hours later, he walked her to her home in a well-maintained brownstone. He took her hand and began to say good night, and suddenly found himself leaning forward and kissing her gently on the lips. She smiled, and went inside.

A good-night kiss was nothing for the girl, but you can

imagine what it was like for Larry! Feelings he thought
nonexistent were coming alive in him. Whatever the reason, he knew he had to try to make love to this girl.

He dated her three more times. He kissed her again before her door, and then he kissed her at greater length on
her couch, and the third date he held her in his arms and
stroked her body and saw her passion mounting. And
said he had to leave; he was going out of town in the
morning; he'd be gone for several weeks.

He hadn't felt any life in his genitals, despite the fact
that he truly liked the girl and found her very good to
look at and to touch. He contacted the Foundation the
next morning.

This case was to run a full two weeks. Anywhere
from twelve to fourteen meetings, with an additional one
or two possible in case it was absolutely necessary. I
couldn't complain, since I'd had such a short case with
Wallace, but because of Greg, I could see complications
on complications! And I wasn't wrong.

Greg phoned me at work the next morning. I again
pleaded illness, and when he said he would come to my
home, I said I wanted another long night of rest. He was
definitely cool when he said good-bye, and he didn't
mention seeing me for our usual Saturday-night date. So
when Gini called to say Larry was pleased with me, I
reminded her of the promise to allow for my personal
life this time. I wanted Saturday night off. She quickly
said she would make Larry's an afternoon session. I then
said that, in addition, I had to have all day Sunday for
myself. She was sure it would be all right, since Dr.
Masters felt I needed extra time to recover from my severe
cold.

I began to feel better. Besides, it was the first week in
May, and truly beautiful weather—the warmest we'd had
in years. Almost hot, which suited my fading cold just
perfectly. I called Greg back, and apologized for the way
I'd been acting, and said I hoped we would be seeing
each other Saturday night. He warmed a bit, but asked
why not Saturday afternoon as well? I said I didn't think
my health would allow it, but that I hoped by Sunday to
be well enough to spend the whole day with him. That

seemed to make everything right again, and I worked happily the rest of the day.

I arrived in front of the Forest Park Hotel at seven. Larry was waiting, and said he'd heard of a restaurant on Lindell that had excellent French food. I tried to talk him out of it. He said, "All right; there's the Nantucket Cove just down the street. . . ." What reason could I give for not going *there?* It wasn't the *restaurants* I disliked, it was the *neighborhood*—Greg's neighborhood, where he might be walking, or eating.

Still, we couldn't always be driving downtown: It was much too far away, much too inconvenient. We went to the Nantucket Cove. It took a while, but I finally relaxed and stopped expecting to see Greg pop up. We talked easily and well, and I found I was beginning to like the man. We walked back to the hotel—it was only half a block —and went into the lobby. Now I began to cringe. It was Friday night, and the hotel bar was booming, and there were so many people around. . . .

In the room, we sat on the davenport and continued to talk. With Larry, one didn't have to force the conversation. We agreed on many things,—and disagreed—but in friendly fashion—on many things, and there was never any dearth of subjects. At an early point, I put my hand on his thigh, very lightly, and began to move it back and forth. He paused in his flow of talk, and then continued. A few minutes later, I turned to him, lips close to his, and said something. He leaned forward the few inches, and kissed me. It was all very gentle, very sweet . . . and very asexual.

I moved my hand higher up on his thigh. His hand came to my knee, and stroked up lightly. We talked awhile longer, and that was it. He was relaxed, and I left him that way.

Our next meeting began, again, at the Nantucket Cove, and within two hours we were back on the davenport. We talked, kissed, and again I stroked his thigh. The conversation went on, and we kissed occasionally, and his hand went to *my* legs. We both stroked higher and higher, but I stopped short of his genital area. My instructions were to proceed *carefully,* and since I felt no heat, no

passion in him yet, I felt that touching his penis would
be a mistake.

He, however, finally got his hand up around my
crotch, then withdrew. I made believe I hadn't noticed,
because the touch had been so light and quick. He also
touched my breasts several times, almost as if by accident.

I smiled and suggested we lie down. He froze. I mean, his
entire body actually seemed to go rigid! But it was for
only a moment, and then he rose and went to the bedroom, *ahead* of me, as if to say, "See, I'm not afraid."
But he was. His pallor and trembling showed it.

I didn't undress. I made the decision right then and
there to keep this third meeting minimal. We lay down
in our clothing. He seemed surprised, and also relieved. I
talked about the pleasures of touching, the tactile sensations that led to sensual stimulation. I stroked his face,
his neck, his arms through his clothing. I kissed him, and
held his hand. He rubbed my fingers. He kissed my hand.
He looked at me and kissed my lips.

I said we'd had enough for tonight. He asked if it was
going badly. I said, "It's going exactly as planned."

Saturday afternoon, I was in his room at three. We had
a drink: he had no hard liquor, just a bottle of Cinzano
sweet vermouth. I guess he'd decided not to tempt himself with whiskey, and I was just as glad, since I was seeing Greg at six-thirty.

We sat on the davenport. We kissed, stroked each other's legs, and went to the bedroom. He decided at the
last moment he wanted another vermouth. I said nothing, but smiled a little. He stopped and smiled weakly in
return and said, "I guess I'm rather transparent."

"I'm going to undress," I told him. "Will you help me,
Larry?"

He didn't seem to know a thing about undressing a
woman; or else he was just too nervous. The blouse came
off all right, but he couldn't unhook the brassiere, and I
finally showed him how. Then I turned. He looked at my
breasts, and then quickly away, as if it weren't allowed.
I unzipped my skirt, and when he made no move, I removed it myself. Then I asked him to take off my panties.

He drew them down, kneeling, mouth inches from my crotch. He put them on the chair and wet his lips and cleared his throat. "You'll have to forgive me. I'm rather . . . unsettled."

I began to undress him. I touched him and kissed him. When he was naked, I drew him to the bed, and we lay down. I told him there could be no genital play. *Verboten.* He didn't look disappointed. He was as limp as I've ever seen a man, his penis drawn far up into his body. He looked at himself once and laughed nervously. "You'll have to take my word for it; I'm not considered small." He seemed to relax after I laughed.

I went through the touch-and-feel process, encouraging him this time to touch *me* a little. He did . . . very little. But he desperately wanted an erection, because at one point he began manipulating himself. Then he stopped and said, "That's wrong, isn't it? I mean, the doctor said no masturbation."

I said that Bill meant no masturbation when alone, and to orgasm. Here, anything that helped turn him on was all right. But he didn't go back to it, and since we'd had about twenty-five minutes in bed, I said we'd finished our session. As we dressed, I told him he was coming along well, and he said, "I don't mean to be insulting, but I know that's not true."

I looked him full in the face. "It *is* true." And it was. We had no set schedule of reaction from this man who'd been ten years a homosexual. How could we?

My date with Greg wasn't a roaring success. Somehow, he seemed standoffish. Even dancing, he kept himself further away than usual. But in bed, he once again became my wonderful lover. And how I needed that!

Sunday was all ours, and still I felt something was wrong. When I questioned him, he said there were problems at the office, but he gave no details. We got home rather early—before nine—as he said he was beginning to feel a little under the weather. I accepted it. Despite near-summer temperatures, there was a lot of flu going around St. Louis. He didn't ask when he would next see me, and I said I would call to find out how he was feeling. Which I did the next afternoon. He said not too

well, and he planned on going to bed with a hot toddy
and a good brief.

That evening I went out to dinner with Larry and felt
almost no tension. Greg was at home in bed, right? An
hour later, I was on the davenport with Larry and asked
how he felt after a full week at the Foundation. He said,
"Well, it's hard to decide. I mean, I look forward to my
morning sessions with Dr. Masters, and also to my meetings with you . . . but I really don't feel anything; physically, that is. You must have noticed my lack of response?"

He meant no erections. I said that would come, in time.

"But we don't have that much time, do we?"

"Yes, we do. As much as we need; perhaps more. You
might be good and sick of me before this is over."

He took my hand and said quietly, "I doubt it. You're
. . . most pleasant; most attractive."

"As attractive as your bookstore girl?"

I meant it as a joke, but he answered seriously.
"You're different types. She's not quite as . . . well,
sensual."

As he stopped speaking, he suddenly took me in his
arms and kissed me. And he did it with fervor. Either he
was beginning to feel something, or he *wanted* to so
badly he was pushing himself. Then he said, "You know,
I kept thinking of what we did Saturday; being naked
together in bed. I know I didn't seem excited—and I
wasn't, at the time. I was too uptight to be excited. But
later, after you'd gone, I actually had an erection thinking of it."

My hand was moving up and back on his thigh. He
kept his arms around me and kissed my cheek and then
my neck. One hand came to my breast, exploring with
trembling light touches. I put my lips in his way, and we
kissed, and for the very first time *I* felt something—
pleasure in being with a man. And whether this was what
did it, or whether the time had finally come—as Masters
and Johnson had hoped it would, after several nonpres-
sure meetings—he sighed and moved his bottom in a way
that told me there were stirrings in his genital area. I
moved my hand farther up, and brushed a length of hard-

ness that hadn't been there before. His sigh was deep then, and I quickly took him to the bedroom.

We didn't talk. I think we were both afraid to! We didn't want anything to change. He undressed me, and did it competently. He kissed me a few times; my shoulder, my arm, once a deep kiss to the belly, which felt quite lovely. (I couldn't help wondering if he wouldn't be great at oral love, once he got used to doing it to a woman. After all, he'd used his mouth so much as a homosexual. The thought gave me a definite tingle between the legs!)

When I was naked, he took me in his arms for a long, tender hug, and one hand slid softly down to caress my bottom. I smiled at him and murmured, "Mmmm, how nice!" He caressed the cheeks again, and his fingers crept into the cleft, and one seemed ready to probe my anus. (Again, I had a thought relative to his being gay. He *would* know how to play with a behind, wouldn't he!)

He let me go and began unbuttoning his shirt. I stopped him by saying, "Let me," but it was a good sign. He was beginning to *want* to be naked with me, *want* to get to bed with me. No great surprise, you say, thinking of men in general; but think again of homosexuals in particular!

In bed, I went through the touch-and-feel process, this time kissing his chest, nibbling his nipples, caressing his belly and thighs quite close to the genitals. He'd had a semierection when I'd taken off his shorts. Now he was almost completely hard, though it rose and fell by the second, depending upon how close my mouth got to his cock.

I led him to caress me. I had him rub and kiss my breasts, run his hands over my arms and sides and belly and legs. Once he murmured, "Smooth as silk," and went back to the high insides of my thighs for more of that "silk." I sighed, moved lasciviously (it was partly natural and partly by plan), and whispered, "Kiss-kiss."

We played with each other, and I kept skirting his semirigid cock. Finally he grasped it himself, looking at me. I smiled and nodded. He began stroking it, still looking at me, touching my breasts and belly with his free hand. I could see it growing, thrusting itself farther up out of his fist, and then he really turned on, really pounded his meat . . . and I stopped him. I took it in my own hand, stroked it, kissed him hard. He maintained the erection for about a minute, and then it began to soften. I kissed his belly, his thighs, tried stroking faster to see if I could bring it back, and he whispered, "Could you—your mouth?"

I knew that had to come sooner or later, and I had my answer all ready. It was not an answer Masters and Johnson had given me, but it was one they accepted, because they knew how I felt about sucking Larry, or anyone who had experienced anal intercourse over a period of years. I just couldn't think of taking that penis in my mouth when it had been up so many male rectums! Illogical for a sexual therapist? Perhaps. But I never claimed to be free of hangups.

Even normal intercourse with Larry worried me. By this time I knew of E. Coli. It's a serious infection that *can* take place when a penis picks up certain bacteria from anal intercourse, then transmits it to a vagina. It can render a woman incapable of bearing children. How could I be sure he wouldn't give in to an overpowering need for homosexual pleasure and have rectal intercourse shortly before being with *me*?

I said, "It's not allowed because of its close association with homosexual love."

The session ended on a negative note with his penis almost all the way down, but I said it had been a great success. This time he believed me, and this time I felt I was wrong. But when I spoke to Gini, I heard my own words repeated. She reminded me that this man had not been with a woman in any sort of sexual situation for ten years. The fact that I, a woman, had given him an erection, no matter for how short a time, was a breakthrough.

The next day I called Greg. He was not at the office, having phoned in ill. I called his home. No answer. I decided he had either turned his phone down so as to sleep or had gone to the doctor. I tried calling at four and again at six, both times without success.

Larry and I went to the French restaurant on Lindell. Except for the first few minutes, I wasn't too uptight, and a good meal and interesting conversation soon had me relaxed. Larry and I agreed about almost everything that night. I asked if he'd been thinking again—going over last night's events in his mind—and he nodded. "It was terribly exciting, Val."

I was Val now. We were growing close.

It was a warm, overcast night. It actually was getting up into the eighties during the day, and not much lower in the evening! So I blamed the weather for a sudden, strange, unhappy feeling as we walked across the dark parking lot. I felt as if . . . well, someone or something were close behind me, threatening me. I didn't want to give in to the foolish feeling, but as I entered my car I glanced back. Nothing but parked cars, empty, of course.

The feeling weakened on the way back to the hotel— and then I was too busy to think of it.

After some petting on the davenport, Larry looked down at himself, smiling. His pants were obviously distended. We went to bed, and his erection weakened. He began to look uptight, so I went to his genitals. I played with his balls and kissed him and put my tongue in his mouth for the first time. I encouraged him to put his hand on my cunt. He fumbled awhile for the slit and found it and inserted a finger. He didn't seem to know what to do then, and I whispered instructions to him. He began moving his finger, found the right spot, played with it. I began to get hot, and acted even hotter. His erection mounted steadily, and when I grasped it, I suggested he put his hand over mine and show me the movement, the rhythm he preferred. He did, and it was a slow stroke with increased pressure toward the glans.

He didn't make me come, but I faked it. I went through a complete gasping, writhing orgasm, without the orgasm. (Later, he would return the compliment!) He didn't come either, but he desperately wanted to; and when he gave up, he twisted over on his side, away from me. "Oh, God," he said, voice shaking.

I took him by the shoulders and turned him back to me and kissed him—and noticed that there were tears in his eyes. I kissed him again, and because of the way he was lying and because of a sudden hunch, I moved myself atop him, lay stretched out full length on his body, kissed him with open mouth and all the feeling I could muster.

It was the right way to end this session. I felt his cock come up between my legs. Before it could go down, I said I had to leave.

We dressed. He walked me to the door. As I put my hand on the knob, he spoke quickly, blurting out the words: "I have to tell you—something happened this afternoon. Something that disturbed me, and perhaps hurt me in bed tonight."

He'd been approached in the lobby by a homosexual youth! The boy hadn't been *sure* of anything, simply trying several men in hopes of making a quick dollar. He'd asked if he could "wash up" in Larry's room. When Larry shook his head, the boy said, "I'm so broke I'd do *anything* for twenty dollars," and licked his lips and moved his ass—and Larry had run from a sudden vision of getting sucked off and penetrating that nice young ass; had run from a need to ejaculate, to rid himself of sexual tension after eight days of concentrating on sex. (Now, this was exactly what I'd worried about when I mentioned E. Coli.)

I said I was sorry he hadn't mentioned it earlier. I suggested he tell Dr. Masters about it. And then I took another chance. I turned and patted my rump and said, "You'll soon get all the nice young ass you can handle."

He laughed—a good, loud, tension-reducing belly laugh—and kissed me good night as if he didn't want me to go.

I left quickly then, feeling my gamble had paid off. Still, everything I did in the area of saucy femininity was risky. This time it had worked. The next time it might not.

Greg was in his office Wednesday morning, but said he couldn't talk, as he was in the middle of a client conference. He would try to call me that night. I hesitated, and then said I had to work late but I'd call *him* by nine-thirty or ten. "Won't you be at your phone?" he asked, casually enough.

"No, honey, I really don't know just where I'll be. One of the administrative offices. So let me call you."

He said, "Fine," and hung up. I thought of what would

happen if he ever found out what I was doing—and felt
sick. He'd never forgive me! No lover could accept such
"work"!

I was still feeling a little of that when I came to Larry's
room, and as a result asked if he wouldn't order something from room service. He was obviously disappointed,
and said he'd been looking forward all day to going out
with me.

It helped me get rid of the guilty, ugly feeling. He
really *enjoyed* being with me. So I said all right, and we
left. And I was glad I did, because tonight's dinner was
a very special event he had arranged with the management of a fine English-style restaurant in Ladue, St.
Louis' most prestigious suburb. He'd used the yellow
pages, calling several places until he found one that
would prepare Beef Wellington.

It was a wonderful surprise, though he murmured that
he'd tasted better. I hadn't! We didn't get back to the
hotel until almost nine, and I was very aware of my
promise to call Greg between nine-thirty and ten, so I
maneuvered us both into bed in the shortest time possible, hoping it wouldn't bother Larry. It didn't. He'd been
"thinking" again, and was anxious to play—and came up
good and hard as soon as I stroked his cock. He put his
hand on mine to remind me of how he liked it, then lay
back, a hand on my bottom and a finger creeping into
my anus. And before I knew it, he was gasping, "Faster!
Val . . . please . . . faster . . . oh, God, oh, God!" Spasms
shook his entire body as I pulled him off. There was an
impressive amount of semen! When he finished, he
looked at me. "I'm going to make it," he said, voice low.

I kissed him, and he grabbed me so hard I squealed.
"I'm going to make it!"

He went to the bathroom to wash, his face aglow, and
I swear that his walk was different! I mean, he was actually swaggering a little!

When he returned, I was dressed, and his face fell.
"Must you?" he asked.

I told him it was best. We'd had a marvelous triumph.
One of the reasons was that he had thought back to the
previous night and evaluated it and grown hopeful and
excited. I wanted him to relax now, with a book or TV

or just sitting around. "And think, honey. Think how far you've come."

I called Greg from a lobby phone. There was no answer.

I called him again when I reached home. Still no answer.

I reported in to Dr. Masters. He was delighted with Larry's progress, and congratulated me on how I was bringing him along.

I lay down and closed my eyes; just for a few moments, I told myself. I fully intended to stay up until midnight and call Greg then, but I fell asleep. I was exhausted. You have to remember that I had a heavy schedule of work every day at the medical complex, and that I was undergoing considerable tension—whether or not I was always aware of it at the time—most nights. And that bout with the flu had taken its toll. Anyway, I overslept and was late at work Thursday morning. There was a message for me: "Call Greg."

He asked if he could see me that night. I hesitated. Was there still time to get to Dr. Masters before he saw Larry? I glanced at my watch. Nine-forty. Larry's appointment was at ten. If I asked for a night off . . .

Greg said, "You still there?" He didn't say it too pleasantly.

"Yes, honey . . . and all yours."

No laugh. No response of any kind. I decided to see him, and said how about eight, eight-thirty? He said, "Right," and I said good-bye and phoned Dr. Masters. I couldn't get him; the receptionist said he would call me back.

I waited and waited, and called again. He was still unavailable. Finally, at eleven, I called Gini. I said I had to have the evening off. She didn't think it was possible; Bill Masters had already finished his morning therapy session with Larry, and they'd decided that if things went well, we could try sexual intercourse tonight. He was all primed for it. Canceling out could be damaging.

I began to sweat.

Gini asked if an early appointment, with no dinner, would help? I said yes; I wanted to go directly to the hotel from work. She said they'd call Larry and tell him

I'd be there at five-thirty. But if he wasn't in his room, and if he didn't return until six or later . . .

I jumped at the phone each time it rang. Finally, at two-thirty, Gini called back to say it was all right. I was expected at five-thirty. I sank back in my chair, exhausted all over again. What a morning—trying to keep my love life and my secret profession from clashing! But everything looked fine now. I'd leave Larry no later than seven, race home, dress for my date, and be waiting for Greg whether he came at eight or eight-thirty. And since this was my seventh session with Larry, I was half through with the job; maybe even more than half through. It looked as if I'd be able to keep both my lover *and* my standing at the Foundation.

It wasn't going to work out that way, but I didn't know it when I entered Larry's room. He'd been thinking again, and was anxious to get into bed. His erection came quickly, and I stroked it until it was red and throbbing. He was gasping, his face buried in my breasts, finger wriggling up my ass—and that bothered me just a little. It seemed to me that he'd been avoiding my vagina; that he'd gone there reluctantly when I'd directed his hand. He had to get acquainted with cunt sooner or later. It was going to be either his salvation or his Waterloo!

("Vagina" and "cunt," Herb. I felt *he* felt it was a vaguely unpleasant anatomical area, and so it was "vagina." But what he had to grow to love was "cunt"!)

I felt he was ready to be mounted. I said as much to him and felt no reduction in the strength of the hard-on in my hand. But I also whispered that *I* wanted to be ready, and took his hand and moved it between my legs. He fumbled; I directed; he then did well, as he had the last time. I began to feel it; I began to turn on, to pant, to move, to *want*—and I rolled over onto him and straddled him and got him into me.

It didn't take half a minute for him to go absolutely soft. And no matter what I did afterward, he stayed soft.

He closed his eyes. "I'm so sorry," he whispered.

I told him it was expected. He looked at me. "You can't mean that."

I said that there was usually a point where the patient, no matter what the specifics of his problem, failed, and that most often it was at the first attempt at coitus. The absolute despair on his face eased a little. I said that if he thought this evening over, carefully, unemotionally, he would see the good points: he had attained an erection quickly, on his own. It had grown more intense in *my* hand, without any help from *his* hand. He had entered my body without trouble, and remained hard for some time. Only when he'd *looked,* only when he'd become a frightened spectator at his own mating, did he fail. The next time, or the time after, he wouldn't fail. We had many meetings left . . . as many as we needed. It was still going far better than anyone had a right to expect.

I dressed and left. I came down in the elevator, congratulating myself on turning disaster into something that might very well be as positive as successful intercourse would have been. Because if he could bounce back tomorrow and screw, he'd have proved that one failure didn't mean the ballgame. Smiling a little, I walked through the lobby and out the doors, *and came face to face with Greg!*

"Thirty-five minutes," he said, face white, eyes terribly cold. "That was a quickie. The last time it was closer to an hour and a half. And no dinner tonight? He must be taking you for granted . . . or can't you wait to climb in the sack with him?"

I moved my lips. His face suddenly twisted, and his arm rose, and I waited for him to slap me right there in the street. "Don't try any stupid lies on me! I've been following you for days now! You even sneaked in a matinee before our date! You dirty, dirty bitch!" His hand clenched into a fist, and I knew he was going to hit me, and I cried out, "It's my job! My *job,* Greg! I swear!"

People were looking at us. A man seemed about to come over, as Greg's fist was still poised over me. I took that fist, lowered it, kissed it. I was crying, but I knew I had to talk, and talk fast if I wasn't to lose what I'd waited a lifetime to find. I led him away from the lobby, holding tightly to his arm. I don't remember how I said it, but I told him the truth. The words ran over each other because I was afraid he would pull away at any minute and leave me forever. And he would be right, because how would *I* feel if *he* were "treating"

women, if *he* were a therapist to women as I was to
men? I'd have hated him! But even so, he had to know
that I hadn't been cheating on him!

I saw his face begin to change. We reached his car,
and he opened the door, and I got inside, still babbling
away, afraid to stop. He got in beside me and turned
to me. My throat went dry, and I coughed. He said,
"You don't expect me to believe this nonsense, do you?"
But I saw that he already believed it. I told him I would
bring him to Bill and Gini if I had to. And then I said,
"Just don't leave me. Please, honey, I love you, and I'll
do whatever you say."

But what if he told me to stop working immediately?
How could I leave Bill and Gini up the creek this way?
And more importantly, from both Masters' and Johnson's viewpoint, and my own, how in the world could I
leave Larry halfway toward manhood? Yet I wanted to
stop—to give up all wife-surrogate work—to marry Greg.

We looked at each other, I crying and he simply staring. Then he said, "Tell me how it all began."

We drove. I talked. We went to a restaurant and had
dinner. I talked. We went to a cocktail lounge and drank.
I talked. Outside, he took my hand. And drew me close.
And murmured, "Poor baby." In the car, he kept touching my legs, my breasts. He couldn't wait to get me
to the apartment, and into bed. His lovemaking was more
violent than it had ever been.

Afterward, he asked for more details. He wanted to
know about my work as a therapist, day by day, session
by session. And I told him what I could without mentioning names or identities. What he really wanted to
know was about my feelings: whether I'd been hot,
whether it had felt good, whether my guilt was real—
and he made love to me twice more. I finally pleaded for
rest! I told him what should have been obvious; I'd had
a terrible emotional shock. He had too, and while I
didn't say so, I couldn't understand the intense physical
performance that night of all nights.

He drove me back to my car, kissed me, said he
wanted to spend tomorrow evening with me. I was to
cancel out of my appointment with Larry. I nodded, and
realized he hadn't said to cancel out with the Foundation

completely. But he'd get around to that tomorrow. Anyway, I was too exhausted to think straight.

At home, I called Dr. Masters and said I wasn't feeling too well and he would have to cancel out tomorrow's session. I couldn't bring myself to say that he might have to get someone to take over for me. He asked a few questions, and I felt that perhaps he'd begun to sense trouble. But he was very soft with me, very gentle, and said that I'd done and said exactly the right thing after Larry's failure, and that a day's rest would do us both good. He would schedule the next session for Saturday. Perhaps the afternoon, so that I could take Sunday off and go somewhere with my boyfriend for a short weekend?

I muttered yes, that would be nice, and I'd speak to him again tomorrow. Then I fell into bed and passed out.

The next day, Friday, Greg called to say he'd be by the hospital to take me to lunch. He sounded normal, even cheerful. For some reason, it didn't make me happy.

At lunch, he said he was sorry he'd been so emotional, and that he was trying to "adjust to the idea." He asked if we could spend the weekend together. I tested him, now that he was so goddamned understanding, by saying I would probably have to finish out Larry's case, and had been asked to conduct an afternoon session on Saturday.

He sighed. He nodded. He said, "A wealthy client is flying his own jet to Las Vegas, five o'clock Saturday. He wants to take us. He'll be back in St. Louis by one A.M. Monday. We could have a ball. Try to make it, will you?" And he called for the check.

I spent the day in a daze. We had a date for eight that evening. I didn't know what was eating at me; or rather, I *did* know, and told myself it was absolutely ridiculous. He was a marvelous man, my Greg! A civilized, understanding man! No male chauvinist he! I was a free agent, as long as I didn't involve myself emotionally. Who could ask for a better lover? Women's lib would be *ecstatic* about him.

That night, he continued his questioning of me as wife surrogate. I answered as briefly as possible. Then I decided to test him further, and when he next asked a

question, I admitted I'd been really turned on with
Wallace. He asked for details. I gave them. The end
result was that I got laid three more times that night!
And afterward, he said he not only loved me, he *respected* me.

I took a sleeping pill the minute I reached my home.
I told myself to cool it. Everything would soon fall into
place. Everything would soon make sense to me. I just
had to finish with Larry, and then concentrate on Greg.

The night's sleep did me good. I arrived at Larry's
room refreshed and quite cheerful. I was a little late; it
was three. I'd have to hurry to make the flight to Vegas.

I was glad to see my patient. I kissed him with more
warmth than at any time previous to this. I touched his
body with more real affection and desire. I was less
guilty about being with him. And it got through to him,
as it will to any man. Finally, I forgot my hangups long
enough to go down on him, although briefly. He loved
it, and reciprocated by burying his face between my legs
and tonguing me until I was ready to come. I tried to
disengage, wanting to save my fire for coitus, but he
read me, grasped my hips, held me there, and brought
me to orgasm.

Beautiful! It was better than anything I'd felt with
Greg the last two nights; and once I realized it, I realized something else, something I wasn't ready for. So
I shoved that realization away, and went to work on
Larry. *Larry* was my man right now. He was my patient,
and he was my responsibility, and for the moment he
was my lover. I had to get him ready for that bookstore
girl. I had to make sure he'd give her what she needed
to love him, stay with him, help him make a new life.
And I wasn't going to check my watch while doing it!

Larry was still up. I stroked him. I kissed his lips and
whispered his name and said he'd become "dear to me."
He grasped me tightly, and I rolled onto him.

This time he stayed hard, but I don't believe he came.
I can't be sure, because he went through all the motions,
yet he had no ejaculation. So he either faked it, for me,
or, as Dr. Masters later suggested, he had something I'd
never heard of, a *dry* orgasm. My own feeling is that he

faked it, to make me happy, to show me he was a successful patient.

I left without mentioning it. I took my time driving
home, and called Gini and chatted at length with her,
and then realized it was too late to make the flight to
Las Vegas. (Or had I realized it all along?) I called
Greg and apologized. He said, "No problem. My client
decided to wait for us, no matter how long. Pick you up
in an hour. Bye!"

That short weekend was much too long for me, though
I did find Las Vegas exciting. Greg wanted more details,
and turned on with every one, and gave me love—if you
can call it that—until we were both exhausted. When
he dropped me off at my home early in the A.M., he
kissed me good night, happy as could be. He didn't have
the faintest idea that our love was finished, but it was. I
wasn't quite ready to say good-bye, to give up on the
dream, but love was something I no longer felt, only
remembered. Funny, he'd accepted what I was doing,
and I couldn't accept his acceptance!

I was very tired the next day at work, and even more
tired when I came to Larry's room at seven o'clock. And
it was hot. I mean *hot!* Only the second week in May,
but a real freak heatwave. When Larry tried the window
air-conditioner in the bedroom, he discovered it was out
of order. I guess the management hadn't gotten around
to checking them out for the summer.

Larry remarked that I wasn't looking up to par. I said
I'd had a hectic weekend. He said that perhaps we
shouldn't go out tonight. He ordered two chef's salads
from room service, and we had tall glasses of iced Vermouth and soda, while sitting on the davenport. The
salads were brought up, but we ignored them, chatting
in desultory fashion about the weather, Las Vegas—
which he felt was overrated—and ourselves. He asked,
for the first time, whether I had a strong personal at-
tachment. Without even thinking, I said, "No. I did, but
it's about over." I'd been leaning back in the couch,
eyes half-closed, but hearing myself, I lifted my head
and came fully awake.

He leaned toward me and barely touched my lips with
his. "Beautiful Val," he murmured. "Until now, you've

been . . . my doctor, my priest, my . . ." He waited to
see how I would react. I simply waited. "Now," he said,
"you're a woman . . . a woman I want . . . a woman
I wish were mine."

"And the bookstore girl?"

He smiled. "But I wish you were *both* mine."

That was a very manly thing to say, a very male thing
to want! He took me in his arms and kissed me, and his
hand went under my dress, and didn't take long to find
its way into my pants. I caressed his thigh, and soon felt
a hard-on.

We forgot the salads, and the heat. We went to the
bedroom and undressed each other and stood there,
nude, playing. He pressed his erection into me, and it
felt hard as iron. We got into bed. He kissed my breasts
and my belly and my thighs, and then ate me again. I
stroked his cock and played with his balls. Since he didn't
need it, I simply forgot to use my mouth.

We were man and woman together in that bed. As far
as I was concerned, the issue was no longer in doubt. I
could *feel* his maleness, *sense* his changeover. It had
happened, and Larry was a man, and he was going to
function as a man.

However, I wasn't sure that *he* knew it; or if he did,
whether he knew it strongly enough. It would, of course,
have to be proven now, and more than once. And I
wasn't going to worry about E. Coli, not with that stiff
cock throbbing in my hand as we lay *pied-à-tête* and he
brought me closer and closer to orgasm with his mouth.

He stopped this time. He came back up to me, and
looked at me, and I knew he wanted to get on me. But
I regained caution. If he went soft . . .

I got on him. I put him in me. I watched his face,
and there was no sign of fear. He'd been "thinking"
again. He'd remembered he had *not* gone soft the last
time and had gone on for a good five minutes and had
failed only to ejaculate. I sank down on him, began giving him a grinding, swiveling motion. And saw something I hadn't seen the last time: his eyes literally rolled
back in his head. He was feeling ecstasy. There would
be no need to fake tonight.

Neither of us had to fake. I came before he did by at

least five minutes. We went on about ten, all told, and
when he clutched my breasts and lunged up under me,
shuddering, I knew he had come.

He begged me not to leave. I closed my eyes, and we
lay there, holding hands. He told me how marvelous it
had felt. He said he knew it would get better and better
as he lost every last bit of fear, as he gained every last
bit of sensation. I smiled, but I was falling asleep. I
didn't want to think—about Greg. Larry brought the
salads to the bedroom. I sat up and ate a little, and then
said if I didn't leave I'd have to sleep here all night.

"Could you?"

I smiled at the excitement in his voice, and explained
about my mother.

At the door he said, "Let's not go out tomorrow night
either, all right?" I nodded. He said, "Come as early as
you can, please?" Again I nodded. He took me in his
arms and held me, and I felt him getting stiff! I
stepped back and touched him lightly there. "And I'll
stay late," I said. I left to the sound of his laughter.

I called the Foundation. Neither Gini nor Dr. Masters
felt there was any need to change plans. I was to continue on as before. If Larry could attain and maintain
a good erection at tomorrow's session, I was to see if he
could mount me, male-dominant position. If I felt any
weakening on his part, I was to repeat the female-
dominant position. What they wanted were two or three
male-dominant sex acts, to convince this "homosexual"
of ten years' duration that he could enjoy making love
to a woman.

Greg called while I was away from my phone Tuesday. I didn't return the call.

I came to Larry's room at six-thirty. We went right
to bed. We played for almost an hour. He never once
lost his erection in all that time, and took my hand away
from him twice in order not to have an orgasm. But he
waited for me to climb on him, and when I drew him
toward me and spread my legs wide, he said, "Should
I? What if . . ."

I reached out and grabbed his cock. It had begun to
wilt a little. I said, "You want me. I want you. There
are no more what-ifs. Whether you do it now, or an

hour from now, or tomorrow, or the day after, you know you're going to do it. Sooner or later, you're going to fuck me, Larry. I haven't the slightest doubt of that. It might as well be now."

He stiffened as I spoke and as I rubbed his cock with my fingers. And he moved onto me as I continued to speak. And when I finished, he was between my legs. I put him in, and he moved a little, and then he moved more strongly. I began to move under him, pacing him, and then we were fucking, man and woman, and he came. Not prematurely; just rather soon, about two or three minutes. I'd begun mounting toward orgasm myself, but I didn't let him see my disappointment.

I doubt he could have seen it anyway. He was in heaven! I then realized that we were both covered with perspiration. It was the hottest night yet—but neither of us had felt the discomfort until now.

We had salads again, and cold beer, and he said, "Do you know, this is our tenth session? In ten meetings, you've changed ten years!"

I think he could have gone again. Perhaps I should have tried him, but I was beginning to feel what I call the "withdrawals." Larry was a success, and would soon be gone. I would then face Greg; face my feelings for Greg.

Wednesday Greg called and asked why I hadn't gotten back to him. I said I hadn't received the message. He asked if we could get together tonight. I said, "I'm sorry. I have to see my patient. We're finishing up in the next two or three days." He asked what I meant by "finishing up." I acted a little coy; he pressed me; I said, "Well, he's quite functional now. We're hammering home, if you'll pardon the expression, the lesson."

Greg pardoned the expression, and everything else. He said he was looking forward to the weekend, when I would be definitely finished and we could "discuss the case in detail."

I arrived at Larry's room at six. We went to bed and made love until seven-thirty. I was deeply depressed, and yet I managed a healthy orgasm. He had *two*.

Reporting in to Masters and Johnson that night, I indicated I felt the case was as good as over. But we all agreed it would be useful to go on, as previously decided, for another male-dominant act or two.

I was at his door at six-thirty the next night. There was no answer to my knock. I went downstairs and called the Foundation from the lobby, thinking there'd been some mixup in timing. Gini couldn't understand it. I decided to check the desk. Larry had left an envelope for me; it contained a letter. He thanked me, said he'd been struck by a sudden urge to go home and see his bookstore girl. "But I'll never forget you, Val. I wonder how many grateful souls have said that to you? No matter—none can mean it more than I do."

In retrospect, it's almost funny. I worried so much about sex with Larry because he was a homosexual. He worried so much about sex with me because I was a woman. But once he began heterosexual activity, the problem simply ceased to be. And he married the bookstore girl eight months later.

Anyway, end of Larry.

And a few weeks later, end of Greg. He never did understand why. I saw him every so often for another five or six months. But I wouldn't go to bed with him. I'd simply ceased to care for him. It didn't hurt as much as it would have had he ceased caring for me. And I must say he tried and tried, and gave up with obvious pain. But there it is.

I worked. I dated. I went to bed with a date every so often, and usually enjoyed it. I liked a number of men, and loved none. I slept well and ate well and learned to play golf and to skin-dive. I had a ten-day vacation in Bermuda, courtesy of a very nice doctor, and a long weekend in Las Vegas, courtesy of my skin-diving instructor. The emptiness wasn't noticeable, except on rare occasions when I awoke before my alarm went off and wondered why I bothered to get up at all.

I never cried anymore. What was there to cry about, except, perhaps, my continuing money problems. But adults don't cry about things like that, and I was twenty-five, going on twenty-six. I still looked for that perfect lover, but I didn't really expect to find him anymore. I was a woman with quite a past, and I refused to dwell on the future.

In September Gini contacted me. They had another case. I grew cold inside, even as I asked questions about the patient.

I hit it lucky for a change. The patient was a movie star. A real live movie star, whose name I would recognize instantly if it were mentioned! And not a Boris Karloff type, either. A leading man. Tall, fair, and incredibly handsome. Roughly forty years old. Married to an actress of lesser fame, but still known to many. And it was the wife to whom I owed this chance. She had been at the Foundation as a patient with her husband for six days, and then decided she had to rejoin the road company of a Broadway show with which she'd been touring. It was felt that this was an excuse, that she hadn't been able to take to the method of treatment. Also, she insisted that he functioned well enough with her.

Actually, this wasn't far from the truth. He had never failed with his wife. The problem was, he didn't enjoy it at all with her! And what she didn't know was that in his extramarital affairs he was failing steadily. So this might be a rough case, since he wasn't a man who would automatically turn on for a different woman, a young and attractive woman, as would a man with little opportunity for such goodies.

When I was finally given his name, I gasped!

I was to come to the Foundation for a briefing at five this afternoon, and meet the actor I'll call Brent at seven-thirty . . . if I accepted.

Of course I accepted! Hadn't I always fantasized myself opposite the leading man in the movies I'd seen as a girl? This was a chance to make at least a third of those dreams come true!

5

The briefing for my fourth case was short and sweet. Brent was at the very top of his career, and at the very bottom of his joy in life. He was an internationally known screen lover, and had been close to that in real life until five or six years before, when he had begun to fail in his extramarital affairs. And these were more frequent, in terms of actual intercourse, than the sex in his married life. Also, very important to him.

He had become progressively more fearful, and therefore progressively less capable. He was now totally unable to function with anyone but his wife. And the way she managed sex was so cut-and-dried as to preclude pleasure on his part. As described to me, she would make love once a week, as a matter of principle, and had actually told him she did it to keep him in good health. She would frequently discuss their peers, other actors and actresses, and show contempt for their "filthy" affairs and messy personal lives. She told him they were lucky to have such a "tidy" life; and that is just what it was.

He could always tell when she was about to bestow a sex act on him; she would spend a very long time in the bathroom and would return to sit in bed and read awhile, not speaking at all—she usually talked a great deal—preparing herself for the trauma, no doubt! He would then prepare himself in a manner he had learned was helpful. He had a collection of pornographic books, photographs, slides, and films, and would manage to look at some part of it before joining her in bed. Then they would kiss, pet for a while, and though she didn't stop him from doing whatever he wanted to, it was so obviously planned, so lacking in need and spontaneity, that all the fire and passion went out of him. There had been a time when their lovemaking had been good, if not wildly erotic. He wanted not only to regain his manhood with the girls he had at his disposal, but also to regain some element of pleasure with his wife.

And he had a special problem. News of his failures had been getting around certain Hollywood circles. There were always girls—many called themselves "starlets"—who dated widely among the famous; and inevitably, friends of his would end up with girls *he'd* been with. When he suspected what was happening, he began refusing to go to parties, premieres, anyplace where he might be laughed at.

This was a man with enormous pride, and the pride was being systematically destroyed. Not only was the ability to make love his personal life, it was also in a sense his professional life! So life itself was being destroyed, and he admitted to Dr. Masters that he had considered suicide more than once, and had actually made an abortive attempt—taking five or six sleeping pills from a supply of forty. He smiled as he said this, and stated he knew it was idiotic, but there it was. If there wasn't some change, soon, his next attempt might not be abortive.

Despite this, Dr. Masters and Gini felt that it might not be too difficult a case. This man had been jumping into bed, *expecting* failure, then running off in a panic to leap on another starlet, compounding the failure—on and on, until he'd come here. He'd forgotten the basic principles of touch, feel, play—and especially *choice* and *need!* He seemed to feel that he should want (and therefore perform with) any and all women who were, as he put it, "reasonably attractive." He didn't seem to realize he had inner preferences, unconscious likes and dislikes; that there had to be some chemistry between him and a partner. He had to be slowed down; had to learn that only when he *strongly wanted* should he make any sort of a sexual move; had to be taught all over again to enjoy a woman without haste and without fear.

Also, there was obviously some hidden background of morality, though he insisted he had been on his own in all ways since he was sixteen, had "laid a thousand women, easily" and had never believed in sin or the like. But there simply had to be guilt involved with these other women; otherwise why continue to perform—no matter how joylessly—with his wife? (Though I felt that could also be explained by the long history of *success* with his wife—no news of failure with her could reach his friends! And the success might be explained by the total lack of pressure with her: he neither wanted her very much nor feared failing with her.)

On the most obvious level, his problem was that he lost his erection at some point between petting and putting it in, and never regained it. My job was not to see that he *didn't* lose his erection—but to make sure he *did*, and then to bring it back and have him use it. Tonight, if possible. We had between four and six meetings, and because of his depressed mental state, he might cut out and run at any time.

I drove home at about a quarter to six, showered, and tried to think of what to wear. I considered a two-piece pants outfit, a jumpsuit, a knit mini, several other outfits that played up my figure. But I was going to meet a man who dealt with the most beautiful women who wore the most daring clothing. It would be a mistake to compete in that way. If, on the other hand, he started out feeling somewhat disappointed and then could be made to feel delight and excitement at the right moment . . .

I chose a navy-blue suit just back from the cleaner. It had seen plenty of wear. The skirt length was barely mini; the jacket was full enough to effectively hide my breasts; I added a pair of medium-heeled black shoes that did little for my legs. No makeup, no jewelry, a gray band to pull back my hair . . . and Miss Prim was ready to go on the town!

I parked in front of the Foundation and went up in the elevator to the third floor. When I entered the outer office where the receptionist normally sits (she was, of course, off duty by now), I saw a man slouched back in a chair, riffling through a magazine. He glanced up, then looked back at the magazine . . . and I suddenly regretted dressing as I had. Because this was the most *beautiful* male I'd ever had the good fortune to meet! He was even better-looking in person than on the screen, and I was suddenly a little girl wanting to impress the big movie star. I understood why he had his pick of the world's women, and for both the first and last time, all regret at being a wife surrogate disappeared—and didn't return until this case was over. From here on, it was a love affair!

I walked over to him, feeling a big, foolish smile spread across my face. I said, "You must be Brent Warren," and babbled on about having seen his movies and enjoyed *all* of them. He smiled and nodded and murmured a few words when I gave him the chance. I was just so . . . *enthralled*. Here I'd been feeling as old as the hills, and now I was a naïve, bubbling little movie fan again!

After a while I heard a stirring in back, and out came Dr. Masters and Mrs. Johnson. Dr. Masters said, "I see you two have already met," and then hesitated, wondering, I think, whether or not I'd introduced myself. He finally introduced us: "Valerie, this is Brent."

Dr. Masters didn't ordinarily do the introducing—at least not for any of my other patients. I think he was acknowledging Brent's position as a superpersonality, and giving his ego the boost it needed. Dr. Masters and Gini made a few remarks, and only then did Brent seem to realize that I was his wife surrogate, the girl who was supposed to fire him up and solve his problems. And while he didn't do anything obvious, he most definitely did *not* look happy!

We chatted awhile, and I cursed myself and wished I could leap into a nearby room and, like Superman, emerge with a new outfit. But Brent was rising and shaking Dr. Masters' hand, and we were on our way out. Because he was so well known, so easily identifiable, he had rented a furnished apartment, rather than risk walking in and out of hotel or motel lobbies. And yet, when, in line with this, I suggested buying food at a nearby delicatessen and eating at his place, he said that he

wanted to try several St. Louis restaurants. I looked
surprised, and he said, "You *expected* to meet me, and
so you recognized me. But people rarely do—on the
street, in a store or a restaurant, I mean. If I'm in a
television studio or entering a theater for a premiere,
it's different. Besides, I have a little kit here . . ." And
he reached into his breast pocket and came out with
hair. That's right, he had a hairpiece and a moustache,
both dark, and using my rear-view mirror, put them on
in a minute. And he did it well. I mean, it was convincing. But, of course, he was an actor.

I had to laugh. He grinned back at me. He looked so
different with that pencil-line moustache and black wig.
I asked how they stayed on, and he said with a special
kind of adhesive tape. "But let's forget that and find a
place to eat. I'm starving!"

We went to the Nantucket Cove, the best seafood
house in St. Louis, and had lobster and a half-bottle of
white wine (he wanted a full bottle, but I cautioned
him). He didn't talk too much, and I was too confused
by that wig and moustache, and by being with him, and
by wishing I hadn't made myself look so drab, to create
conversation. But little by little, we did exchange some
words—and finally, over coffee, he looked at me, looked
hard, with those wide-set, pale-blue eyes that have stared
at women for twenty years out of Technicolor movies,
and he said in that honey-rich voice that has melted
women's hearts from New York to California, "Forgive
me, Valerie, but I don't think you do yourself justice,
the way you dress." And I began to nod, and then broke up.
I laughed, splattering bits of seven-layer cake across the
table.

He stared. I shook my head, trying to speak, and
laughed some more. Then I saw a faint flush beginning
to move up from his neck to his face, and realized that
with me he wasn't the great actor but a very fragile male.
If he thought I was laughing at *him* . . .

I already liked him more than any man I knew at
that time. I mean, he was just so good to look at and
listen to—what little he *did* say was bright and interesting—that I felt I could fall in love with him with no

effort whatsoever. *And that's exactly what I told him, once I stopped laughing.*

When I'd finished my little speech, I dropped my eyes and sat there. And sat there, and sat there—and nothing happened. So I had to look up. He was staring again, but there was no longer any faint flush. "Would you mind if we left now?" he asked.

The first thing he did on entering his apartment was to remove the false hair. He had three rooms—bedroom, living room, and large kitchen—furnished rather drably, and with nothing but the TV less than fifteen years old. I felt it was a good match for the clothing I was wearing! And when I looked at the bed, I wanted to ask, "Will it hold up under therapy?"

He caught my look and my expression and murmured, "Did you ever treat a patient on the floor? You may have to this time." I laughed, and turned, and he was suddenly very close. I think he was going to back off, but I bumped into him, deliberately, and let him feel my superstructure. He looked down at me—he towered over me from his height of six-two or six-three—and slowly, reluctantly, I'd say, put his arms around me.

I gave in to the dream right then and there—the dream of kissing Brent Warren, the movie star. I let myself go, and soon I was enjoying not only a dream, but the reality of a big, beautiful hunk of man moving his hands over my body, his tongue into my mouth, and once he'd felt my bottom a little, pressing his stiff cock into my belly. And what I felt through both our clothing was no semi or partial or weak erection, but a powerful hard-on. I mean, it really made its presence felt, and in a way that I truly couldn't remember with any other man.

We never went to the davenport. He began undressing me right there—and I didn't have to lead him, or instruct him. Not that I should have expected to with Brent Warren, but, after all, he *was* a patient. (I had trouble remembering that all through this case. And that's why I broke rule after rule.)

When he got my blouse and brassiere off, he simply stared. Then he put out his hand and touched first one breast and then the other. "My God, Valerie, where have you been hiding these all evening?"

My tension ended, and I laughed. He took off the rest of my clothing, and kneeling to remove my panties, stroked and kissed my bottom, calling it "classic." Then he said, "You're not a member of some religious order, are you—wearing that *habit?* Because, honey, you'd do better going nude!"

It was my turn to undress him. Though he was probably forty-five or close to it, he had the body of a young athlete—not the heavy bulging muscles, but the long, hard ones of a swimmer. Anyway, every part of his body was tight, hard, delineated in muscle and tendon. And when I took off his trousers and saw how his shorts were bulging . . .

He'd been surprised when my brassiere came off, and I was stunned when those shorts came down. There I was, kneeling about two inches away from the most enormous hard-on I've ever seen! I know I've said that size doesn't count, and normally it doesn't. Had he been someone I disliked, it certainly wouldn't have made any difference. But here was the dream lover who turned out to have the dream cock!

I said, "My God, and where have you been hiding *that* monster?" We both laughed. He said that my breasts and his cock were well matched, and I said *that* wasn't the match we were looking for. His hand went between my legs, and we strained our naked bodies together, kissing, and I swear, I've never been kissed like that, ever.

We fell into bed, and he wanted to get right on and in me. There didn't seem to be the slightest fear in him or the slightest chance that he could fail with that enormous, steel-hard erection. But even as I was melting under his caresses, feeling my legs parting as if by their own will, I realized that disaster might be just a moment or two away. His failures came *during* coitus, not before it. And there was a pattern which usually preceded failure that I don't believe I've mentioned before. His wife, as I've said, would give him time to prepare himself with pornography. But if he was with a "starlet," and *she* took off for a moment, as many of them seemed to have done when with him (to wash, I guess, in preparation for this paragon of lovers), then he invariably went soft while waiting, and never regained his erection. For he'd become convinced it was impossible to make love once he'd lost his erection, and he lost it between petting and coitus—or during coitus.

He was rolling over on me, pressing me down, kissing my face and neck, his tool rubbing between my thighs. Another moment, and I wouldn't be able to control myself, and so I said, "Excuse me a moment, would you, Brent?" and slid away and got off the bed. I was going to walk right out, but I heard a sound, and glanced back. He was shaking his head, sighing, all the joy gone from his face. "It'll go away," he whispered, holding his cock, stroking it in an obvious attempt to keep it hard.

"And that's just what we want, so we can bring it back again."

"It won't come back, Valerie."

I smiled. I said we'd see how nicely it came back in a moment or two. "If you think I don't want that fantastic thing, if you think I'm going to leave without sampling it . . ." and I didn't have to fake the pouty-mouthed, heavy-breathed, hip-swinging exit. I was *feeling* it.

I goofed around in the bathroom awhile, running the water and flushing the toilet and doing all the things that had turned him off with other women—or was it simply having a few moments alone in which to worry about his performance?

When I returned to the bedroom, he'd covered himself with the blanket. He watched me as I came toward him, his eyes going to my breasts, my crotch. And then he flung aside the blanket, shaking his head and laughing. "It didn't happen," he said, holding out his arms—and there was that incredible hard-on, and I didn't know whether to feel delighted as a woman or disappointed as a therapist. Then I was in his arms, and there was no longer any room in me for the wife surrogate, no longer any thought of applying the squeeze technique to make him go down. Because he was feeding that huge tool into my body, and he was saying he loved me—over and over, just like that, "I love you, Valerie, I love you, honey!"—and for the moment it was true and for the moment I believed him and for the moment I said it too, panting, gasping, groaning the words into his mouth: "I love you, Brent, I love you!"

And all the time he was pounding me with that incredible cock, which, like his career, like the dreams he created, was bigger than life size.

I came so hard it seemed to reach my brain. I was dizzy and exhausted—and unable to do very much for Brent. But he didn't mind; he was down to the short strokes, gripping my ass and biting my neck, and then going off like a cannon. His shudders, his deep-down-in-the-throat cries, went on for what seemed a long time, a long, beautiful time.

Afterward, we talked. I asked about his childhood, his youth, his life before he became an actor and a public institution. He'd had what amounted to one long success story. He'd been a precocious and athletic child in grammar school; less the great student in high school, but still well up in the B's, compensating for any loss of scholarship by making just about every team in the school, with football his specialty. He was All-American in college, and it was here he did his first acting—a drama-club play. He'd been bitten rather severely by the show-biz bug, and after graduation—as a business administration major—he went to New York to try the stage. Even here, in traditionally difficult territory, he made his way easily and well, landing a small part in a Broadway musical within a week after arriving!

Four more roles, the last a solid dramatic part, followed, and he was spotted in that last play by a Hollywood producer. His screen test was for a small part opposite a sexpot star—he was to play her young lover, who was killed within the first ten minutes of the film—but his part was padded when the producer and director saw how the sexpot and other women on the lot responded to him. From there to his starring role took only nine months, and he'd never been headed since.

And women? He'd been seduced by a neighbor, a housewife with two children, who hired him to mow her lawn when he was sixteen and then had him take care of a few jobs inside the house . . . and who finally had him do a job on her. She walked in on him, stark naked,

one Sunday afternoon when her husband was off playing golf and the children were out in the backyard. He was repairing a kitchen cabinet, rehanging the door, and she acted as if she'd forgotten he was there and gasped and turned her back—displaying, he said, her best feature, "a truly *gorgeous* ass"—but remained there. Finally, he approached, touched her, and she whirled on him and simply gobbled him up. He was in bed and on her about half a minute after he touched her shoulder!

He banged his Mrs. Robinson a few times a week for almost a year, and even here his luck held good. No one ever gossiped or suspected. And then he met a girl in school, and she became his steady, and he dropped his housewife. The housewife, however, claimed she loved him. She managed to get him into her home just once more, but he played immovable object, and she had to be satisfied with falling to her knees and blowing him as he stood there, arms crossed. He said it was a "great kick," and he stood still long enough for a *second* blow job!

In college, he had many girls, none really important to him. In New York, he fell in love for the first time, with an actress two years older than he, and he eventually married her when she too came to Hollywood. That was his first wife. He divorced her after seven years of marriage: "And they were good years, Val. It's just that she was making it with too many other men on the side, and while I was doing the same, I somehow couldn't accept it in her. She was a lot better in bed than Cleo —that's my wife, now."

He'd stayed single for three years, then married Cleo. He'd been attracted to her by her looks—she was a beautiful woman, tall and full-breasted and "regal"— but it was more than that. They slept together only after a full year of courtship (unusual in any case, and *most* unusual in Hollywood!), at which time he discovered she was a virgin. And even during their courtship, she never once dated another man. And after marriage she was "absolutely faithful" to him, which was such a great contrast to the other women he knew, and especially to his first wife, that it kept him reasonably happy despite their

not-so-great love life. What he had begun to realize only recently was that Cleo didn't play around because Cleo's need for sex was minimal.

At first, he was faithful in return—except for, as he put it, "an occasional piece, when it was inevitable." But then his erotic needs reawakened, and he began to indulge himself in starlets again. About ten years later, he had his first failure.

End of story, he said, but I'd noticed one blank spot. Parents.

"What were your mother and father like, Brent?"

He'd begun touching me again, playing with my breasts, and now he leaned over me, kissed me, stroked my hips and thighs. I wondered whether he was avoiding answering my question. Then I forgot everything but what he was doing—which was reversing himself over me, bringing that huge tool to my mouth, sucking at my vulva with his mouth and probing inside with his tongue. It went on until he jerked himself away, and by that time I'd had one fantastic orgasm, and knew I was going to have another as soon as he plunged his cock into me. I came again in no time at all, and was still excited as he went on and on, until he threw my legs up over his shoulders and thrust into me a few times and began to groan and shudder.

When it was over, I went to the bathroom to wash, and he followed, and we washed together. I remember being surprised at how small his penis was when limp; no hint at all of the enormous potential there. We returned to the bedroom and lay down again and held hands, and he asked about *my* life.

Trying not to weaken my position as wife surrogate—supposedly calm and assured and always in control—I talked about Mother and my job at the hospital and my lack of ambition. Finally, I told him about Greg. He found it funny, and soon had me laughing too! But then he kissed me gently and said I deserved better and that he wished . . . He stopped then. He'd been about to say something foolish, and how I would have loved to have heard it!

We were terribly tender with each other for about half an hour, simply touching and kissing and talking,

with practically no passion involved. Which was just as well, because we'd broken enough rules already without risking failure due to exhaustion. I'd been supposed to put him down, bring him up, and then mount him for one copulation, never risking a possible failure on a second try. Instead, he'd never gone down, and I hadn't had the objectivity to use the squeeze technique, and *he'd* mounted *me,* and we'd had two copulations.

I explained it to him as I rose and dressed. He laughed and said, "I won't tell if you won't." I said, "It's a deal." We sealed it with a kiss, but of course I knew I was going to tell Dr. Masters when I reported.

He lit a cigarette and sat on the couch. I was dressed, and hesitated, knowing it was time to leave. Always before, in this postcoital situation, the patient would plead with me to stay, and I would want to leave. This time, he said nothing, and I wanted to stay. Finally I said, "Anything to drink here?"

He had vodka, and we made bloody Marys. Sitting on the davenport, I turned to him. "You're not *avoiding* talking about your parents, are you, Brent?"

"Of course not!" It was said a little too sharply.

We sipped. I said nothing. He cleared his throat. "Wonder what's on television?"

"Maybe an old Brent Warren movie."

He chuckled.

I said, "Have you discussed your parents with Dr. Masters?"

"I guess so. I really don't remember. I discussed everything else with him."

"What did you tell him about your earliest memories?"

He got up and went to the TV and put it on and switched the dial to every channel, then turned it off and looked at me. "You think it's important?"

I nodded.

He sighed. "I really don't think it has anything to do with why I'm here."

"Then why avoid talking about it?"

"Because . . ." He waved his hands. "They're both dead, and the manner of their deaths pained me . . . especially my mother's, six years ago."

"Your sexual trouble started when?" I murmured, looking down at my glass.

"Look, tonight has been wonderful, and I haven't felt this good in years, but I'm simply out of steam, physically and emotionally, so could we drop it?"

I went to him and kissed his face and touched his hair. "Good night, dear." I was afraid I'd pushed too hard, and that Dr. Masters would hear of it the next day and feel I'd overstepped my role. But more than that, I was afraid that I'd hurt my lover. "I'm sorry if I upset you."

His nod was barely perceptible. He didn't move from his position near the TV as I went to the door. I let myself out and drove home, fighting tears.

I was worried when I spoke to Gini later, telling her about how quickly we had moved to male-dominant coitus, but she wasn't at all disturbed. She and Dr. Masters felt that because Brent had had his wife here awhile, he was probably primed and ready for intercourse. Besides, whatever worked was acceptable. (It would have been a different story if I'd *hurt* the patient by allowing him to rush!)

At work the next day, I borrowed a *Post-Dispatch* and turned to the entertainment section. Sure enough, Brent had a movie downtown. The rest of the day I played a little game with myself, trying to imagine the reactions of various individuals to my having made love to a world-famous movie star. Kid stuff, I know, but it was fun.

As five o'clock approached, I became more and more excited—and worried. We hadn't parted very well last night. Would it change things?

I wanted to call him, but of course I couldn't; it wasn't part of my job. I wanted him to call me—I'd told him I worked at the medical complex—but why should he?

I left at ten to five, in order to avoid the jam of cars leaving the Forest Park area for Kingshighway Road.

I drove home and got into my maroon jumpsuit, a knit that clung to every little curve and crevice of my body. It was, by far, the most daring outfit I owned, and among the most flattering . . . and I hoped it would please Brent, and I feared *nothing* would. I began the drive back to the Forest Park area at six-fifteen, much

sooner than I had to, since I was due at Brent's place at
seven-thirty.

Something strange began to happen as I drove. I was
thinking of Brent, of his body, of his huge cock, and I
began to turn on in a way I never had before. I mean, I
was getting terribly excited merely *thinking,* just *remembering* what we had done last night; so excited that I
could feel the moisture between my legs. I began to
move, at first uncomfortably, and then with erotic purpose. The vibration of the car, a section of bumpy road,
my own movements all combined to bring me to fever
pitch. Finally, I pressed my hand to my crotch and
rubbed up and back on the seat—and I came! Right
there in the car, exiting at Kingshighway Road, I had
an orgasm! It's lucky I wasn't killed, because I think I
closed my eyes during the few seconds of actual spasm
and ecstasy.

I parked to catch my breath. I was shocked at myself!
Not that I hadn't masturbated before. Since Abner, and
his making me do it in front of the mirror, I'd occasionally relieved myself that way, but never without being in my bed and working at it for a good ten or fifteen
minutes.

It was only seven o'clock. I had a half-hour to waste.
I wanted to go right to his place, but that might catch
him before he was ready for me—and he *was* a patient.
I repeated that to myself several times. "He *is* a patient!"

As soon as I began to drive, I felt the heat rise again.
Every little bump, every vibration, seemed Brent's fingers, Brent's tool, working on me. I refused to give in to
it, though, refused to touch myself. But it made no difference. I was driving toward his apartment, thinking
ahead and visualizing how I would draw down his shorts
and grasp that beautiful cock and caress his big balls and
kiss them, kiss and suck everything I could get in my
mouth. And how he would put my legs up over his
shoulders and *slide* into me; how I would feel every inch
as it entered. And then that first sliding out, almost to
the knob. And then that sudden stroke in, all the way in
. . . it was just too much, and I spasmed, came, had an
orgasm without touching myself!

I parked in front of his apartment house and leaned

back, eyes closed. My panties were wet, and I was afraid
I'd soak right through my jumpsuit. I was gasping for
breath, utterly knocked out. And wasn't I the fool, I
thought, to use up my passion and cut down on the wonderful sensation of *actually* making love to Brent.

But I needn't have worried about *that*. As soon as he
opened the door to my knock, as soon as I saw him
standing there in lean slacks and short-sleeved shirt and
suede loafers, as soon as he smiled and held out his
arms, I was ready. So was he—because he barely paused
to kiss me before undressing me. I did the best I could
to undress him at the same time. He finished up for himself, and picked me up like a baby, one hand under my
back and the other under my knees, and groaned softly,
"Oh, Val, what I'm going to do to you!" Then both his
arms moved. The one under my back reached around,
and his hand grasped my breast, and the one under my
knees moved up, and the hand grasped my buttocks. I
began slipping out of his arms, but slowly, and as I did
I turned to face him, and then we were glued together,
body to body, mouth to mouth, and he was sucking
the breath out of me and backing me toward the bedroom, step by step, never pausing in his kissing, his caressing. My body felt like one large cunt—hot and wet and
aching.

I didn't think of the squeeze technique and how I was
supposed to make him lose his erection. I thought of
nothing but getting him into me and satisfying my terrible
need.

It was last night all over again; *better*, because there
wasn't even the slightest pause between wanting and loving; no bathroom and no talk and no thought of "treatment." We did everything. Sixty-nine and doggy fashion
and on our sides and Mamma-Papa. We finished with his
favorite position: my legs over his shoulders. I came
twice before he finally reached his orgasm. He went to
wash up. I lay there, trembling like a leaf. I'd had four
orgasms tonight, and I think I'd been mounting toward a
fifth when he came!

He brought a wet towel to the bed. He washed me
gently, first between the legs, and then, turning me over,
between my buttocks. He kissed my face and my belly

and my back and my behind. He repeated what he'd said during our lovemaking, but very, very softly now: "I love you, Valerie."

I smiled and touched his face. "I love you too, Brent, and isn't it silly, when you'll be leaving in a few days?"

He'd been smiling, but at that his smile began to fade. I quickly said, "But it's true anyhow. I *do* love you. I feel you *do* love me. For the time we have, darling. Just that little time. And it's better than if we were going on together. Because every love I've ever had has died when it went on. Yours too, I'll bet."

He nodded slowly.

"And this won't have the chance to die, will it? This will retire, like a smart boxing champion, untied and undefeated."

He bent to my lips and kissed me; and I felt something against my leg. It was his cock, slowly lengthening, slowly stiffening as he gave me his tongue and ran his hands over my breasts.

I got up, saying I was hungry.

"That's right, we never thought of dinner, did we? Now that you've reminded me, I'm starving!"

We dressed, and he put on his dark hairpiece and moustache. We went back to the Nantucket Cove and had lobster again—lots and lots of fresh broiled lobster. I'll never forget that dinner. We kept touching hands. Once he leaned across the table and kissed me, and I kissed him back. I never thought about the other people—though the place was jammed—all I thought of was us in bed, and I was coming on strong again!

He talked about Hollywood, inside talk, and I laughed a lot, and once I was surprised and dismayed to learn that a comic I loved was a lecher who used his position to pressure women who worked in his films into his bed. And once I was upset to learn that a manly he-man was addicted to teen-age boys and regularly went to Mexico for homosexual orgies. And once I sat absolutely still, enthralled by the story of an old man who lived in a weird little cottage in Santa Monica Canyon and drank nothing but bourbon and ate nothing but raw eggs and whole-wheat bread and staggered out into his front yard on certain days to ask passersby if they remembered

certain films—*silent* films—and certain leading ladies.
"We had *such* a success," he would say in a cracked,
ruined alto-tenor that had never been much better for
talkies. "*Such* a success, and such a love afterward." And
once Brent leaned forward and used his napkin to wipe
away a trickle of melted butter on my chin, and then
touched my lips with his finger.

Back at the apartment, we undressed and got into bed.
I made as if to suck him, getting down there and stroking his shaft and kissing the knob a few times. But what
I did was to murmur, "Please don't be upset. This
might hurt a little, but it's necessary that you go soft,
so as to see that you can regain your erection."

"Valerie, no . . ."

I was already digging my thumb into the underside
of the glans in the discomforting—for some men *painful*
—squeeze technique. "The doctor feels it's necessary," I
said, "and so do I."

He grunted a little as my thumb went in deeper. *But
he didn't go down.* I really gave it all I had, and he
said, "Ouch!" and laughed, because that cock was nowhere near losing its rigidity. No matter how hard I
squeezed and how long I kept it up, he just wouldn't
soften. And then we were both laughing, hysterically,
and I fell back down beside him, and we laughed to
think that anyone—least of all Brent Warren—should
think he had any problem relating to sex, and to think
that I was anything but his willing paramour, his panting
piece of ass, his desirous lover.

After laughter came passion, and we made love and
he cried out in orgasm and I was a few seconds behind
him, coming as he shuddered into stillness. Then we
slept.

When I awoke, it was midnight. He still slept, and I
got up carefully and tiptoed into the kitchen, where there
was a wall phone. As I dialed my home, I kept thinking
that I had to try the squeeze technique again. It was
dangerous to allow him to go on without losing and regaining an erection. We'd obviously hit it off tremendous-
ly well—one of those rare cases of perfect chemistry—
but that wouldn't help him the first time he got into bed
with one of his starlets.

And then I thought: To hell with his starlets, and his wife too. He was *mine*. But of course I stopped that nonsense short. He was mine for another two nights—he'd told Bill he planned to leave Sunday morning, and it was now Thursday night. I had tomorrow and Saturday with him, and then it was finished.

I spoke to my mother's nurse. She was upset. I'd promised to be back at ten or ten-thirty. I told her I'd had car trouble and asked if she could stay on another two hours. "I know it's a terrible imposition, but I'll drive you home. . . ."

When I entered the bedroom, Brent was just stirring. I kissed him, and he came fully awake and stretched that magnificent body. He smiled at me and drew me down for a sweet, sweet kiss.

We got up, and he rummaged in the refrigerator and made a plate of cheese and cold cuts, and brought out a bottle of Mumm's champagne. We sat at the table, he in a short robe, me in one of his shirts, and ate and drank and talked. He was a marvelous raconteur, going on about his experiences. He told me about shooting on location in France some years before, and driving into a little town in the evening with the chief cameraman and being recognized while eating at a little outdoor café. The waitress who recognized him was short and plump, "with enormous breasts and an ass to match," and pitched him as hard as she could with her English, "both body and broken." He had experienced only a few failures at this time, hadn't had a woman in almost a week, and the waitress was "low and slutty enough to set me off in a very basic way." The cameraman, however, turned out to be interested less in girls than in boys, and the owner's son, a faggoty kid of fifteen or sixteen, responded to the waitress's whispered excitement by approaching the table and trying his luck. He didn't make out with Brent, but the cameraman was most interested. Anyway, they all ended up in a big bed in the waitress's room—a *ménage à quatre*. Brent had no problems that night, giving the waitress a good, long go, but felt that might have been due (in part at least) to his watching the other couple. He admitted he was turned on by the cameraman's sucking and sodomizing the boy . . . and

by the boy taking the opportunity to touch Brent's cock
every so often. Eventually the boy became a third party
to Brent's second go with the waitress, putting Brent's
penis into her for starters. Then he worked with his hands
and mouth at everything he could manage to reach
while Brent screwed the girl—licking his anus, reaching
down to touch his shaft as it slid in and out of the girl,
pushing his stiff little prick between Brent's buttocks.

Brent felt that this kind of stimulation might help
him, so when he got back to Hollywood, he tried it,
using a good-looking young faggot and a hefty young
starlet.

"Nothing. What worked for one crazy, magic night
in France never worked again—even when I went back
to the same town and tried the same combination!"

We'd finished the champagne, and it was after one,
and I had to be going. He asked me to call the nurse
and offer her double time for sleeping at my home. He
would pay the bill.

God, how I wanted to, but Mother always got up early
to see me before work. I said it was difficult to arrange,
but I would try for Saturday night. Brent said, "At least
give me Saturday, *all day?*"

I nodded, so delighted I couldn't speak. He wanted
to be with me, and not just in bed. Four-day romance or
not, it's what I'd been aching to hear!

I dressed. As we went to the door, he said, "I haven't
forgotten your question about my parents, Val. I'll get
back to it before Saturday, I promise."

I told him to get back to it first with Dr. Masters,
and we kissed good-bye. The drive home through deserted streets and roads was heaven!

The next night we ate at a fine Italian restaurant
called Angelo's. Back at the apartment, we undressed and
played with each other, both eager to get at it, but first
I grasped his cock and applied the squeeze technique.
Again I exerted all the pressure I felt I could without
damaging him, and again failed to weaken his hard-on
in the slightest! And again we laughed and made love.

Immediately afterward he began to talk about his
parents, as he had to Dr. Masters that morning. He'd
been born in Cleveland, where his father had owned a

luncheonette, but before Brent was old enough to absorb much, the business had failed and they'd moved to a small town in Arkansas. His mother's parents lived there, and they kept the destitute family for almost a year, during which time a second son was born. Brent was three and the brother six months when they moved into "a big old house with a backyard a mile long." He was happy there, though his parents began quarreling about money. The father was now operating a snack bar on the main highway leading to Little Rock, but it wasn't doing well. After the birth of their third child, a daughter, the quarrels became more frequent.

The snack bar finally failed, and the family picked up stakes once again, moving this time to Wisconsin, another small town, where the *father's* parents lived. They helped him get started in still another business—a good-sized tavern-restaurant—in partnership with a well-to-do cousin. Brent's father owned a third of the business, and was expected to do most of the work, since he'd invested none of the cash. For a while it went well, the third share providing sufficient income to support the family—which soon had an addition, another daughter.

Then Brent's father began quarreling with his partner, demanding a full half share because of the amount of work he did, and eventually agreed to being bought out for a lump sum. He invested this in a roadhouse-nightclub, borrowing heavily from the bank to make up the remainder of the purchase price, and almost immediately was in trouble.

These were Brent's teen-age years, and because he was a successful student, athlete, and human being, he managed to be happy despite his family's financial problems. He took part-time jobs when in high school—which led him to his first sexual encounter with the neighbor housewife—and gave most of what he earned to his mother.

He paused in his story at this point, and I asked whether his parents got along sexually. "That's just it," he said. "They were always at each other—or my father was always at my mother. I don't know how she *really* felt, inside that is, but I know she was convinced it was her duty to serve her husband in bed. Maybe she enjoyed it too; I certainly hope so, since she was on her back just about every night! We kids were always hearing them banging away. Their bed squeaked, and I'd put cotton in my ears so as not to hear them. Also, on Sundays, when the tavern was closed, my father would be around the house all day, and I caught him trying to get her into bed more than once."

Again he paused, but went on before I could say anything. "I remember that my mother was always washing herself. In the middle of the night, on Sunday afternoons, whenever she'd been with my father, she would go to the bathroom and wash. My God, she washed—showered and bathed and scrubbed at the sink—before and after and in between! I think she spent as much time in the bathroom as she spent in the kitchen! And remember, she had a family of five to cook for; six including herself!"

This time he paused and looked at me as if expecting something. He then said, "Aren't you going to make the obvious psychological deduction? My mother kept washing, and it was connected with sexual activity. So when a woman washes before sex with me, I remember my father's defeat as a man in the business world, and as his son, successful in my own business, I join him in failure the one way I can—in bed."

I said I wasn't a psychologist; and even if I had been, I wouldn't make such pat and flat-out assumptions.

He was quiet awhile, then asked if I would like a drink. I said I would like the rest of the story. Hadn't he said that both his parents were dead, and that the manner of their deaths had "pained" him, especially his mother's?

He went to the kitchen and made two bloody Marys anyway. We sipped awhile in silence. Finally he spoke, very quickly, as if to get it over with as soon as possible.

What it amounted to was that his father had killed himself, though no one was ever able to prove it, and the insurance company eventually had to pay off. He drove his car at ninety miles an hour into a concrete abutment on his way to work one afternoon. Brent had just left for college. Since he had a football scholarship that paid not only his tuition but, in one of those under-the-table deals that are far from uncommon, his living expenses as well, he was no drain on the family. His mother had the insurance, and she also was able to sell the roadhouse-nightclub and regain part of the initial investment, so she wasn't too badly off financially. But emotionally, she was coming apart.

She blamed herself for her husband's death, reliving their money quarrels with anguished guilt. At the same time, she began missing the nightly bouts in bed. Whether or not she had wanted the man when he was alive, she definitely wanted some man after he was dead. Still, she had a family to raise, and no practice in going out and picking up men, so she simply accepted anything that came to her door—the Fuller Brush man, the fruit peddler, the Great Books salesman, and so on. More than accepted the occasional proposition—began actively enticing and seducing. This became known around the neighborhood, creating shame for Brent's brother and sisters, and the brother eventually wrote him in New York about it. Brent couldn't do anything at the time, but once he began earning heavy money in Hollywood, he asked the entire family to come to Los Angeles, where he would get them a house and see that the kids went to college—and that the mother met some eligible men.

The mother was no fool; driven, yes, but not dumb. She understood, finally, that she had humiliated her children and demeaned herself, and so she began to drink, substituting alcohol for sex. And she refused to go to the West Coast. The family remained in Wisconsin, but she completely isolated herself from everyone but her children. And even with them she was withdrawn and silent, preparing their meals and keeping the house clean, but otherwise staying in her room with her bottle.

One by one, the children went to college. Each was capable and attractive, so, as Brent put it, "Mom and Dad must have done *something* right." Eventually the mother was left all alone. She sold the house and moved into a small apartment above a grocery store. By this time Brent was a famous actor, the other children were married and on their own. Both daughters, as well as Brent, tried to get the mother to move in with them. Brent pushed especially hard for this, but the mother refused all invitations. She stayed in her apartment. She became a neighborhood curiosity—the movie star's mother who was a drunken recluse.

After a national magazine ran an article on her, with photographs and neighbors' comments, Brent's studio said something had to be done about her. Brent himself was convinced it was time to take legal steps, and so with the help of studio lawyers he had his mother adjudged not of sound mind and himself named her legal guardian. Whereupon he moved her out to his home in Los Angeles. He was already married to his second wife, Cleo, and they had a room prepared for her, and a servant assigned to see that she didn't drink.

The mother went swimming one humid evening in the pool just behind her room and drowned—or so the story released to the press stated. Actually, it was at three in the morning and she left a note stating that her life had ended many years ago, so why bother going on with the farce? At the funeral, the other children commended Brent on his treatment of the mother. No one blamed him for a thing—no one but Brent himself; he'd been left with a huge guilt complex.

That had been six years ago, Brent concluded. He didn't feel guilty anymore.

"And you're not sexually hung up anymore, either," I said.

He smiled, looking down at his hands. "With you," he murmured.

"I'm nothing special. The beautiful actresses you know . . ."

"I'm not so sure you're not special," he interrupted. "The minute you took off your clothes, I knew it was going to work. Not that I knew it would work as *well* as it has."

"Why should it be different with me than with a beautiful starlet?"

He shrugged. "I don't know. Maybe because you're my therapist, my confidante, as safe as Cleo to my ego, yet an exciting new lover too. And because you can't have me and I can't have you after Saturday."

My insides jolted at that. He saw it and reached for me. We kissed for a very long time, and then made love again. And it was marvelous again. Our parting was full of love, full of sadness, and no one could fake such a thing: not he, the actor, and not I, the therapist. We held to each other, we touched hands as I went through the door, we touched eyes as I went down the hall. And looking back, I saw him still watching me.

I was beside myself with joy, and with sorrow. I was going to spend all Saturday with him, and lose him forever on Sunday morning. I kept trying to be realistic, to tell myself there was no *true* love involved here—just a lovely fantasy, a beautiful game. But while my brain knew the truth, my insides, my guts, my heart if you will, wouldn't accept it.

We met at ten Saturday morning and went driving, out beyond the city limits. I showed him Clayton and Ladue, the very best suburbs St. Louis has to offer, and he tried to act impressed at the homes and scenery. But finally he responded to my constant, "Isn't *that* lovely?" with a flat, "No, not really. This is plains country, grassland originally, and at best cropland. It was never forest, never mountain and valley and lake, never beautiful in the way the East Coast and West Coast are. No Hudson Valley here, and no Beverly Hills or rugged Big Sur. No Utah forests, Wisconsin lakes, Gulf beaches . . ." He gestured. "The closest true scenic beauty is in the Ozarks. For me, St. Louis offers little for the eye"—then he touched my hand—"except Valerie."

The day passed much too quickly. We stopped at a motel near the airport, and he rented a room, and we made love for two hours. We had dinner and talked and went to the apartment and made love again. We slept. I gave him my surprise: I'd told Mother I was going out of town and wouldn't be back until Sunday afternoon. The nurse was staying the night.

His reaction was pure joy. He grabbed me and held me. After a while we both fell asleep. At two A.M. I awoke, and he was lying on his back, arms outflung, the covers bunched around his feet. That beautiful body lay open to me—for the last time. I kissed his arms, chest, belly . . . and then his genitals. I nuzzled his penis, his testicles, kissed and licked them, handled and caressed them. He sighed; his penis lengthened; it began to rise, to grow toward its full size. I took it in my mouth and sucked it. I wanted to take *all* of him into my mouth—wanted to swallow him and keep him.

He awoke. He tried to stop me, said he wanted to make love again. But he had no strength to pull away, he was enjoying it so much, and so I refused to stop. I held his balls with one hand and stroked his lower shaft with the other and sucked the top two or three inches of cock. He began to gasp, to writhe and cry out. I sucked harder, and took the full discharge, swallowing with a feeling that this was the most I would ever have of him.

He went down on me. He made me come once that way and once with his fingers, and by then he was hard again. He made me come with my legs up over his shoulders, and I went on for the considerable time it took him to have his third orgasm.

After that, it was breakfast and packing, and I drove him to the airport. He said he would be in touch with Dr. Masters and Mrs. Johnson, as they requested all their patients to be, for the full five-year period. He also asked if he could "contact Miss Valerie Scott."

I was stunned. Where, I asked, had he learned my last name? He smiled. I'd given it to him the first time I'd met him, in the waiting room, without even realizing it.

I said yes. Then we were parking, and checking his bags, and walking to the gate. He got his boarding slip. Until this moment, I'd managed to laugh and talk and and be the perfect little therapist. But now it all changed. Now it was the end. Now my eyes burned, and when he wiped my face with his handkerchief, I realized the tears were streaming down my cheeks. I walked him to the exit door. He kissed me and said, "You'll hear from me," and was gone.

I never heard from him, but I heard *about* him. He succeeded for a short time with several starlets, then began to fail again. He found one studio secretary who liked it slam-bam-thank-you-ma'am, and it worked that way for a while. He would go to her place, quickly drop his pants, get her pants down and her dress up, and make it. But that too failed when she became emotionally involved and wanted long, loving evenings. As for his wife, it never did change. They separated twice, and only the fact that he had no one else to turn to kept them married.

His career still flourishes. He looks the same. I never miss his new pictures, or the old ones on TV. But I often miss him. And I often wonder about him.

Why should he have been so right with me those beautiful four days, and so wrong with the rest of the world of women?

If it was my being a wife surrogate—neither whore nor lover—and thereby freeing him of fear, of crippling hang-ups, why then didn't he try to see me? Why didn't he try to make something of our relationship, since it might have saved his manhood, his joy in life?

One answer always presents itself, an answer I myself had given: "Every love I've ever had has died when it went on. Yours too, I'll bet. And this won't have the chance to die, will it? This will retire, like a smart boxing champion, untied and undefeated."

I met a very nice young doctor, and he became my steady for a while, but then we quarreled about his watching professional football on the weekends, and I stopped seeing him. I guess I used the argument to cover my failing interest. I met another doctor, not so young, and very married. I had an affair. It was satisfying, and he began to fall heavily, and to talk divorce. I thought that was what I'd been waiting for, but I ran. I began to feel that I could no longer work at the medical complex with all the loves and ex-loves wandering around there!

A medical group in the Forest Park area advertised for an experienced paraprofessional. I really wasn't qualified, but it was time I grew professionally, and time I made more money. This job paid a full third more, to start, than my hospital job, and it went up into respectable professional income levels.

I got the job. For two months I was too busy, first bluffing and then learning, to bother with much private life. Then, quite suddenly, I realized I was running the place efficiently. I'd done it! I'd broken out of my non-professional status.

A month later, Gini called. Another case.

No chills or fears this time. I could still use the mon-

ey, because Mother's illness—her care and medication
and occasional hospitalization—simply devoured money.
But it wasn't just that. I'd been lucky in my patients
until now. Even Glenn hadn't been all *that* bad, and
Wallace and Larry had been fine; and as for Brent . . .
And Christmas was coming up, and I wanted to fill my
days and nights completely to avoid the blues.

And so I didn't press too hard with questions. All I
was really interested in was the patient's age: no sixty
and overs, please. He was twenty-seven, a successful
curio-shop proprietor, college-educated, and very artistic.
I asked whether that "very artistic" had any implications
of homosexuality. Gini said definitely not. Then what
exactly was his problem? The answer was, primary orgasmic dysfunction.

"You mean he's *never* had an orgasm?"

It turned out he had, but not with a woman. He'd
had three while masturbating.

That gave me some pause. Gini said she and Dr. Masters were looking forward to seeing me at five-thirty. I
said all right, because I thought of something else, something I'd decided would happen the next time I was asked
to take a case. I felt I had grown to the point where I
could become an associate: not just an in-bed therapist,
but an in-office one too, conducting interviews as Gini
and a male-female doctor team did. Perhaps they would
pair me with an M.D. I would be willing to leave my new
job for that, once it worked out.

It was with high hopes and no real misgivings that I
went into my fifth case.

6

It was felt that David would need as long a period of treatment as possible, perhaps two full weeks on my part. Because of his complete lack of sexual experience with women, the Foundation felt that my part of the therapy —the in-bed variety—was even more important than in my other cases (in relation to the interview-type therapy). I was asked to remember that not only had this twenty-seven-year-old man never been in bed with a woman, he had never touched a woman's body or been touched by a woman. He was possessed of an enormous and deep-rooted lack of confidence.

I was told to go to his room, and take him to my car instead of meeting him on the street. So I walked into a room at the Forest Park Hotel and looked down at my patient. That's right, I said looked *down*. He'd been described to me as rather short, with a thick head of hair, long sideburns, and a moustache. "Rather short" was rather an understatement: David couldn't have been much more than five feet tall! And he seemed even shorter, since he was also very stout—a fat little butterball of a man. The considerable amount of hair he wore did nothing to help; in fact, it gave me the insane feeling that I was in a grammar-school play and that my leading man was about twelve and made up as an adult! He had black hair worn long in back—almost to his shoulders—and over his ears at the sides. The sideburns came down to meet the moustache, which in turn was full and bushy.

Out of this forest of hair peeked two tiny little gray eyes, a stubby little nose, and a pouty, red-lipped mouth. He wore a tight-fitting gray suit with vest, striped shirt with black velvet tie, black shoes with an alligator-leather finish.

"I'm Valerie," I said, to say something, to cover the sinking feeling, to stop my mind from leaping ahead to all the horrors to come.

I'm sorry to show again how dependent I am upon a man's looks, and on the chemistry set up, initially at least, by those looks. But all my self-confidence, all my professional strength, disappeared instantly on seeing David, and I was more or less the same Valerie who had suffered through her very first case.

He still hadn't said a word. He simply stood there, those little eyes blinking at me. I forced a smile. "Aren't you going to offer me a drink?" He then seemed to awaken, said, "I . . . I'll call room service."

The door was still open. I turned to it, and he scuttled past me to shut it. And I do mean *scuttled!* He had these tiny little legs coming out of that rotund little body, and when he walked . . .

Oh, Lord, it was certainly a greater affliction to him than to me, and yet again I found I was raging at myself for getting into these things!

He closed the door, went to the phone, then turned to me. "Exactly what do you prefer, Valerie?"

His voice suited my concept of the little-boy-playing-adult: it was high-pitched, and at the moment quite quavery and unsteady (though that lessened in time). How in the world would I ever get this . . . this *child* to make love! And *should* I? Wouldn't I be arrested for contributing to the delinquency of a minor?

I told him a double Scotch and water, and he spoke to room service. His own choice was cream sherry on the rocks.

We were to go out to dinner. *Out* to dinner, and no bones about it. It was important, the Foundation felt, that David get accustomed to a woman in a social sense before attempting anything sexual. I nursed my double Scotch as long as I could to put off the moment of leaving for a restaurant. We sat on the davenport and drank and spoke very little. He kept glancing at me, and I kept glancing down into my glass. Finally he said, "It's rather mild for December, Valerie, wouldn't you say?"

"Yes, but then again, you come from Chicago, and I believe your winters are more severe there."

"Yes, they are."

"Not that we don't have severe cold weather here . . . and snow too."

"I wouldn't doubt it."

We both nodded. We both drank. And I tried not to notice that his feet didn't quite reach the floor. He sat on the couch, his head not too far above my shoulder, and his tiny little feet in their tiny little shoes swung a good inch or more off the carpeting. It upset me terribly, it was all so grotesque!

And then he did something that showed he knew what I was feeling, and that he wanted to help *me*, something that almost broke my heart.

Quite suddenly—I guess he could do it no other way —his lips touched my cheek in the lightest of kisses. When I turned to him, truly shocked, he said, his child's voice trembling, his eyes downcast, "You're so very beautiful, Valerie, and I'm so sorry . . . sorry that I can't be . . . what you would like."

How I wanted to come up with a strongly reassuring answer, but at the moment all I could say was, "You're going to become what *you* would like to be. That's the important thing."

He smiled then, a very childlike smile, and nodded. I had been about to ask for another drink before that kiss and heartbreaking statement. Now I rose and said we should be leaving for dinner.

When he put his overcoat on, he looked like a fat little teddy bear—except that I had no desire to cuddle him! Walking out of that room with him was murder; and when we reached the elevator and a waiting couple, I simply could *not* look up. We walked through the bustling lobby and down the street to my car. As we pulled away, I asked for his preference in food. He said anything at all would do, and I searched my mind for the darkest restaurant in St. Louis. One I'd used before had closed, and the only other spot kept dark enough was a cocktail lounge that served only sandwiches.

Again I was ashamed of myself, and again I couldn't help a chill of horror at the thought that I might meet someone I knew. I finally chose a little steak house on the other side of Forest Park, a place not highly thought of around the hospital and therefore not generally patronized by most of my friends. I was pleased to see that their parking lot was sparsely populated, but even so, the walk to the entrance was terrible. He gave me his arm, and of course I took it, and it was like walking with a child. Worse—it was *dating* this child, and knowing I would eventually have to make love to him. . . .

I guess I've said enough about my feelings. I'm not proud of them, but there was nothing I could do to change my gut reactions.

I wolfed down a small steak and salad, hoping he too would eat quickly. But he was finicky and meticulous and cut small pieces and chewed slowly and halfway through the meal commented that he'd had better food. I agreed. I said we wouldn't return here—and wondered how I would live through two weeks of eating out.

People looked at us. It wasn't my imagination this time. Several people actually stared, and every time I got the courage to look up, it seemed I met someone's eyes, someone who glanced quickly away. Our waiter was young, rather good-looking, and I could almost read his eyes: "What's wrong with you that you have to date a man like *this?*"

David tipped so heavily, about twenty-five percent of the bill, that I just had to tell him it wasn't necessary. He sighed and nodded. "I always do," he murmured. "A sign of inadequacy, of insecurity, I suppose. When I was a child . . ." He stopped. "But you wouldn't be interested."

"I certainly *would.*"

But somehow he managed to change the subject as we went out to the car. And since I wasn't going up to the room with him tonight, and since I was now simply *dying* to say good night and get away, I didn't bring him back to the subject.

At the hotel, he thanked me for a most pleasant evening, and hesitated and then touched my hand. I wasn't able to bring myself to do more than squeeze his hand in response, though a gentle kiss would have been right. Still, he reacted with a big smile and said, "I can't *wait* until tomorrow evening, Valerie!"

Tomorrow evening. I couldn't even *think* of it!

I called Gini from home. I reported the evening's events quickly, without emotion. She said Dr. Masters had suggested that tomorrow I advance to some minor kissing and nongenital caressing. I said nothing. She said good night. I hung up. I wasn't going to complain. She knew what David looked like, and I'm sure she must have known what I was thinking and feeling. But the important thing was to help the patient.

I took a sleeping pill. The next day seemed to *fly* by, and before I knew it I was home and dressing. And then I was driving to the hotel. And then I was entering the room, and David was there, smiling an excited, totally pathetic little smile.

I went to him and bent and kissed him on the lips.

"Oh," he breathed. "Oh, Valerie!" A little boy receiving a present at Christmastime. A little boy with eyes opening wide.

We went to dinner at the Red Brick Inn. I ate, and died inside as people looked at us. But David was delighted with everything, and talked and talked. He told me about his curio shop, and about his trips abroad to procure *objets d'art*. He ordered a red wine called Lafite Rothschild, and though he said it wasn't a very good year, I found it very pleasant. I drank far more of it than he did, and found I was beginning to enjoy his conversation. When I'd had five glasses, I began asking questions. And eventually I brought him back to the statement he'd made last night about always overtipping, and that aborted revelation, "When I was a child . . ."

He grew quiet. He sipped his wine. Then his little gray eyes rose to mine. "I've told Dr. Masters all about my life," he said, his voice a delicate whisper. "You must have been told. . . ."

I nodded. We returned to the hotel. We rode up in the elevator. A young couple glanced at us and grew uncomfortably silent. It wasn't lost on David. In the room he said, "You're a very lovely woman, Valerie. It must be hard to . . . deal with some of your patients."

I said it was the patient's feelings that mattered, not mine.

He shook his head. "No. I can't accept that. If your feelings are in turmoil, then how can you properly work with a patient?"

My feelings were *now* in turmoil! He was getting too close to the heart of the matter! I said he shouldn't think that way. He was here for treatment. I was his therapist, not too different from Dr. Masters and Mrs. Johnson. Again he shook his head. "They don't have to deal with me socially . . . and, soon, sexually. You do. I know I'm abnormal. . . ."

"Of course," I interrupted, desperate to stop him. "That's why you're here. Every patient is *abnormal* in the sense that he doesn't function normally."

"I'm abnormal in many ways," he whispered. "I'm convinced my body never matured. I doubt you'll be able to do anything to help me, but I wanted to make this last effort. I can live well enough the way I am. I just decided to cover every possibility. To know love—a woman's love . . ." He turned away. "I've always wanted that. I've never dared . . ." He went quickly to the bathroom and closed the door.

I stood there, shaking inside. I was certain he'd been crying, and now I had to begin to help him. But who would help *me*?

It was David himself who helped me that night. He came out and said, voice low but quite distinct, that I would have to excuse him. "I . . . I need a little time to myself, Valerie. I just can't face anything tonight. Would Dr. Masters be very angry if we just ended it here and picked up again tomorrow night?"

I was going to try to talk him out of it; I really was, no matter what my own feelings were—and they were pure relief. But looking into his eyes, I saw that he wanted out right now. So I nodded.

But before I left, I went to him and stroked his cheek and kissed him on the lips. And said, "It's going to work out, David. I promise you that."

No one at the Foundation seemed too surprised at what

had happened, though they were not exactly overjoyed. And I was told to persist—gently, of course—at tomorrow's meeting.

David was ready and waiting when I knocked at his door the next night. This time I managed to keep my eyes up in the elevator, and the operator kept his eyes forward. In the lobby, we got some looks, but generally people were interested in their own business. And on the street, I said, "Let's try the Nantucket Cove . . . it's just down the street."

I hadn't been there since those wonderful dinners with Brent, and at first I thought I'd made a bad mistake. I couldn't help comparing what I'd felt then with what I felt now. But eventually it was that very comparison that helped me. Both Brent and David shared the dubious distinction of being patients, and both deserved the same treatment.

I had lobster, and David had a mixed seafood platter. He proclaimed the food "superior," and I was as proud as if I were president of the St. Louis Chamber of Commerce! He ordered a white Chambertin, a delightful wine, again new to me. One thing about this little man: he knew his food and wine as well as anyone I'd ever met! And his conversation was interesting and involving; he made me respond and discuss and contribute.

But when we were back in the room, I had an impulse to give him a quick kiss and say good night. I would be easy enough to tell Gini that once again he hadn't been ready for anything more. . . .

It would be a terrible cop-out, a destructive and irresponsible act. I went to the davenport and sat down. He asked if I'd like a drink. I said we'd had our limit of alcohol. He said he hadn't been aware the limits applied to me, and I had to smile, because I'd certainly put away the lion's share of the wine at our two dinners. I patted the cushion beside me. He hesitated, then excused himself and went into the bathroom. The water ran; then there was silence for a minute or two. When he came out and sat down beside me, his hair—head and face— was perfectly arranged, and he smelled of a good men's cologne.

I asked him a few questions, trying to lead him into talking about himself, but he was evasive, and generally silent. He didn't want *talk*. And he was medically correct in his attitude. He'd had nothing but talk, all his life, and for the six days he'd been in St. Louis.

He was sitting facing forward, his feet off the carpet but not moving as they had yesterday. He was breathing heavily, and there was perspiration on his forehead. As I put my hand on his shoulder, he went absolutely rigid!

I stroked his arm. I said, "Nothing very much can happen tonight, David. We're going to move along slowly, but I'm sure we'll eventually find that you have little or no problem. You've never *failed* with a woman; simply not had the experience. . . ."

"That's not quite true." His little boy's voice was quavering badly.

"Oh? From what Dr. Masters told me . . ."

"It's all in how you define failure with a woman. I failed many times, *fantasizing* about a woman—or women—with pornographic photographs and literature. I couldn't . . . achieve manual orgasm."

"But you *did* masturbate several times, didn't you?"

"Three times . . . but not in the last five years."

"You've had erections?"

"Mornings, yes, but they don't count, do they?"

"Of course they do. If it happens in the morning, it can happen anytime."

"But . . . I'm almost dead down there." He was still rigid, still speaking in that shaky whisper. "Take right now, for example. There's no feeling, none at all there. And I'm with a beautiful woman. . . ."

"And you're anticipating some sort of sexual test and anticipating failure and growing more and more uptight by the second. And nothing will happen, and all your nervousness is wasted."

He digested that, and finally looked at me. "But Dr. Masters said . . ."

"That you *might* have some light physical contact. I'm the one who makes the final decision, and I don't think you're ready for it yet."

His expression was a mixture of relief and disappointment, and I felt an immediate lessening of his body rigidity. Again I asked him questions about his child-hood, his personal life, and squeezed his shoulder lightly where my hand still rested there. He began to talk. His high-pitched voice steadied, and he spoke quickly and well—and what he said was in a way a gentle tale of a gentle upbringing, and in another way a horror story that made my blood run cold. But I never stopped rubbing his shoulder, and later his back, and finally his neck. And he loosened more and more.

David had been born in Chicago, the only child of then-poor parents who ran a small grocery store and lived in two rooms above it. His mother and father were both religious Protestants, extremely ethical, moral people, and David's earliest memories concerned bedtime prayers. "Almost the first words I learned to speak after 'Mamma' and 'Dada' were, 'Now I lay me down to sleep, I pray the Lord my soul to keep.' And almost from the beginning, I didn't really believe there *was* a Lord to keep my soul. That's because almost from the beginning I began to suffer indignities from everyone outside my own little family circle."

He was an incubator baby, and always smaller than other children. In kindergarten, the teacher was so concerned for his safety—she said he looked like a child of three—that she more or less isolated him from the other children. She was soon proven not to be too far wrong in her fears. The Southside neighborhood was a near-slum and surrounded by ethnically and racially mixed areas, high-crime areas. In the second grade, carrying twenty cents for his lunch, David was robbed by a boy his own age, who then proceeded to beat him into bloody hysteria to prove the point that he could do it "with one hand tied behind my back." Word got around about this exploit, and several other children decided to try it, "including one girl who enticed me into a backyard where three other little girls were waiting, and where she not only beat me but finished by taking down my pants and spanking the baby. After this, I wouldn't go to school for a week. My mother finally took me to the principal, and he promised to do everything he could to protect me, but he admitted that in an area like ours it wasn't really possible to guarantee anything, short of assigning me a full-time guard. Well, my father took on this job, walking me to school each morning, waiting for me after dismissal. I spent recess in the nurse's office, where there was always someone on duty, and did homework and read and day-dreamed. As a result, I was soon the best student in the entire school—and this too didn't endear me to my class-mates. But it's wrong to call them class*mates*. They despised me, and I feared them. However, I did have *one* friend. . . ."

A girl two years older than he, crippled by polio, lived in the tenement beside the store. She was a great reader, a great dreamer, and together they spent many pleasant hours.

And David was quite happy with life *within* his home. Those two rooms over the store were a sort of paradise for him. His parents were religious, yes, but not fanatic, and never forced him into anything more than the mini-mal prayers—grace and bedtime and Sunday church. Even here, when they realized he had little true faith, they didn't overreact.

They never had any other children, and gave him all their love and attention. His father was ambitious, and the store prospered. His mother was artistic and took David to the public library and to museums and art gal-leries, and eventually to concerts, plays, ballets, and op-eras. She always said *he* was doing *her* the favor, as her husband never had the time, and not too much inclina-tion, for such entertainments, and she had wanted "a suitable escort" all her life.

David withdrew entirely from the life of the streets. Denied stickball and touch-tackle and clubs and the com-radeship of boys his own age, he immersed himself in books, the excursions with his mother, and the hours of play—almost entirely mental—with the crippled girl next door. There were several more incidents of violence and humiliation—his father couldn't be with him *always*—but he wiped them from his mind almost as soon as they happened. Or so he insisted; yet he was able to describe them in detail. They ranged from such minor acts as be-ing shoved out of line—minor for a normal child, but full of trauma for one who had no hope of striking back —to being challenged by a child three years his junior who then knocked him around in the schoolyard until a physical-education teacher intervened. The teacher chided David for not fighting back and insisted he spend several recess periods learning the manly art of self-defense. If David had actively *sought* the instruction, it might have been good for him; but he was forced into it, and it turned into yet another area of humiliation as he stumbled around an improvised ring, red-faced and inept, hearing the laughter of spectators and, incredibly, of his instructor. After this he was challenged by half a dozen boys and beaten half a dozen times.

David's father intervened, threatening to give the gym teacher some instruction of his own, and since he was big, with arms hard and muscular from lugging cases of bottles and cans, the gym teacher admitted he might have made an error in judgment.

Shortly afterward, the father decided he'd saved enough money, and had a good enough offer for his store, to make a move into the near Northside, a far better neighborhood and a far better store. David was told the news on a mild Friday evening in early June. The move would be made after his graduation from grammar school—just two weeks away. He was delighted at first, but when he'd run next door to tell his friend—now fifteen and "perfectly lovely, with long black hair and big eyes and a swelling bosom"—and saw her sudden pallor, he realized he was going to lose his only friend. He was thirteen, and had already begun to feel the first stirrings of his sexuality. That evening, in her room with their books and their daydreams, he was led to touch her hair, and then her face, and finally her breast. She broke into tears, and he begged her to forgive him. She shook her head, and he ran away, hating himself and feeling ugly and sinful.

The next day she told him she'd shaken her head not because she couldn't forgive him his touches, but because she couldn't forgive his leaving her in two weeks. Their last three days together were spent in increasing sexual exploration, with the girl leading him to put his hand inside her blouse and, finally, under her dress to feel her thighs. At thirteen, and backward as he was, it was no more than playing doctor for David; but for the girl, he realized much later, it was a move toward love with the one boy who came to her, locked as she was into braces for her shriveled legs.

He never forgot her, and thought of her even today as his lost love.

He spent the summer helping his father and mother establish their "fancy grocery" in the near Northside near Lake Shore Drive. Things went well right from the start, and David was delighted with the new, roomier apartment a block away from the store. He was certain that things would be different in high school, because the students were more mature. Also, scholastic achievement was bound to be more highly valued than in grammar school, since good grades were needed for college admission. And in a way he was right, but in another way he was very, very wrong.

He was then about four feet tall, a head shorter than the shortest of his classmates, and felt his inferiority *increasing*. Also, he was very babyish in form, feature, and voice. Except for his first term, when he was bullied by another very small boy, none of the students bothered him in a physical sense, but high school introduced him into another area of inferiority and pain: the social area. Boys and girls began dating in high school, and the big heroes were not, as he'd hoped, scholars, but athletes. David excelled in his studies. He made the honor roll and strove to be head of his class. He came close, but was topped by an all-around success who captained the basketball team and beat David out each term by a point, or fraction of a point. This boy, Clyde, was David's ideal, and truly deserving of hero-worship. He did his best to introduce David to his friends and to get him into at least a few social activities.

David was terrified of girls, and of parties, but he finally allowed himself to be persuaded by Clyde to attend a small gathering of honor students who were also very active in various groups and clubs. Clyde felt that by meeting and mixing with these boys and girls, David would be drawn into extracurricular and social activities. But the others did not take to David except in an obviously embarrassed, pitying, or patronizing manner. One girl spent some time chatting with him, and he took the desperate gamble of asking her out. She said she was busy. He tried twice more. She remained busy.

David's father was doing so well with his grocery, he opened a branch not too far away, and after a three-month trial period, hired a manager to run it for him. David was given a generous allowance, and found himself with considerably more money than any of his peers. He then began doing what he'd alluded to in the restaurant last night—trying to *buy* friendship. At first, it took the form of lending change to classmates in the lunchroom and later refusing to accept payment. Then he found a way to get an occasional date. He would buy the best seats to the most popular stage show in town, generally a high-priced musical (though he detested most musicals, raised as he was on opera and ballet), then would casually mention to a girl that he was stuck with an extra seat for Saturday night and ask her to accompany him, *just* for the show. He always had to "go somewhere" immediately afterward, and this was the clincher for those girls who wanted to see the show without actually dating him.

Most often, he felt that he had to stick to his pretense of leaving the girl immediately after the show: her attitude, her discomfort at being with him, made this clear. But once in a while he would take the chance of changing his story and quickly offer dinner at an expensive restaurant, one so desirable and so far beyond the girl's expectations that she would be seduced into acceptance. And at the restaurant, he would tip heavily to get proper attention and to impress the girl further.

One girl dated him five times, and after their last date actually kissed him on the cheek. It stimulated him to dreams and fantasies, and led to his first masturbation. He was successful in masturbating because he felt he had a chance to be successful with the girl. But the very next time he asked her out, she said her "steady" was getting angry and that she wouldn't be able to see David anymore.

End of fantasy, and end of ability to masturbate for several years—though he tried twice, pulling his penis until he broke down in tears.

In his third year, he decided he would look up the crippled girl from his old Southside neighborhood. His mother thought it an excellent idea, and together they drove in the family's new car to the narrow side street where the old grocery store still did business—in a neighborhood now so run-down and slummy that the mother feared getting out. And when they did, they learned that the crippled girl and her family had moved a year before, and no one knew where.

End of the lost-love-regained dream. David continued to try his "extra-ticket" trick to get dates, but by this time everyone in school knew it *was* a trick, and David knew they knew. He got an occasional thank-you peck on the cheek, but it meant nothing. Toward the end of his senior year he joined the Class Night Committee and helped write a satire on high-school romance. He attended the play, along with his proud parents, but he was at home reading, telling himself he was perfectly content, the night of the prom. At graduation, he learned he had come in second in his class to Clyde, but he was still in line for several excellent scholarships with his 95.8 average. He chose one of the most highly rated universities in the nation . . . in California.

His parents begged him to reconsider, pointing out that he would be more comfortable at the University of Chicago or the University of Illinois, Chicago campus branch. They said that being able to live at home would help him in his studies, but David understood the *true* motive behind their plea. They were afraid for their little boy. And he shared that fear. But he had another, stronger fear, one that was beginning to devour him—the fear that he was abnormal in more than his diminutive size. He was beginning to believe that he was a child sexually, and therefore forever impotent. There was only one way to prove this wrong—get far away from the protection and comfort of his home, leave his loving and protective parents. If he was to change, to become a man, it wouldn't be with Mother and Dad, and it wouldn't be "comfortable."

It was an act of true courage when he kissed his mother and father good-bye, took a taxi to O'Hare Airport, and then a jet to California. His parents had offered him enough money to pay for an apartment of his own, but that would be a cop-out, he reasoned, and he went into a dormitory.

Just as high school had held less physical terror than grammar school, college held less than high school. In fact, with men of superior intellect and generally fine upper-class background, there was no problem at all in that area, and he made quite a few friends. He attended bull sessions in the rooms, drank beer at a local pub, quickly joined a number of scholastic clubs, and was eventually invited to join a fraternity. But again, as in high school, there was an acceleration in the social area, and in college the social is also strongly sexual.

He couldn't pull his "extra-tickets" trick here; he was in strange territory. He concentrated on his studies, and his male friendships. Weekends, he saw movies, read books, took long walks. Holidays, he flew home. And despite continuing high grades, he became increasingly more lonely, increasingly more depressed.

His roommate finally got him a date. They went out double. David's girl was tiny—barely an inch taller than he in her flat-heeled shoes—and quite lovely. They had dinner, went dancing—and David managed reasonably well, having taken lessons while still in high school—then drove to a lovers'-lane spot. The roommate and his date took "a little stroll." David was left in the back seat with his date. His inclination was to talk incessantly, to fill the time until the others returned, but he fought his fear of rejection. He had wanted to find just such opportunities as these in order to become a man. He couldn't back out now.

How he managed to make himself put his arm around the girl, he never knew, but he did. And when she turned to him, he refused to read her expression (it was a mixture of shock, revulsion, and pity, he later admitted to himself), and kissed her lightly on the lips. When she didn't push him away, he intensified the kiss. And when she still did nothing, either positive or negative, he hugged her and placed one hand on her hip. The softness and warmth of the flesh under her dress, the feel of a woman's body, finally overcame his fear, and he reached for her breasts, feeling the beginnings of desire. At this point she gently disengaged herself and said she too would like a little air.

They met the other couple returning to the car, the boy smiling to himself, the girl rumpled and smoothing out her clothing. As for David, he was in seventh heaven. He walked the girl to her door, where she gave him a good-night kiss and thanked him for a lovely evening. He asked if he could see her again. She hesitated, then said, "Call me." That night he masturbated into a towel while in bed. His orgasm was strong, and he began to doubt his own analysis of abnormality.

A second date, doubling with the roommate and his girl, seemed successful, though David was unable to get any further than that hand on the hip. His try for the breast was firmly blocked, but he told himself that was only natural in a nice girl. At her door, she accepted his kiss, and again said, "Call me," when he asked for another date.

Again he masturbated in bed, though not quite as easily or with as much pleasure as the week before. Fear was returning, though he fought it by telling himself he was going to see her again.

She turned him down three straight times, and when he tried to discuss it with his roommate, he got a muttered "Beats me" and a quick withdrawal.

That was his last date. He completed the year, and transferred to the University of Chicago. He lived with his parents, made a few halfhearted efforts at dating, then gave up completely. He also tried masturbation with pornography, failed every time, and eventually gave that up too. His mind, his *heart,* he said, ached for feminine companionship, for love and sex, but his body had withdrawn from the fight. He had erections in the mornings, before urinating, and no other times. He made excellent grades and attended operas, plays, ballets, and concerts with his mother. On Sundays, the entire family would take outings to various parks, country inns, and restaurants.

The next summer, he took his first trip abroad, with his mother—a month of hopping from city to city all over Europe. The summer after that he went alone, and concentrated on France and Germany. He returned with

several *objets d'art,* and with an idea of what he wanted
to do.

After graduating with his B.A., he talked to his father
about opening a curio shop. The father was doubtful and
suggested he go for his master's degree and teach. He
agreed to get the degree, and *then* decide.

Again he went to Europe, for almost two months this
time. Again he returned with various bits of art—and
with the beginnings of his moustache. He and his father
examined art catalogs and talked, but he was persuaded
to return to school. At twenty-two, he received his master's in history and began teaching at a Chicago high
school—where he was immediately made miserable by a
nickname, Little Big Mouth, and by memories of his own
high-school days. "I wasn't sure which side of the desk I
belonged on. I was younger-looking than most of my students in the junior and senior classes. I dreaded each
morning."

He began to be troubled with a buzzing in the ears. He
mentioned it to his department head, and was sent for an
examination. The report indicated he had a forty-percent
loss of hearing on the right side. He used this as an excuse to take a sabbatical for medical treatment. As soon
as he stopped teaching, the buzzing went away. His
parents realized what he was going through, and the father agreed to advance the capital to open a curio shop.

That was five years ago. The shop had prospered; he
had paid off his father; he was now a successful business-
man. He had resigned himself to a life without passion.
Then he learned of Masters and Johnson, and decided to
give it a try, just to be certain he was passing up no opportunity. He still lived with his parents, "and with a
beautiful Persian cat I call Kitty, not to infringe on her
rights of self-determination."

He paused briefly, and then added, "Oh, I was approached several times by homosexual persons. They
sickened me, so even that is denied me." He smiled wan-
ly. "So you're my last chance, Valerie. After you, *le
débâcle* . . . or rather, emptiness. Comfortable emptiness,
of course." His eyes sought mine, and there was a terrible
fear in them. "I'm twenty-seven," he murmured, "and already growing weary. Please . . . please . . ."

I was kissing him, my eyes closed against his physical presence, my heart opening to his agony. I was fighting back tears and stroking his head. And when he returned my kiss, I *made* myself open my lips and feed him the tip of my tongue.

His head actually jerked, but then he was touching my tongue with his own, tentatively, cautiously. His arms came around me, and he held me, and we kissed for a long time—and one part of me was sickened and another part of me fought it.

I felt one arm leave me. I felt his hand on my knee, and then on my thigh. I forced my mouth open still wider and dropped a hand to his thigh and stroked up and back. I wanted to go all the way up to his crotch, wanted to touch him and give him excitement, wanted to make him hard and suck him and fuck him and give him everything he'd missed, wanted to do it all at once, now— and at the same time dreaded it!

Terribly dangerous. Pity was making me forget what Gini had said about going *very* slowly. Another long kiss, and I said I had to be going.

Mother wasn't feeling too well. She complained of a bad headache, and I stayed up until after midnight with her, wondering whether I should call the doctor. Finally she fell asleep, and I was able to go to my own room. I was too exhausted to think, and the next thing I knew, the alarm was ringing.

Friday on the job was hectic, but toward five o'clock I had everything under control, and I considered calling Dr. Masters to tell him I wanted to become an associate in the Foundation. Then I decided to wait until the conclusion of this case. If I could successfully treat David, there would be little doubt of my ability to handle just about anything!

When I entered David's room, he presented me with a nosegay of white carnations surrounding a deep-red rose. It was a fragrant little bouquet, and touched me deeply. I bent to kiss him, and he seized me by the hips and crushed me to him fervently. I pulled back, surprised. He flushed and muttered, "I *am* sorry. I really didn't plan on doing that."

"But it's a very good sign," I said, recovering; and

trying to recapture the sympathy, the *feeling* I'd had for him yesterday.

And then I made a sudden decision. Tonight, at least, we would *not* go out to dinner, this despite the instructions I'd received from the Foundation. Valerie Scott needed to be manipulated, needed to be brought along and put in the proper mood. If *I* could be made to feel right, if *I* could relax and grow tender and warm, then and only then could I help him.

He was delighted with my suggestion that we eat in, and we pored over the room-service menu for ten minutes before making our choices. During that time I brushed his shoulder with my breasts and touched his hand several times.

We had steaks and salads and red wine—a "quiet" Beaujolais, to quote David. We ate in the little dining area—same as you had, Herb—and I got up several times to get things and then to clear away the dishes, but actually to let him look at me in a tight mini-skirt and tighter sweater. And he looked and looked, as if he couldn't get enough. And his story came back to me, his tortured, tormented life came back to me, and after several glasses of wine, I began to feel the right way, the necessary way.

We went to the davenport. I put my hand on his thigh, and following my established technique, moved it back and forth. He took my other hand. He was trembling violently, and I again said there was no need to feel uptight, to be tense, because nothing much could happen tonight. But he picked up the "much," and when he looked at me, he was frightened.

I leaned forward, inviting his kiss. He hesitated. I leaned further, and his lips touched mine. First that gentle, frightened kiss. Then a pressing and a parting of lips. And finally his arms came to me, his hands came to me, and he touched my breasts, lightly, and he touched my thighs—more firmly, more demandingly.

After a while I stood up, holding his hand, drawing him up with me. I walked to the bedroom, and felt resistance. He was actually hanging back—and the image of a little boy being taken somewhere he feared to go

was so strong it turned me off. How was sex possible
with this hairy-faced infant!

But when I stopped, he moved forward on his own and
whispered in a voice trembling like a vibrator, "Please
. . . be patient with me, Valerie." And I was ashamed
of myself.

I asked him to help me remove my sweater. He unbuttoned the back more easily than I'd anticipated, and was
at my brassiere hooks in no time. He removed sweater and
brassiere, and I turned. His face was white, and his little
eyes glittered and his little hands trembled. He said,
voice so low it didn't qualify as a full-fledged whisper,
"Oh, Valerie, how beautiful!" He stared at my breasts,
and it was as if his gaze had *substance,* that stare was so
strong. I began to feel warm, began to experience the excitement of a woman being adored.

"My skirt," I finally said, and now my own voice was
barely a whisper.

He bent and unfastened and unzipped, and the skirt
fell around my feet. I stepped out of it as his eyes
fastened on my panties, on the bulge of my crotch. He
was breathing like a steam engine, and when his hands
came to the elastic panty top, they made me jump, they
were so icy cold. He pulled them down, and I kicked
them away, and he was looking at my pubic area, staring
at it with an unblinking, fixed gaze.

Then he leaned forward, and I thought he was about
to kiss me there. Instead, he kissed my thighs, up and
down, and along the insides. "Silk," he whispered. "Warm
silk."

All his facial hair, soft though it was compared to
some men's moustaches, tickled and made me giggle. He
straightened abruptly, face flaming, and I knew I was on
the edge of a gigantic blunder. "Do it again." I murmured. "I love the soft, scratchy *tickle.*"

He blinked, and then smiled—a radiant, little-boy
smile. He kissed my thighs again, and one small hand
crept around to caress my buttocks.

I stopped him. We were getting too specifically sexual,
and he might soon begin to feel pressure, a need to perform, and that might frighten him and lead to failure.

He rose, and I began undressing him. He allowed me

to remove his jacket, vest, and tie, but when I began unbuttoning his shirt, his hands came to mine, covered mine, made me pause. I said, "Would you rather do it yourself?" He didn't answer. He *tried* to, his lips moved, but he said nothing. His hands fell away, and I took off his shirt. He was wearing a T-shirt, and I pulled it up over his head. When it came off, his eyes were closed.

He stood there, shutting out my reaction to him. He had a plump little torso, hairless and so very childlike that, even though I expected it, it shocked me. His arms were soft and seemingly without muscle—a little girl's arms rather than a boy's. There was baby fat on his shoulders and chest, and a childish bulge at the stomach.

It turned me off terribly hard, but I knelt and unbuckled his belt and drew down his trousers. His legs were more of the same—short, plump, hairless, seemingly without muscle enough to keep him upright. His shorts were boxer type, and absolutely nothing but a round tummy showed behind them.

I drew down the shorts, trying not to see his genitals. And that wasn't too difficult! I mean, they were practically nonexistent! The testicles were almost completely drawn up into the scrotum, but that might have been partly from tension. As for the penis, it was just a tiny little tip showing from the foreskin—perhaps an inch of matter all told!

Again, I'm reminded of what I said about penises—that they don't vary all that much in size, and that even when they do it isn't size that makes the difference, but the *man,* the personality, the lover behind the tool. In Brent's case, an enormous cock made *quite* a difference because of the man, the beautiful, exciting man. In David's case, whatever would emerge in erection—and I couldn't foresee more than three, three and a half inches—might also make a difference to a woman, a depressing and negative difference.

This man didn't have a thing going for him.

No, that isn't quite right. He had *several* things, if they could be freed from a vast inferiority complex: intelligence, gentleness, and *savoir-faire* in much excepting women.

I'd omitted something I'd done with all my other patients, and now I tried to rectify it. I hadn't kissed and caressed him while I was removing his clothing. I'd been so engrossed in the spectacle of this child-man, in the struggle not to allow my complete lack of sexual feelings to show, that I'd stripped him as quickly as possible. Now I rose and stroked his arms and murmured, "David, look at me."

His eyes were still closed against what his intelligence told him would be a bad reaction. He said, "A moment," voice shaking. "A moment, please."

I bent and kissed his neck, his shoulder. I stroked his chest, and fought a sudden tickle of revulsion at the unmanly softness. Then something else began to happen. He smelled exceptionally sweet and clean—a *baby* sweetness of flesh and body. He *felt* the same way, and while it was a turn-off in one sense, it was . . . well, pleasant, in another.

I began to think of him in a different way. This was a little boy, in truth if not chronology. This was a young and virginal boy, and I was his seductress, his first woman, if I could manage it.

To be the very first sexual partner in a man's life is, quite obviously, a big kick for almost any woman. To be the temptress and seductress of a child who is yet not really a child, well, there's a Lolita-like thrill there. It began to worm its way into my mind, my feelings, and then, as I pressed my naked body against his, against that small, tender, babyish form, it also wormed its way into my crotch. He was so much smaller than I, softer than I, so delicate in bone and tender in flesh, and he huddled against me not like a man but like a frightened baby, with no life at all in that tiny penis.

It was beginning to help me in my need to approach David with some degree of excitement and desire! I wanted his little hands to move over me, to touch the sexual parts of me. . . .

I drew him to the bed. I told him we could only touch each other a little tonight, but I planned to go as far in the touch-and-feel process as he seemed able to accept. He again closed his eyes. I spoke softly, explaining that he should relax and give in to the warm, pleasant sensation. I stroked his body—arms and sides and chest and belly—and heard him gasp as I approached his genitals. Still, there was no sign of life in that diminutive penis.

I skipped the genitalia and went to his legs, rubbing up from the ankles to the knees, from the knees to the thighs and again heard that gasp as my fingers barely touched the sparse nest of pubic hair. This time there *was* movement in the penis. It stirred, and emerged a bit from the foreskin. I was as excited as if I were seeing a half-drowned man responding to artificial respiration! And when I glanced at his face, his eyes were open and on me . . . or rather on my breasts, swinging, as I bent and moved over him.

I changed position so as to kiss his lips. I pressed my breasts against that soft chest and felt the breath rushing in and out of him. I tongued him, stroked his belly, and felt, finally, one hand touch me, so very, very tentatively, on the hip. I lay back. I smiled and murmured, "Your turn."

He came up on an elbow. For a moment he looked down at himself, at his penis, and he said what so many other men say. "It's . . . so small, isn't it?"

I was about to say it would grow bigger in full erection, and then saw that it was up, standing stiffly. He was in full erection, and even the three and a half inches I'd thought would be his were denied him.

I murmured that size didn't matter; he had enough to satisfy any woman; enough to make love and have orgasms and give orgasms and make babies. He said, "Really?" and one hand moved to my belly and trembled there, and the other hand brushed over my breast as if it were a hot stove.

Now, there was to be no genital touching, including the breasts, at this session, but as I've done before, I took it on myself to change the plan. I murmured, "Yes, more," and closed my eyes. That little hand stroked more strongly. That little hand grasped a breast and rubbed the nipple. I sighed and squirmed, acting, yes, but also feeling . . . well, an evil little thrill. I was robbing the cradle!

He began to warm to his work, and I opened my eyes a slit, watching his cock. It was red and throbbing. It was a young man's hard-on, Lilliputian or not, and it attracted me mightily. I wanted to get my hands on it.

I pulled him down to me for a kiss. I tongued him. He kissed back with energy, and then with passion. He said, "Oh, Valerie!" in that toys-at-Christmastime way of his. His hands roamed from my breasts to my thighs, and touched my pubic area.

I considered stopping him there. He might grow frightened if he got involved with cunt at this early stage of the game. But I parted my legs, inviting him with sighs and squirms to get to it. He came close, but then withdrew. He did it again and again, until I actually itched for his little fingers to plunge in! That perverse excitement really had me now. I was stroking his head, murmuring, "Sweet baby," the way a woman does with a man—only my meaning was *literal!* I just *had* to take that tiny red cock in my hand, and I did, and his sudden groan and "Valerie!" frightened me, they were so intense.

I let go. He said, "Please, please," and took my hand and brought it back. No woman had ever stroked his body. No woman had ever soul-kissed him. No woman had ever allowed him to see, not to say touch, her naked body. And no hand but his own had ever held that burning little tool.

I grasped it. It disappeared in my fist. I squeezed it, stroked it. He came down with his lips on my breasts, gasping, crying out, saying, "Oh, Valerie, Valerie!"

Suddenly, surprisingly, he pulled away, took his cock from my grasp, shaking his head and saying, "Wait, no, wait. . . ."

I asked why he wanted me to stop. He was lying back, head on the pillow, panting. Then I noticed that he was dripping sweat, and was quite white. He said, "Faint . . . please . . . sick. . . ." I got up, about to get him some water . . . but he jumped from the bed and ran for the bathroom. I heard him vomiting.

When he came out, he was terribly embarrassed. I said, "It's natural, reacting that way. We covered about ten years in ten minutes, David. What you might have experienced little by little over the years since you were seventeen, you had all at once. But it went marvelously well."

"Did it? I . . . really have no way of knowing."

I smiled. "You certainly must have known how excited *I* was?"

He didn't return my smile. His gray eyes fell away. "You're my therapist."

A bright man; an adult, and a sensitive one when it came to his mind. "Yes, I'm your therapist. Yes, you wouldn't know if I *wasn't* excited. But I was, David. And if you'd put your hand between my legs . . ."

He actually blushed. He murmured, "But *why,* being the way I am?"

"The way you are? You're a small man, but a man. And very bright, and very sensitive, and very nice to be with. And once you accept the fact that being small, even *quite* small . . ."

"*Abnormally* small," he interrupted, determined to put it all on the line.

"No, not abnormally small. Small and delicate. But that erection you had was pulsing with maleness. And I wanted to touch it. And I'm going to have it in me, once *you* want it in me."

He was staring at me, desperate to believe me, yet unable to because of his life's history of rejection. We'd covered much ground during our ten minutes in bed, but not enough, not nearly enough, to overcome those ten destructive years; or rather, those twenty-seven destructive years.

I got off the bed and came to him, pushing my breasts out, walking with a roll of buttocks and hips, wanting to be all woman—and grateful that part of the perverse excitement, the strange desire for this child-man, was still alive in me. I came right up against him, and put my hand around his waist and low on his soft backside. "Tell me I'm lying, David. Go on, tell me."

He said, "Valerie," his voice breaking, and I felt that little cock stir against my thigh.

I stepped back. We'd had enough, more than enough, for our fourth session.

I called Gini from home. Tomorrow, Saturday, she

wanted us to go out, to spend time together eating, perhaps even having a drink in a lounge with music and
dancing. She wanted him to feel that he was out on a
date. I said I already had a date for the evening; that
I'd counted on an afternoon session, as had always been
the case before. She said all right, we would go out for
lunch. But Sunday, she wanted us to spend the entire
day together, outdoors if the weather held nice. Forest
Park Zoo would be perfect. My heart sank. . . .

I was dating an anesthetist. I'd had four previous dates
with him, and we'd gone to bed together the last time.
He was thirty-eight, tall, and good-looking despite thinning hair and a perpetually glum expression. He spoke
well, was ardent in bed, seemed easygoing and undemanding, though that glum expression was matched by a rather cynical approach to life. As he'd told me, he'd been
disappointed in most people, especially women, and so
didn't expect very much from any of them. "And that includes you, sweet Valerie," he'd said, smiling slightly.

It suited me fine. I liked him, but he didn't kindle any
fires in my heart.

Mother was still complaining of a severe headache
when I dressed at eleven Saturday morning. The nurse
said she felt it was because of too much television. I
again asked whether we shouldn't call the doctor. The
nurse said it wasn't necessary; she would administer a
mild sedative and then a neck and back rub, which should
do the trick. But I was still worried, and said I would
call in an hour to see if the pain had decreased.

David was all spruced up in a gray tweed suit, with
vest of course, and had his coat on his arm and a little
tweed cap in his hand. He said he was in the mood for a
brisk walk, and when he put on that little cap, I thought
I would die! A brisk *toddle* was more like it!

I know it sounds cruel, but that's the way he looked,
and that's the way I felt, and liking him in some ways
and feeling some strange turn-on with him and admiring
his perception and intelligence didn't change my gut reactions.

Again I suffered through the elevator ride and the
walk through the lobby. And this time there was no kind,
covering darkness outside, but one of the clearest skies

and brightest suns we'd had in weeks. He asked me to choose a restaurant in the neighborhood so that we could walk there. I immediately suggested we go again to the Nantucket Cove because of its excellent food—but actually because it wasn't quite a block away. And that block seemed like a mile!

I refused wine and dessert to shorten the meal. He went along with this, and we returned to the hotel in just about an hour. In the room, he excused himself and went to the bathroom. Again, when he emerged, his hair was damply neat and he smelled of cologne. He sat right down on the davenport.

I asked if I could have a drink, thinking he would call room service, but he'd been up early that morning and visited a local liquor store. He had sherry and Scotch. I chose the Scotch, he had a sherry, and we sat there sipping, continuing our conversation about Chicago and his trips to Europe to purchase items for his shop. At this point he rose, went to the bedroom, and returned with a small package. "Something I brought with me from home, on the chance that I'd want to give it to my surrogate. I thought to keep it for the last meeting, but I simply can't wait, Valerie. Not after . . . the *wonder* of last night."

So he *had* been left feeling happy and triumphant! It gave me a warm glow, and I squeezed his hand as I took the package. I removed the wrapping paper, opened the box—and gasped. It held a small statuette, no more than five inches high, perhaps two inches wide at the base, of a man and woman embracing. The figures were beautifully made—not idealized, but quite natural —and the material was a green, jadelike stone. But it couldn't be jade; that would be far too expensive.

I looked up at him. He smiled. "Do you like it?"

I nodded. "Is it . . . ?"

"Jade, yes."

"But I can't . . . "

"After what you've given me, and what I hope you're going to give me . . ."

I put the statue down and rose, and we came together. Again, he was so pitifully small and delicate, so soft and plump and unmanly, and again, as I undressed him, I began to feel that perverse thrill, that devilish turn-on. This time I kissed each part that I exposed—shoulders, arms, stomach, thighs. This time his little cock was up by the time I took down his shorts, and I kissed that too. His "Oh, Valerie!" seemed mostly shock. I looked up and murmured, "You don't like it?" His little nod made me smile. I rose to allow him to undress me, and directed him to kiss and touch each part he exposed of *my* body.

In bed, we went through the petting, the touch-and-feel process, but then he asked a question, and I answered without thinking. "Are you going out tonight?"

"Yes, but we have plenty of time."

Almost immediately, I saw him going limp.

"Just an old friend." But why should I be lying to a patient about a purely personal matter? I stopped, and said, "That's not important in terms of the two of us, David."

He nodded, but briefly, abruptly.

I went back to touching him, kissing him. Nothing did any good. "It's wrong," he finally said. "I mean, to take your weekend, your Saturday, when you want to be with someone . . . you love."

I sat up. I said, "David, there *have* been times in my life when I've been with a patient and wanted desperately to be with someone I loved. But I love no one now, except dear old Mom. . . ." At that, I remembered I was supposed to call to find out how she was. I explained about her sickness, and asked him to excuse me while I phoned. He began to leave the room. I pulled him back down, reached to the nightstand for the phone, and called home. The nurse said my mother was much better. I thanked her and hung up. I asked David to lie down beside me. He said, "Valerie, could we . . . skip the therapy today? I don't know why, but I'd . . . just like to have another drink."

I got a hunch then. His putdown wasn't really because of my date. He'd felt something and not in the room. His life of rejection had made him supersensitive to slights, and that brief walk and quick meal had gotten to him: he'd assumed, correctly, that I was rushing to get out of the public eye.

I began to feel a sort of panic. I'd have to go *out* with

this man for at least another week. In the room, it wasn't too bad, but outside I simply couldn't control my feelings of shame because of his incredible appearance. How was I going to operate successfully with him if he persisted in reacting to *my* reactions?

I couldn't push him. He was really *down* now, in all ways. But I asked him not to dress, said we would sit and drink as we were, nude. He hesitated, then agreed. On the davenport, I examined the statue and expressed my delight. He told me where he'd bought it and took it from me to point out certain details. I leaned against him, pressing my bare breasts into his arm, and then kissed his neck. He stood up. He was ridiculous in his nudity, this little barrel, this little teddy bear, but he had a certain dignity as he said, "I'm sorry, I just must . . . cover myself."

We dressed. He said there was a movie he wanted to see.

He was asking me to leave.

I put on my coat and went to the door. He accompanied me, always the gentleman. I turned to him. "David, I'm sorry."

"Whatever for?"

"I think you know. Please be patient with me."

I'd reversed our roles. And it worked. He came up against me, leaned his head on my bosom, murmured, "I didn't think it was going to be easy. In fact, I didn't think it was going to be *half* this good. But . . . I do so like you, Valerie. I know it's the patient-nurse syndrome, and even more so in my case. You'll have to tolerate it. You're my first real . . . girl. I'm falling . . ." He stopped himself then. We kissed. I left.

I had tears in my eyes as I drove away in my car, but still, I was glad to get home and dress and meet my date —my big, manly, horny, not-so-gentle-and-sensitive date.

He wanted to go to bed with me. I wasn't in the mood. He looked at me strangely and said, "I called your home this afternoon. Your mother's nurse said you were out on a date. You really pack them in, don't you? Did the afternoon male wear you out?"

I had to laugh. First the patient had been uptight

about the boyfriend; now the boyfriend was uptight about the patient.

James didn't seem to like my laugh, and I couldn't very well explain it to him. In fact, he got downright sullen, and took me right home. As I opened his car door, he said, "If you don't like the action, let me know. I'll stop *bothering* you."

He surprised me. There was real heat in that statement. I hadn't thought he was all that involved in little Valerie. And, of course, it made me a little more involved with him. I said, "I hope you keep *bothering* me for quite a while, Jimmy."

He took a deep breath and slid across the seat and pulled me to him. When he came up for air, he smiled that grim smile of his. "Just watch it, Val-baby. Just don't get *too* deeply under my skin."

A tough-guy anesthetist? Not quite in the tradition of the gangster movies *I'd* seen, and I laughed and went into my home. And realized I hadn't called in to report to Dr. Masters on my session with David. I guess I wasn't anxious to say it had been a failure. But when I did call, I was simply told to try again tomorrow. They hadn't expected *this* to be an easy case. The erection was a triumph in itself.

The first thing I did the next morning was to look out the window, hoping for rain or snow or anything that would give me an excuse not to spend the day outdoors with David; but it was again clear and bright.

Mother made it to the breakfast table, and complained in her usual fashion about my never being home lately, so I felt she'd recovered from her headaches.

At eleven-thirty I knocked at David's door . . . and he was ready to leave. We went down to my car, drove into Forest Park, found a parking spot, and walked to the zoo. He was once again wearing that gray tweed suit with vest, and little tweed cap, and I told myself it looked as good as anything else would look on him—and wasn't comforted much. But I'd made up my mind not to look at other people and not to feel shame and not to fear being seen.

I failed miserably to control my feelings, but I think this time I managed to hide them. The three hours we

spent in the zoo and close to two hours we spent in a
French restaurant on Lindell are beyond description—or
maybe I just can't allow myself to describe them. I want
to forget the people who came up behind us, thinking I
was with an overdressed child, and then turned and stared
and hid their laughter; and being at the monkey cage,
where a child spent more time examining David than he
did the monkeys; and all the happy couples, the normal
couples, holding hands or holding babies.

I was back to hating myself, my life, everything and
everyone. I hurt so badly I was close to tears half a dozen
times. And yet there I was listening to a man react with
excitement, pleasure, and intelligent comment. He talked
about the London Zoo and how much more humanely
animals are confined there. He described a trip he'd
taken to South Africa for tribal wood carvings, and a
side trip to Krueger National Park where the animals
are free and the visitors in effect caged. He never once
said anything dull or insipid or in bad taste, as more than
one of my dates has, and still I was drenched with perspiration by the time we returned to the hotel—a cold,
enervating sweat of repressed emotion.

I said I had to shower, and did, and came out wrapped
in a towel. David had prepared two drinks, mine Scotch,
and I took it down quickly. I felt exhausted, but I helped
him undress and led him to the bed, fully intending to
get into touch-and-feel and then to whatever more he appeared able to handle. But as soon as we lay down, my
eyes closed. I asked him to touch me, took his hands and
directed them over my arms, sides, belly—told myself I'd
rest a few moments and then take a more active part.

I fell asleep. When I awoke, it was dark; I'd slept
more than three hours. I didn't move as I awoke, simply
opened my eyes and tried to remember where I was.
Then I moved my head, looking for David, and saw that
he was down at the foot of the bed. He had parted my
legs, and his face was about an inch away from my vagina. He was examining me, sniffing me, touching me
very, very lightly around the mons and labia. He was
doing something he had never before been able to do—
examining a woman's private parts to his heart's content.

It may sound funny, but it made my insides ache for

him. Again I was reminded of his terribly deprived and lonesome life, and I sighed and spread my legs even farther and said, "David, touch me there. Put your fingers in me, please."

At my first movement, he'd started guiltily and begun to rise. But when he heard me out, he went back down and began to play. I helped him, instructed him, and soon he was fingering me with enthusiasm—and soon I was feeling that rising heat, that mounting need.

When the heat grew too much, I tried to stop him. I said, "Let me touch *you*," but my words were weak, smothered in gasps, and inexperienced though he was, he read the signs correctly and intensified rather than stopped his movements. With my help, he'd found the clitoris, and his little fingers played around it perfectly. Looking down at him, I was again swept by that perverse pleasure of having a child-man, and I reached for his head and stroked it and moaned, "Baby, faster . . . yes . . . yes. . . ."

I was writhing, humping up and down, and his free hand went under my body and squeezed and probed and played with my anus—and I came hard, and continued to come as his fingers worked on and on.

I finally had to pull his hand away. I was weak, drained, and satisfied. I drew him to me for a long, sweet kiss, and felt for his cock, and it was up and oozing precoital fluid. I squeezed it, stroked it, even though again I was going ahead of schedule: if he again withdrew and was sick, it could establish a dangerous pattern of self-rejection, self-induced failure. But he seemed ready, and so I kept stroking, kept kissing him.

He was moving his fat little hips in the unmistakable rhythm of coitus—and I was suddenly moving over onto him, wondering if I could get that baby prick up me. And then I was straddling him, hunching down as hard as I could, and small as it was, it went into me, tickling my clitoris and bringing a return of heat. I couldn't rise and fall very much, or I'd have unsheathed him, but I swiveled and ground and rotated, and he said, voice almost conversational, "What . . . what are you doing?" and then, "Valerie, my love, Valerie . . . please . . . don't . . . Valerie. . . ."

He screamed, Herb. I mean, he really screamed, so that anyone in the next room could have heard! It scared the hell out of me. I didn't know if I'd hurt him, or whether he'd suffered a traumatic shock that had flipped him out completely, or what. I rolled off him and took him in my arms and rocked him. He was crying. His body was wracked by sobs, and the tears poured from his eyes, and he kept shaking his head, back and forth, back and forth. "David," I kept saying, "David, honey, what is it? David, please. . . ."

His arms came around me, and he gripped me and said, "I'm a man, Valerie. I'm a man at last. I know it, and I will never go back to the way I used to be, the horrible way I used to be. I'm a man, and I'll never forget it again. I'm a man . . . I'm really a man . . . I'm not abnormal that way. I'm a man. I'm a man. . . ."

I couldn't stop him, and after a while I didn't try to. He went on that way, hysterical with happiness. When he finally ran down, he kissed me and kissed me and said, "Will we do it again? You won't tell the doctor it's finished now, will you? I want to do it again. I want to do it other ways, Valerie. Promise me we'll do it again, other ways? Promise?"

He was a child again, and I promised and rocked him, and we stayed that way for about half an hour.

We dressed and had a drink on the davenport. He had Scotch this time, and said that while he didn't like the taste, he *did* like the hot, burning feeling. I remembered those lines from the Bible: "When I was a child, I spake as a child. . . . When I became a man, I put away childish things."

Gini and Bill were pleased with David's progress. In fact, they felt he was far ahead of schedule, and they wanted me to go along just as I had, moving toward male-dominant intercourse at whatever speed I felt was right for the patient.

We had ten or eleven more sessions scheduled, and I knew I was in for hell outside that room, and success inside it. Monday I went down on him for a few minutes, and he insisted on doing the same for me, and while he wasn't too good at it, I warmed enough so that this time, when I mounted him, I achieved orgasm, that tiny prick acting something like a finger on me.

Tuesday he met me at the door with a down expression, which certainly was a surprise, since he'd been the happiest man in the world the night before. "I have a confession to make," he muttered. "I . . . I kept thinking of you, and this morning when I woke up I had an erection, and even after I went to the bathroom it wouldn't go away." He took a deep breath. "I masturbated. I didn't tell the doctor. Will it spoil things tonight?"

I smiled and shook my head, and we left for dinner. He was turning into a horny little so-and-so. A morning masturbation wouldn't do anything but whet his appetite for the evening's sport, when I was going to try to get him into male-dominant position.

On returning to the room, my smiles were used up from being out with him. But once in bed, we got going nicely, and he wanted to try sixty-nine, and we did so well and he struggled so hard when I tried to end it that we both came; and his discharge was far from childlike.

I promised myself that Wednesday, for sure, we'd have male-dominant sex, but Wednesday we had no sex at all. Late Tuesday night, Mother's headache returned. Three A.M. Wednesday, she cried out my name several times. Luckily, I awoke and came to her room. She was half off the bed, her head hanging to the floor.

We had a contract with a private ambulance service, and by four A.M. she was in the local hospital. I stayed at her bedside until she regained consciousness at nine A.M., and then she seemed to have just about as much movement and control as she'd had before. Except for her eyesight, and even that was not affected as much as we first thought.

I called the Foundation and said I didn't know when I'd be able to continue with David. I suggested that, since it might be several days, perhaps a week, they get a substitute surrogate to take over. Everyone was upset, but they said they would speak to David and see what *his* schedule was.

When I went home at five that evening, I called the Foundation again. David had refused to consider a substitute. He would reschedule his business arrangements and have the man he'd hired for his shop stay on an extra week if necessary.

It wasn't necessary. Mother recovered completely by the next morning, and was already insisting on coming home. The doctor wasn't *that* complacent about the stroke, but said a day or two and she could be discharged.

I decided I could spend a few hours with David Thursday evening, but told the Foundation that dinner was out. I'd grab a quick sandwich at home. . . .

They told me not to bother, that we would wait until I could do it right—the social and the sexual, together.

I realized then that I was using Mother's illness as a cop-out, and that if I could give David two hours, I could give him three. I said all right, dinner too.

The patient . . . always the patient! But then again, that's what doctors and therapists are all about. Let me say this for Gini and Dr. Masters: however tough they may have seemed at times in regard to my feelings, they never once would consider short-changing the patient. I didn't always like them for this, but I always respected them for it.

David suggested the Nantucket Cove. He knew about my mother, and he wanted to save as much time as possible.

Back at the room, he quickly said, "If you're too distracted . . ."

I took his hand. "No, she's quite all right."

"But if you don't feel up to it, I'm perfectly willing to *say* we did."

He was offering me professional protection. He was willing to give up what he most wanted in all the world. I took him in my arms and kissed him. We went to the bedroom and undressed each other, and when I took down his shorts, I licked his balls and cock, and when he took down my panties, he tongued my cunt, and when we got into bed we wanted each other—yes, I really wanted that gentle little man; he had become dear to me, and so, simply, naturally, I spread my legs, and he moved onto me. For a moment he hesitated, unsure of what to do, and I said, "David, baby, now," and fed that little cock into me and began to screw.

He slipped out. His face was agonized, but I quickly

grabbed a pillow and put it under my ass and said, "Many men use this method," and I again grasped his tool and put it in me. This time I watched my movements, and the pillow helped, and we went on, and he began to get to me. I wrapped my legs around him and whispered his name, and his "Oh, Valerie!" was continuous. I made it, but he was still going on.

He took awhile. I thought perhaps we were going to have a failure, but he later said he had actually stopped himself from coming once, "because it felt so marvelous, so tremendous!"

When I left, he was sipping a Scotch and smiling and looking . . . different.

From then on, each meeting developed more confidence, more manliness, more technique. He went at me from the rear, and though he was barely able to get the head of his cock in that way, it worked for both of us. All it takes is friction in the clitoral area for the woman, and friction on the glans for the man.

It never got better for me when it came to being out with him, but I certainly covered up far more effectively than I had at first.

Mother came home Saturday morning. I saw David Saturday from two to five, and then went home, and the nurse said everything was fine. I phoned Jimmy, my anesthetist boyfriend, to say we were on for tonight. He said, "Right," and hung up. I didn't think much of his terseness at the time, but later that night, after a movie and dinner, he seemed particularly tense, and I said, "Anything bothering you, Jimmy?"

"You." It was said unsmilingly.

"In what way?"

"You're running around with other men, aren't you?"

"Running around?" I laughed. "I didn't realize we had reached . . ."

We were in his car; he was driving; he suddenly backhanded me across the mouth.

I'd never been hit by a man—not in anger. Abner, as you know . . . but this! I felt a trickle of blood from my cut lip, and all I could do was whisper, "Why? Why did you do that?"

"You're either mine, or you're not! I won't share! And

as many times as I call evenings . . ."

I finally came out of my shock. I swung back at him, even though he was speeding now. I hit him and hit him, and he pulled to the side of the road—Lindberg, not too far from my home. As soon as the car stopped, I had the door open and was running.

It was a dark stretch of highway. I was sobbing, mostly in rage. Then I heard the car and looked and saw he was driving up beside me. I shouted that if he dared touch me again, I'd go to the police. He said, "Val, I'm sorry. Please, get back inside."

I said no, and began to run again. He got out and ran around in front of me. I swung at him. He took it, and grabbed my arms . . . and that's when I saw he was crying. I grew still. He said, voice thick, "I'm so sorry. I . . . I've been wanting to tell you from the second date—I love you. I just couldn't stand thinking of you and other men."

I stared at him.

"I love you," he said again. "I want you to go with me, and me only. I want us to . . . think of a permanent arrangement. Please forget what I did. It'll never happen again. *Please*. . . ."

When he took me in his arms, I didn't resist. He kissed me there at the side of the road, with cars whizzing by and the tears running down both our faces. I don't think I kissed him back. Being hit that way—maybe some women find it stimulating, but not I.

I still didn't know how I felt when he called me Sunday morning. I was going to spend the day with David; and when he asked me to spend it with him, I said I already had a date.

He was silent a moment. "Okay," he said, trying to sound loose and at ease, and not succeeding. "But you *do* forgive me for last night, don't you?"

I said I wasn't sure; we'd talk again during the week.

"Next Saturday all right?"

"I told you, Jimmy, we'll talk during the week."

"Right. Remember . . . I love you."

I didn't answer. He said good-bye and hung up. He loved me. Out of the blue, the words I'd valued above all others all my life. The most important words in the world to me. "I love you" . . . preceded by a back-handed crack to the face.

And then I knew I would *not* see him, ever again! The decision was sudden, and irrevocable. Violence of this sort was not my bag. Maybe some women like to be brutalized, outside the bedroom, but not little Valerie.

End of Jimmy, despite a need for love, for companionship this last week before Christmas. End of Jimmy, no matter how many times he would call and plead.

I was alone again.

David and I went to the art museum and the planetarium. The planetarium was fine with the lights out and his small, gentle hand caressing mine constantly. Back at the room, we made love, Mamma-Papa, and that too was fine. He gave me another gift, something he'd bought after I'd left him yesterday—a lovely illustrated copy of the *Rubayyat of Omar Khayyam,* and read sections to me, glancing up every so often with the softest, deepest expression I'd ever seen on the face of a man or child. And we made love a second time.

When I got home, Mother complained of a headache. I called the doctor. He said that if it grew worse, I was to let him know. In the meantime, she was to go to bed. She did, and so did I.

Dinners and, twice, cocktail-lounge drinks with David were still rough from Monday to Thursday, but in the room we made love, and he was a delight to be with: his happiness, his exuberance, his continuing change of personality. Even his voice—though it's unlikely, I'll admit—seemed to deepen a bit. What it probably was, I realized later, was the fact that he no longer used as many childish phrases, and had picked up a few erotic words from me during the sex act. And his confidence—that too added a sense of manliness to him.

On Friday, which was to be our last night together, he said he'd bought tickets to a show. We drove downtown, and once the house lights dimmed we held hands and enjoyed ourselves thoroughly. Dinner at a good German restaurant with the rules about alcohol forgotten and lots of wine for both of us . . . and then we were heading back for the hotel.

In the room, he excused himself and went to the bathroom to freshen up. He was still so careful of his hair, of his appearance and cleanliness, before we made love.

He served champagne, and presented me with flowers and an album of Beethoven's Ninth, his favorite; and since then, one of mine. We held our "graduation exercises." He was better than ever, and I didn't do badly myself.

I couldn't help thinking of Jimmy as we lay in bed together. The tall, handsome man was irrational, neurotic, and violent. The fat little barrel of a man was . . . a man. And in the course of proving it, I learned something. Chemistry would remain important to me, but the value I had placed in externals was definitely diminished.

David told me he was going to hire someone to trace his lost love, his crippled Southside sweetheart. He didn't know if it would work; he simply wanted the chance to find out. I felt it was a wonderful idea. We parted with kisses, and on my part tears . . . and a vast sense of relief.

I took a week's vacation. I spent Christmas and New Year's at home, content for once to be alone with Mother and to do a little shopping and watch a little TV.

After my vacation, I came back to work full of energy, determined to become an associate at the Foundation, working with a doctor the way Mrs. Johnson worked with Dr. Masters. I was also determined to be *very* careful before allowing any man to get close to me! No more Jimmys in my life!

I had lunch one day with Dr. Masters, and came right to the point, saying I felt I was ready for associate work, interviewing patients, but that I would also continue with the surrogate work as long as I was needed.

He said he would let me know, but from his voice and expression, I knew right then that the answer was no.

But why?

A week later, he told me. From now on, only M.D.s, medical doctors, would be used as associates. Yes, he felt I might be able to handle the work, after considerable schooling and training, but he also felt that neither I nor the Foundation could take the gaff—the unjustified criticism the professional world leveled against the Foundation for daring to use someone who wasn't an M.D. for psychological interviews. Gini Johnson was that person, and Dr. Masters said she had suffered far too much medical criticism—she *and* the Foundation—for him to ever allow anyone else to go through it again.

I was disappointed. I said so, but I also understood— and in the light of recent publications and statements by self-appointed guardians of the medical profession, I can see how right he was. I also said I didn't think I would be interested in any further surrogate cases.

And so I went into the new year, finished, I thought, with the Foundation.

7

Mother had another stroke after a long series of bad headaches. Once again it seemed mild, with practically no deteriorating effect on her general condition. Only this time, before she could leave the hospital, she suffered a *major* cerebral attack that left her more vegetable than human. A month afterward, she still didn't know me, and the doctor said it was time to consider putting her in a nursing home.

It killed me, seeing her that way and knowing that there was absolutely nothing I could do for her; nothing *anyone* could do for her. The doctor said that, of course, there might be *some* improvement, but the kind of care she needed could no longer be provided at home by a practical nurse.

I had been just about wiped out by the hospital bills—a month of intensive care and daily visits by a specialist and, for the first two weeks, day and night nurses—even though medical insurance paid a considerable portion of the bills. A nursing home would eat up my salary and leave me practically nothing for a roof over my head!

I asked for, and received, an increase in salary. I couldn't get Mother into the nursing home I preferred—one that was clean and cheerful, and not so expensive that it was impossible—for at least two months. That was when they figured the next vacancy would occur. So for two months Mother would live at home, with a registered nurse capable of handling the details of her medication. Those two months promised to be rough.

I'd never exactly enjoyed going home since Mother's first stroke, but now I positively dreaded it. The lopsided blankness of a face I'd loved—of a face that had always shown love for me—was just too much to bear. So when Gini called to say she had a relatively "easy-to-take" case if I had changed my mind about not doing surrogate work again, I didn't hesitate an instant before accepting.

That was case number six. It lasted eight days, and was followed two weeks later by case number seven. What stands out in my mind about them—and you'll have to forgive my selfishness—is that I had an excuse not to go home after work, and I was able to earn some money to help pay for Mother's medical expenses.

Case number six was a twenty-five-year-old boy from a middle-class Jewish family living in a good section of St. Louis. Marv was a graduate of the University of Illinois and had planned to become a doctor. But he had dropped out of medical school the first month he was there, suddenly realizing, he told his parents, that medicine was the last thing in the world in which he wanted to spend his life. When they pressed him to make another choice— law, engineering, dentistry, teaching—he vacillated for three months, doing nothing, until it was too late to gain admission to any professional school for the next semester. And then he came home one evening and informed the family—mother, father, and younger sister—that he had enlisted in the Marines and was leaving for boot camp on Parris Island within the week.

They'd been absolutely stunned. Not only had Marv been exempt from the draft because of his student status (which was supposed to have continued in professional school), but he also had a lung condition from a childhood bout with pneumonia that the family physician could testify about to the draft board should the need arise. The doctor had, in order to reassure the worried mother, already written a letter for the draft board and given it to the family. Now Marv informed the mother that if she dared to do anything to damage his status as a Marine, he would never forgive her.

As a student, Marv had been involved in several anti-war demonstrations, and was much given to attacking the power structure and arguing with his father about the immorality of the capitalist system. In short, he had appeared to be a student activist of the radical left, and now he was a patriot, a Marine!

The family could do nothing, and Marv went off to boot camp, and within three weeks came home on what he said was "emergency leave." But what, everyone asked, was the emergency? He smiled and shrugged and said he'd worked a deal, and went out each morning, in uniform, and came home each night, and became more and more tense as the family questioned him more and more closely.

Finally, after almost a month of this, he broke down one night when alone with his sister—whom he adored—and told her the truth. He'd been given a medical discharge after fainting several times while on forced marches. The fainting, he said, had nothing to do with his physical condition, which was good, but with a *mental* condition that had started in college and grown progressively worse, and which he had thought to cure by going into the Marines.

But what, exactly, was the mental condition, the sister wanted to know?

Marv wouldn't tell her.

And he didn't tell anyone, until two years later, when he came to the Foundation and told Dr. Masters.

He had engaged in sex as a senior in high school, and it had been "reasonably good": after all, having a girl squat on your penis in a car parked in a drive-in movie isn't exactly conducive to a full sexual experience! The same girl had given him the same sexual treatment *eleven* times.

In college, he had sex with a girl in far better circumstances—in her dorm when the other girls were out. Three times, and the third time he had begun to "lose sensation."

Marv was about five-ten, well built, rather quiet, and quite nice-looking. There was no problem with his finding girls, but there had *always* been a problem with his *wanting* girls. This was evident in presexual dating, when he was generally reluctant to date at all, feeling it was a waste of time. Even later, when sex was a definite possibility, he'd had to push himself to go out. He liked sports—played tennis and golf—and books and movies. He liked them "as well as girls," and this, once he realized it, had begun to worry him. When asked to play tennis or see a movie by a friend who didn't have a date, Marv was often tempted to break his own date. This, he began to feel, was a sign of lack of manliness, of "a tendency toward being neuter"—his own words. And even though he had never failed with a girl in his fourteen or fifteen experiences, he began to worry about "just how much I really enjoyed it." And from worry came that third sex experience in college where he began to lose sensation. The time after that, with the same girl, he went soft. And, in classic tradition, from then on his failure was complete—four times, with four different girls.

His fear, his agony, became so great that he barely got through his senior year of undergraduate work. And because an association had been formed in his mind between sexual failure and college—after all, it had all happened while he was at the University of Illinois—he found he hated the academic world, and that extended to médical school. Besides, how could he concentrate on such exacting studies with his mind in turmoil?

The Marines had seemed a logical solution. If he could be a successful Marine, tough among the world's toughest warriors, a he-man among he-men, he might also regain his *sexual* manhood. But the barracks life tore him apart. The main topic of conversation was cunt. There were pinups and pornography and stories of conquests and sexual plans for passes and leaves. From the very first night, he had been subjected to a constant barrage of sexuality.

The fainting had followed. A confession to a camp doctor had followed that. He was so obviously in deep psychological trouble, the discharge had been given in lieu of having "a dead weight around," to quote his commanding officer.

During the period of time when he held off telling his family about his discharge, he went out in uniform to various parts of the city, thinking to pick up girls, looking for a way to break through the agony of failure, but he never once had the courage to approach anyone, though he received plenty of encouraging smiles and glances. Finally, a friend told him of a call-girl operation. He went to the shabby hotel near East St. Louis, and a girl was sent to his room. She was young, not bad to look at, and had "a terrific figure, if you go for the very obvious sort." He failed with her too, even though she got it up by sucking him. As soon as she spread her legs, he went soft. She left, muttering about "damned queers," but this was one area in which he found he had no worries. He had never felt any unusual attraction to males, and no longer wondered what might happen if he were subjected to a homosexual advance, because he'd had such an advance made to him and had allowed it to reach a point where, had there been any weakness on his part, it would certainly have shown.

This had taken place during his first year in college. He'd gone to a "beer bust" and consumed far more than he was able to handle. Out of a group of thirty students, eight had continued on to another town in search of girls —and dozing in back of the car was Marv. They hadn't found girls, and had decided to sleep at a little motel. The manager wouldn't allow more than two in a room, and Marv had stumbled groggily along with a senior who took him in tow. They undressed, Marv fell into bed, and the next thing he knew he "felt something warm between my legs." The something warm was a mouth. He was being licked and sucked by the senior, but Marv was too sleepy to realize it.

He moved around, "stopped the warm feeling," and went back to sleep. Later, he again awoke, this time to find his hand being manipulated. He was holding the other man's penis. Still groggy from "quarts of beer," he shoved the senior away, and *again* went back to sleep.

The third time he awoke, he awoke for good. The senior was again sucking his penis, and this time had inverted himself over Marv so that his own rigid member was pressing against Marv's mouth.

Marv said that for a moment he didn't react. He thinks he was allowing himself a few seconds in which to search out what his feelings were. Every man wonders at one time or another whether he has gay tendencies; Marv was no exception. What he ‘realized almost immediately was that his penis was stiff. What he felt immediately afterward was a softening, as his mind told him it was a *man* doing the fellatio. After that, he found he disliked having a male organ touch his lips. And after *that* he threw the senior off the bed and told him that if · he didn't walk out of the room, fast, he would be *carried* out. End of homosexual experience, with little or no trauma at:ached.

After the whore had called him a "damned queer," he had gone home and the next day asked to be given work in his father's business. He had not attempted sexual intercourse since then, nor even masturbation, which he had done infrequently anyway. He now sold real estate for his father, and was doing well at it. He had a girl friend, whose picture he showed me—a cute little brunette with soulful eyes and solemn mouth—whom he liked well enough, since she shared his interest in books and movies, if not sports, but whose main purpose in his life, he admitted, was to keep friends and parents from wondering about him. Without her, they'd have begun to suspect something was wrong. With her, he was able to go out to dinner once or twice a week, and not have to do much else. "Because she's only eighteen, and she's been strictly brought up and doesn't expect real sex yet."

But they'd been going together for five months, and she was beginning to want something more than the good-night kisses she'd been getting. In fact, it was she who had precipitated his coming to Masters and Johnson, though he'd read about them in a magazine article and had been thinking, vaguely, of looking into the possibilities of treatment.

On their last date, they'd kissed in his car outside her home, and her body had trembled in his arms, and he'd "felt sorry for her." He still wanted nothing more, but suspected he was cheating her out of what *she* wanted, and so he decided that a mild petting session was in order.

He caressed her breasts a bit, and it felt good. She

stroked his thigh a bit, and that too felt good. And suddenly they were straining together, and his hand was under her dress. She wasn't wearing stockings or pantyhose, and her smooth thighs seemed to crack the months of indifference, the period of total nonsexuality. His hand went up farther, to the heated bulge in her panties—and then he again ran full tilt up against his fear: fear of cunt and the servicing of cunt. But she was now wildly passionate, and before he knew it, she'd unzipped his fly and pulled out his cock. It was erect—for an instant. It was hard "while I didn't really know what she was doing, while I was sort of in a daze." Then he pulled away, saying, "I can't let you . . . we're going too far," and she accepted it, hot though she was, because her own training took hold—her youth and her training. But if she had been just a bit more experienced, she would have realized he had wilted during that last second or two in her hand.

That was when he decided on Masters and Johnson, because something struck him—something more hopeful than anything that had happened in the past year. While he'd been unable to concentrate on his fear, he'd been hard, and "it had felt good." If he could somehow learn not to concentrate on fear, on thoughts of being undersexed, of being a "neuter" (a word he used often), he might become a man again.

His treatment appeared to be a matter of several rather simple steps. One, a physical examination to determine if there was anything wrong: hormonal deficiency, for example. Two, the taped interviews and close examination of his biographical data to determine whether he was holding back any information from the past—any deep trauma he might not be able to discuss. And three, in-bed therapy to reverse the process of actual sexual failure that had begun in college.

The physical exam revealed nothing wrong. The interviews indicated he was telling all he knew. Now it was up to in-bed therapy. And because of Marv's youth, good looks, and nice personality, I was certainly not going to do much suffering. But for the same reasons—everything he had going for him, the seeming lack of any *reason* for failure—it looked as if his chances for success were small. All of us felt this might be one of those cases where sexual failure was so deeply interwoven into a subtle and lifelong psychological illness that only long-range analysis would have a chance of success.

We were wrong. Marv *was* hiding something, but because it was such an obvious thing, and because it was based on a fallacy that a man of his experience—an athlete, a college-dorm man, and finally, if only briefly, a Marine—should have known was a fallacy, we all missed it.

He thought his penis was too small to satisfy a woman.

He had never dared discuss it with anyone. He had assumed he was failing to satisfy his sex partners. He had always averted his eyes from other men's genitals. He had looked at himself without any frame of reference, any means of comparison, and decided he was infinitesimal.

It all came out during our second session. The first was dinner, and because of the specifics of his case, some serious petting. He stayed soft throughout. The second session I undressed myself, and then him, and in bed, touching, stroking, unable to get him to react, I finally complimented him on the shape of his limp tool. Sometimes a circumcised penis can have a very shapely head. His did; and besides, I was looking for something, anything, to change that grim, intense expression. His reaction was a sharp laugh and a muttered, "When you can *see* it."

I asked him what he meant, and then out it came. "You know . . . it's so . . . *small*, really. When I was with my high-school girlfriend, she would say she couldn't feel it. She wanted to get it in deeper, but of course . . ." He shook his head and turned over quickly on his stomach. "It's just too small to work."

I couldn't believe it was that simple. I began to talk. I talked and talked, explaining that coitus while seated in a car is different from coitus in bed, with resultant difficulties in gaining full penetration, and that besides, he and the girl were obviously too inexperienced to have gotten all they could have out of such a limiting position. Then I remembered his three experiences with the college girl in bed, and asked if *she* had said anything about the size of his penis.

"No," he muttered, "but I'm sure she didn't have an orgasm, not once."

"*How* can you be sure?" I was stroking his back, running my hand over his strong buttocks, and between them to touch his testicles. "Did she actually say so?"

He was beginning to squirm, to react to my touches. "No . . . but I was sure . . ."

"Some women come with barely a gasp. Some simply sigh. Others tense up their bodies and then relax. Not everyone goes into obvious paroxysms of delight, you know."

He said she'd tensed, all right . . . and then gone limp. Could *that* have been an orgasm?

I said, "Most definitely." I had my hand under his body now, grasping balls and penis both, and the penis was becoming turgid, thicker. I said that even though I'd only seen him limp, he had as large a penis as most, perhaps larger. I got my hand around it and asked him to turn over so I could prove that what I was saying was true.

At least I hoped I could prove it! Was there one chance in a million that it wouldn't grow normally in erection? I suddenly wished I could question Dr. Masters! Perhaps there *were* some rare cases . . . ?

Marv turned over, slowly, reluctantly, and as soon as he did, as soon as I was able to look at his penis, it shriveled again. I kissed his mouth. I kissed his chest and belly. I skipped the genitals and kissed his thighs, teasing him, waiting for some sign of life. It didn't come until I got down and licked his balls. Then he lengthened—but still didn't rise.

I went down on his cock. I sucked him until my mouth was *tired*. I mean, about half an hour steady! And finally it began to happen. And when it did, he was a good five, five and a half inches, which is enough for any woman.

I told him so, and said I would now prove it. I got on him, expecting he would go soft, but he didn't. He looked at his cock, kept looking at it as I slid it into me, never took his eyes off it as I humped up and down . . . and I eventually reached orgasm. I kept going for quite a while afterward before his eyes closed and he began to lose himself in the act. It took some doing; I was exhausted by the time he came. But come he did.

We had six more sessions, each one a successful act, the last four Mamma-Papa, plus variations. He was young and strong, and if not as wildly sexual as some men, certainly capable. And after the last session he told me he'd finally felt "ecstasy." Know how he said good-bye to me? Shook my hand and said, "Thanks for everything." Not a very emotional fellow!

I have some follow-up information on Marv. He got into trouble with his eighteen-year-old girl friend; he made her pregnant. There was family agony and consultations, and finally the decision went against marriage. She had an abortion. Marv went back to school, but even without sexual problems he didn't really want to be a doctor or any sort of professional. He was a good real-estate agent, and that was what he wanted to do—and that is what he is now.

In his occasional reports to the Foundation, he has stated that, except for one failure with a girl he didn't like for her conservative political beliefs, he has progressed steadily and has had many good sex experiences. He still doesn't run around hunting ass, the way so many young men do, but he's found a girl he truly likes, they go to bed once or twice a week, and they're considering marriage.

Could it all have been that small-penis hangup? Could several years of agony, and many more of self-doubt, be based on anything that simple? I don't know. I'll bet you couldn't find a psychiatrist to accept it. But even if it *wasn't* just that, Marv is now a functioning male. Complicated reasoning, and analysis, might have gotten to other problems, but they might not have made him capable of fucking a girl, *now*. That's what Masters and Johnson and their Foundation are all about.

My seventh case was a thirty-four-year-old associate professor at a Midwestern university. He had been brought up in a house full of women, his father having died when he was three, and his mother having moved him, his three sisters, and herself in with a maiden aunt. No other man ever entered the mother's life, and ex-

cept for Thanksgiving and Christmas, he never saw a
male relative, all of whom lived in other towns. He grew
up, as expected, a very gentle, mannerly boy, but he also
grew up *big*, taking after his father, who had been a six-
foot-three all-around athlete in college. Vance went the
father one inch better, but wasn't quite as burly. But he
had always been the biggest boy on the block, and at
six-four, a hundred ninety-five pounds, he rarely had to
explain his soft and gentle ways.

He was an excellent student all through grammar and
high school, and an exceptional one in college. Scholarships and fellowships came his way, and he decided to
enter the academic world. He was very happy teaching.
He wanted nothing more from life, professionally. He
earned sufficient for his needs, and during the summers
organized student bicycle tours of various European coun-
tries, hiking tours in the Rockies, and other group vacations that brought him a little money and the type of
travel he enjoyed. He was popular with his students, close
to his three sisters, all of whom had married, and visited
his mother and maiden aunt, both alive and well, whenever he could.

He had no obvious hangups. He was in excellent
health. There was just "one little problem," as he put it.
He had never had sexual relations with a woman, though
he masturbated regularly and felt there was no earthly
reason for not having a woman and eventually a wife
and family. No reason except one: he couldn't get an
erection when with a real live girl. With a photograph
and his fist, yes, but not with female flesh and blood.

Sexual history? None to speak of. He had not dated
in high school; not at all. In college, he had gone to a
few dances, escorted a girl every so often to a school
function, but again, no real dating. Those few times he
had held a girl in his arms, his genitals had felt dead.
The lone single example of what might be called a sexual experience was when a girl attempted to arouse him
in a car after rather much to drink. She stroked his fly,
and he was still dead.

In graduate school, a teaching fellowship helped him
get his M.A. and Ph.D., and he was so busy taking
classes, teaching classes, and doing research for his sev-

eral theses that there was no time to think of girls. Except that he *did* think of them—or, rather, of why he was incapable of dealing with them sexually.

After receiving his Ph.D., he was appointed to an instructorship, and not the most convenient one at that. His classes were split between the daytime undergraduate school and the adult evening session. This was to last only a short while, he was assured, and was caused by a scarcity of good teachers for the evening session, where students took courses either for credit or for their own personal edification. One of the noncredit students in an eight-P.M. Great Books class was "a quiet, rather frightened girl of twenty-one, extraordinarily good-looking," to quote Vance. "She had little command of the English language, but had been pushing herself to read recently in an attempt to better herself, to gain some understanding of literature and culture in general."

Beth and Vance grew to know each other as the term progressed. She was a shy girl, but there was never an evening that some car or other, driven by some good-looking man or other, didn't deliver her to the school and pick her up afterward. When he asked about these friends, she shrugged and said, "Men . . . you know. But they don't hang around long."

Later, he learned what she meant. She too had a problem, one given her by a psychotically religious and violent mother. The mother had been deserted by her husband after twelve years of marriage—and Beth said she didn't blame him, even though she had no recollection of him and he'd never made contact with her, her mother, or her four sisters. The sisters were older than Beth, and while two were married, all were "loose women," to quote the mother. The two married sisters had managed that state of grace only after becoming pregnant. The other two, while not professional prostitutes, lived very well on the extras they got from men friends. Beth had been the last to remain in the mother's clutches, and bore several small facial scars as a result of beatings with a belt, buckle first. She had also been subjected to wakenings in the middle of the night to hear tirades against men, and to clean her room, which the mother insisted be kept "neat as a pin." If Beth had a date, her mother would wait until the last minute to "ground" her, keeping her in on some excuse, any excuse, in order to punish her for "looking like my father." Church also became punishment, since it was prefaced by lectures on how "evil" Beth was and how the mother knew she was "whoring" with men as her sisters were, and followed by "prayers" on their knees in the kitchen, where the mother asked that Beth "die rather than grow up the way she was."

Because she was five years younger than the next youngest sister, and because the others had left home when sixteen or seventeen, Beth had been alone with the bitter psychopath for seven years. She had stayed until she was nineteen—out of guilt, fear, and a growing inability to believe she could ever be anything other than what her mother said she was. And what was she? A beautiful girl, extremely sexual in appearance, who couldn't tolerate the slightest touch from the boys who constantly begged her to go out with them. A virgin when she was finally driven from her mother's home by a wild night of beatings and accusations after she had returned from a date at "the ungodly hour" of two A.M.

She had lived with her oldest sister for one full year, working as a salesclerk in a local department store, paying for the right to sleep on a daybed in the living room, growing increasingly more nervous over her brother-in-law's "jokes." The man drank, and when he did, he beat the sister, and after he beat the sister, he "kidded around" with Beth. One night his kidding around took the form of a full-fledged sexual attack, which she got out of only when the sister came into the room and murmured mildly, "What's going on?"

For the past sixteen months she had been living alone in a cheap rooming house and had begun dating to get away from her mean surroundings and her depressed outlook. But she still couldn't accept the mildest form of sexual approach, which led to a constant turnover in men friends. Beth admitted she was "fighting to stay alive." By that she meant she was often tempted by the jars of sleeping pills given her by a "pill doctor" who didn't look too closely into her psyche. She was also trying to find a man she could believe in, one who could

give her some faith in herself, some reason for living—
and who also could arouse her sexual feelings without
bringing on the terrible guilt and self-hatred.

Vance learned all this after he began taking her out
first for coffee, then for dinner, and finally for day-long
drives into the surrounding countryside on weekends.
They grew to be close friends, and he forgot his own
problems while trying to help solve hers. He read her
poetry by Byron, Keats, Shelley. And she gave him
much too: female companionship, the first nonfamily relationship of his life, her beauty to look at and, later, to
touch. They held hands. They progressed to gentle
kisses. And one night he took her in his arms and told
her he loved her, wanted to help her in every way
imaginable.

She wept, she was so happy. She asked him to come
up to her room—at which point he panicked. What if
they ended in bed and he failed her? What would she
think, this terribly sensitive girl who so precariously
held to her sanity? If she felt it a rejection . . .

He had only one course: he confessed his problem to
her. At first she didn't believe him, felt it was a "line"
to get her into bed with him—because that was her
training, her mother-inspired faith in the world of men.
Later, when they *did* go to bed together—merely to
hold each other—she realized his incapacity was no line.

Something happened then, something disastrous for
Vance. If she had responded to his problem as he had to
hers, with patience and affection, with *love,* he felt he
would have had a good chance of fighting his way to
manhood. He cared so deeply for her, and felt she cared
for him too, that he was determined to continue going to
bed with her, simply holding and caressing her. He probably would have worked out his own touch-and-feel
process and lost tension, and his love for her would have
carried him through to eventual success.

But she *didn't* respond as he had. She had previously
made friends with a student in Vance's class, a man of
thirty from her own background but now in good financial shape, who wanted to better himself, and who was
attracted to her. She had managed to abort his early

attempts to ask her for a date without alienating him; now she accepted.

Beth and her new friend became serious very quickly, yet she continued to see Vance too, though far less frequently. She began using Vance as a father figure, because he was, as far as she was concerned, no longer a possibility as lover or husband. He tried to hang on in his earlier role, but she now confided every little incident, sexual and otherwise, of every date with her new friend, asking Vance's advice. And he gave it. Agonized, unable to walk away from the impossible situation because he was still in love and still committed to helping her, he went on this way for three months. The term finally came to an end. Beth said good-bye. When he asked if she would be back for the second section of the course, she said no, she was going to Europe with her new friend.

He stood behind his desk, a smile frozen on his face. He wished her luck, and then she glanced around, took his hand, and confided that she had made love with her friend the previous night. "It was *wonderful!* And you helped me get there, Vance! Thank you so much! Thank you for making me *believe* in love. You're my dearest friend. Thank you for everything!"

He taught for two more months. When colleagues remarked that he looked ill, he smiled and blamed lack of exercise. He never complained to anyone, never felt justified in his feelings of anguished loss and rejection. And then he got a postcard. Beth was married and "so very happy, and I feel I owe it all to you."

He took sick leave, and came to Masters and Johnson.

I wondered what *I* could do for him. He needed Beth, not me. He needed time to get over his agony, his love for Beth. But the Foundation had decided otherwise: Masters and Johnson felt he needed a woman, *any* woman, period. And they were right.

Our first session consisted of eating, talking, kissing good night.

Our second of light petting, kissing, more talk.

Our third session was supposed to progress by easy stages to undress and touch-and-feel, and it did, but when he saw me naked, he suddenly began kissing me all over my body. I didn't stop him, because he was calling me Beth and was so fervent I felt it would be another rejection, and rejection was the one thing he didn't need! He used his mouth on my vagina, and after a while I couldn't help responding. He worked me up to fever pitch, and I came.

He was shocked at the violence of my response. I mean, I grabbed his head and pressed hard and cried out and shook all over. He pulled away and leaned back on his haunches, staring at me. When I caught my breath, I whispered, "My God, how good that was!" His sudden flush, and repressed smile, showed his pride and pleasure.

During our fourth session, I sucked him, and he came up strong and had a premature ejaculation. He knew it was premature, but I explained it was a result of his tension and the build-up of sexual anticipation—and his shame lessened and his fear lessened.

Our fifth session began badly. He was speaking of Beth as we sat on the davenport. Suddenly his head dropped, his breath came harshly, and before I could block it with words, affection or sex, he was sobbing. I did the only thing I could; I held his head against my breast and let him cry himself out. When it ended, he showed a great deal of what can only be classified as *class*. He wiped his eyes, looked directly at me, and said, "I'm glad the damned thing broke out; it was killing me." Then he put his arms around me and asked if we couldn't have dinner later and get right to bed.

We could, and did, and this time he didn't call me Beth, he called me Valerie, and we played and touched and felt and kissed and spent half an hour working up to the point where I felt we should stop. Then we went to dinner, and he again talked about Beth, and he said what had been so obvious to me when I'd heard his story: "We would never have been right for each other, even if we'd managed to have sex together—in the long run, that is. My background and hers—just too many miles, light-years actually, apart." It was at that point I felt his fight was won.

The sixth session went easily from touch and feel to genital handling to female-dominant coitus. I came. He didn't. But he didn't lose his erection until I decided it was going on too long and said we'd try again the next night.

The seventh session was a repeat of the sixth, with one important exception. He had an orgasm.

The eighth repeated the seventh, again with an important exception: we had *two* complete bouts, the second in male-dominant position.

The ninth was male-dominant, twice, and he would have tried for a third had I not pleaded exhaustion!

That night I told Dr. Masters I thought the case was over. He asked for one more session. I agreed. It was pleasant enough being with Vance; I had no other man to go to; and waiting at home was the horror of what had once been my mother.

Vance was a completely capable, confident lover that final session. I stayed until two A.M., and our parting was warm, tender, touching. He said he didn't know why he hadn't been able to do this before with some woman, any woman. I guess the answer was that some woman, any woman, wouldn't have worked. It certainly hadn't worked for those tortured, self-deprived males who had tried everything from sweethearts to whores before coming to the Foundation.

Before Masters and Johnson, there just hadn't *been* such women as wife surrogates. I'm not patting myself on the back, or complimenting my co-surrogates; I'm simply stating a fact. The combination of science and sex, of planned psychological treatment and a woman's body, of therapy and passion, had simply not been tried before. There had been great innovators and researchers, such as Kinsey, and there had been women who had tried to help their men in bed, but the putting together of the researcher, the physician-therapist, and the sex partner, hadn't been thought of before—or if it had, had certainly not been offered in the form of treatment to Americans afflicted with sexual dysfunctions.

A simple idea, this combination of science and passion, as all the many critics of the Foundation will tell you. Too simple to be worth anything. But once again, Herb, Vance's case proved it was worth *everything*, because it *worked*.

And it has continued to work for Vance. His reports to the Foundation indicate a growing sex life, and the recent awakening of romantic interest. He's been to bed with this woman several times, and they're beginning to think in terms of a permanent arrangement. Interestingly enough, she's not a teacher, academician of any sort, or a professional, as would seem right for him. Once again, Vance has gone to a rather simple, not-quite-developed personality. She's a hostess in the best hotel dining room in town, a student at the adult-education night school, and interested in bettering her position. Not too different from Beth, but this time with a more stable background, and very much in love with her sexually functional benefactor.

Well, Vance had his happiness, and I had some money to help pay my bills . . . or I'd *had* it, before Mother went into the nursing home and I had to make a substantial down payment. But my worries about raising more money to keep her there were soon over. Nine weeks to the day she entered, she died in her sleep.

I don't really know what I felt at that funeral I paid for with borrowed money. Grief? Well, that had been just about used up after the last stroke, when my mother —the conscious intellect that had been my mother— passed away and left only a vegetable. Relief? Yes, but even the vegetable had given me the *illusion* that I had a mother. Now I was alone, completely. The apartment was too large, and held too many bad memories, so I moved. I took a one-bedroom place in a new development area, a garden apartment in one of those long, two-story brick buildings that manage to retain the feel of private homes, with grass and trees outside and park areas nearby. I had enough furniture, and as soon as I could pay off the bank loan for the funeral expenses, I'd have enough money.

That first evening in my new apartment, I was in the bedroom, arranging things in my dresser, when I looked up and caught myself in the mirror.

Valerie X. Scott, twenty-seven, going on twenty-eight. A little tired-looking around the eyes, but that was to be expected after death and funerals. Valerie X. Scott, who now tinted her hair to keep it as red as it had once been quite naturally. Valerie X. Scott . . .

Then I no longer saw the image. Then I saw the actual situation.

I lived in St. Louis, Missouri, alone. I had no relatives within a thousand miles, and no real friends either. I had no one to love, and no one loved me. I was a capable medical worker and a successful wife surrogate. I could handle just about anyone and anything, and feared no one and nothing. I was a totally self-sufficient entity— and totally empty.

Well, I'd been empty before. Something would happen. Something always happened. Good or bad, it would end the emptiness.

What happened was *you*, Herb. Not right away, but after the passage of several months. I'd gotten through still another holiday season, and while I didn't have anyone special, I did know three or four nice men who kept me very busy—too busy to dwell on not being with anyone I loved on Christmas and New Year's. Instead, I was with *droves* of people on both eves, at real gay, turned-on parties.

When Gini called, I was glad to accept my eighth case.

The way Gini put it, this case was almost a *gift:* a writer. Attractive. Believes he has a physical disability, and hasn't. Should be cleared up in six or seven sessions—one week, tops—and would provide me with stimulating company and conversation.

Now, what would a writer do with my experiences as a wife surrogate?

I laughed at myself, but I asked Gini what sort of work you'd done.

"Ten novels, some film and television, various short stories and articles. A thoroughgoing professional."

You can't know how relieved I was on meeting you, Herb, to see that Gini hadn't held back any "minor" details—as she had when describing David. I relaxed almost immediately with you that first purely social evening. I was, as I've indicated, a little down after the frantic holiday season. And I'd been reviewing my life, asking

myself *"What am I?"* thinking back to my first case,
Glenn, and how I despised myself. And that's why I said
what I did about sometimes feeling more hooker than
therapist.

By the second evening I was feeling a lot better, looking forward to seeing you and continuing our talk about
your background—and perhaps slipping in a little about
mine, to gauge your reaction. I wore a yellow knit dress,
a clinging, sexy thing, and came to your hotel suite. We
were to go to dinner, but we didn't; not for about an
hour. You came on rather strong all on your own, testing, I believe, the physical report Dr. Masters had given
you, waiting to *fail* and so refute that report.

But you didn't fail. I was relaxed as we undressed and
got into bed, and at first I felt you too were relaxed—
the most relaxed of my patients at this stage of touch-
and-feel and undress petting. But then I began to sense
tension. I'd felt it earlier when you glanced at the phone
several times while speaking, and I wondered if there
wasn't some career crisis taking place, which would be
negative in terms of your therapy. I never considered
another woman, since the fact that you'd come here
for treatment would indicate you were going to follow
the rules.

Now, about the idea of your being at the Foundation
under false colors: don't think Dr. Masters and Mrs.
Johnson didn't consider the possibility and discuss it with
me. They did, and in detail. But Dr. Masters felt that
even if you *were* going to write about the Foundation,
your primary purpose was still to solve a painful personal dilemma. There was no way to stop you from writing whatever you had in mind—information could be
gotten one way or another—and refusing you treatment
could be a cruel and medically unethical rejection.

I remember remarking about your glancing at the
phone. You were surprised and said you hadn't been
aware of doing that. "Is it business?" I asked. You smiled
and said, "In a way . . . *unfinished* business."

I told myself that was just the writer playing with
words, but at the same time I began to feel something

working strongly against us as a patient-therapist team.

Still, I had no proof, and we were progressing nicely. And once we were in bed and into the touch-and-feel process, you came up aces. You were still digesting, we all felt, the results of the physical exam, where your one big excuse for sexual failure—physical disability—had been knocked from under you, and it was anticipated that you might take a session or two to accept this and respond properly.

But no such lag was in evidence when I got you up, used the squeeze technique to put you down, and then got you back up again. When I left the bed to dress, you were still hard as a rock, and I remember laughing to myself at the problem you had trying to get into those tight athletic shorts you wear. Though I didn't say it to you, I was sure that if Gini gave the go-ahead, tomorrow could bring coitus. You looked like a four- or five-session case to me, with never a setback. Several cases similar to yours—not among my patients—had responded along those lines. Why should you be an exception?

That was a Thursday night, Herb. I dressed in another sexy outfit for Friday's session, and wore my best black-lace undies. I was going to enjoy this, I told myself.

Then I went to your suite—and you know what happened. I was absolutely unable to make you respond in the slightest! I used my hands, my mouth, everything I knew, to give you the erection you'd attained so easily the night before. *Nothing.* And what really surprised me was that you didn't seem particularly upset.

You asked if we could dress and talk. We sat on the davenport and drank Canadian and soda, and I was brightly reassuring about tomorrow night, and you said, "I'm going to level with you, Valerie. I'm breaking the rules. There's a girl here in St. Louis. She's begun to mean something to me. I was with her today. I didn't make love to her, because I was afraid to, but I wanted to. And I'm confused. I want her, and she's the first girl I've wanted strongly in several years, and then you come here and we get into bed. . . ."

I'd had no experience with such a flagrant breaking of the rules. I said you would have to discuss it with Dr. Masters and that perhaps I should leave. You said,

"Please don't leave. There was a time in my life when having two such beautiful girls available . . . well, it would have been the ideal situation! Make that three, and it would have been even better. But now . . ."

"But now you're shaky, trying to find your way back to sexuality, and you're confusing the issue. It's a mistake, Herb. I don't think we can continue if you go on seeing the other girl."

You nodded. I finished my drink and rose. You said, "I don't know if I'll tell Dr. Masters tomorrow. I don't know if I'll tell him at all."

"You understand of course that *I* will. I *must*."

"Have you always reported such occurrences?"

I replied that I'd never had this experience before.

"In *all* your cases? Twenty or more?"

I knew then you were beginning to probe for information. I sat down. "Eight cases, including yours, over a period of almost four years."

"That's not very many, is it?"

"It seems very many to me. It's not as if I sat in a house and waited for customers to trot up to my room."

You began to murmur a disclaimer then, but I continued. "I lived my life, and the cases came along and complicated that life."

I went on. You asked your sly little leading questions, and I smiled to myself and answered in as interesting a manner as I could. I was beginning to wonder whether you were thinking of writing a book about the Foundation . . . about *me*.

Then you said, "Have you ever thought of writing out your experiences?"

"Not really."

You hesitated. "Have you considered the fact that my breaking the rules was, is, an unconscious or semiconscious way of my testing the Masters-Johnson method? I'm not saying I'm fully in control of this situation. Far from it. That's why I said 'unconscious or semiconscious.' But if I can take what you teach me, and apply it right now to a situation where the woman is of my own choice, won't I then have a far better chance of *staying*, shall we call it, healthy?"

I'd never thought of it. I said I sort. of doubted the reasoning, unless it was a matter of *love*. If you were applying this second-stage method to someone you loved, someone you hoped to be with for a long time, well, then, perhaps. Because I had often questioned the lack of emphasis on the concept of love in the Foundation's treatment of single patients.

You then defended the nonlove approach in such treatment by saying that trying first to define and then to apply—or ignore—love would unnecessarily complicate what had to remain a basically simple approach. You went on to say that you didn't know if you would ever truly love this girl, Gail, but that you certainly were attracted to her, and she to you, and that in your own individual case, by the specifics of your own personality, it was the *only* way you could go at the present.

"If you blow the whistle on me tomorrow, the experiment ends. My chance at arriving at my own personal solution ends." You paused. "And so does our chance to talk about your work."

The next night we went out to dinner, and you were terribly tense and nervous. I asked if you'd seen Gail, and you said yes. You hadn't taken her to bed. You were afraid to, but you wanted to more than ever, and you knew she wanted it too. You ended by saying, "And it's something more than bed: I like her so very much."

We returned to the suite and went through the kissing, the touch-and-feel, and the undressing—because you wanted to know *exactly* how in-bed therapy went. You wanted to know, because you were going to apply it with Gail!

You surprised yourself, Herb. At first, it looked like a repeat of the night before; you remained down throughout the touching, the petting, even my stroking of your genitals. But something happened. The phone rang. You reached across me to answer it, and I lay there with the expansion line on my breast and listened. Your end of the conversation went something like this: First you smiled and said, "Hey!" Then, "About eleven, if you want to make a late-late night of it." You smiled again and listened awhile and murmured, "Yes, fine, 'bye."

When you hung up, you again reached across me, turning on your side, pressing up against me. I felt something on my hip. You had an erection.

I have to admit I felt a little put down for a moment, Herb. That girl could give you a hard-on with her *voice*, while I . . .

But then the feeling changed, and I liked you for it. It was what I, too, believed in—individual choice, love, whatever you care to call it. And I grabbed that hard-on and I stroked it, and when I kissed you I felt response, and I didn't care if your closed eyes meant you were thinking of Gail; I didn't care about anything but getting that tool of yours to feel and to work!

After a while I sensed the beginnings of withdrawal on your part, and I did what I felt would give us the best chance of continuing. I went down on you.

At first you didn't react too strongly, though there was certainly no further withdrawal. Finally you began to move, and to sigh, and to breathe heavily. I normally would have stopped at that point—with another patient, I mean—and tried for coitus. But for you coitus at this point held too great a chance of failure, and so I went on until you gasped my name and came. *My* name, Herb, not Gail's—so there had been no substitution.

A moment later, you said, with a somewhat wry grin, "I think we can call this blowing my date with Gail tonight."

We both laughed. You weren't upset, though you weren't as delighted as any other patient would have been. You *were* surprised at how quickly it happened, and you added that there hadn't been full sensation in the orgasm.

We talked further about Masters and Johnson, and about the wife-surrogate program. You made a few notes. I asked if you were going to write anything about the Foundation, about me. You said you didn't know, and glanced at your watch. I realized then it was ten o'clock and you were beginning to think of your eleven-o'clock date with Gail.

I got up to leave. You asked for my last name. "In case I suddenly have to leave St. Louis and want to look you up again."

I didn't know what to say. When I didn't answer, you smiled and said, "I want to talk to my agent. Then I'll want to talk to you, at length. But I don't feel I'm going to be here much longer."

I said it would be a great mistake to leave without another two, three sessions—to establish what in-bed therapy was all about. You said you'd planned on that.

When Gini asked whether you showed undue interest in aspects of the Foundation unrelated to your own case, I said I wasn't sure.

We were scheduled to meet Sunday at four. I was at your room on time, but there was no answer to my knock. I must say I was disappointed in you, Herb, because I thought you'd taken off. But just to make sure, I asked at the desk. Mr. Lee had *not* checked out of Room 606.

I sat down in the lobby, wondering what had happened to you, and you rushed in through the doors not too long afterward. I stood up, and you came over and apologized. But you were grinning a triumphant grin, and your manner was *exuberant*.

I felt I knew what it meant, and asked if you'd been with Gail. You nodded, and took my hand, and led me to the elevators. In the room, you poured two drinks and toasted me. I suggested you were toasting the wrong party. You shook your head. "No. Masters and Johnson and you. First the authority. Then the physical exam. Then you—the methodology—which I've been following. And today it paid off." You kissed me, and hugged me tight against you.

I wondered if you might be able to go again. I wondered if I couldn't prove beyond all shadow of a doubt that you could function, even without your special-special choice.

You gave me a surprised look when I began to rub against you. But you didn't stop me. We kissed again, and your hands moved over my body. You had previously said you were an "ass man," and that's what you liked in me, too.

We undressed each other. You didn't have an erection to begin with, but one touch of my lips to your penis, and up it came. I got quickly on top. You grasped my hips, and away we went. I came rather quickly, and as soon as I did you reversed our positions, getting on top of me. You went on long enough to give me a second orgasm, and your own was impressive enough to make me take a chance and say, "No lack of full sensation this time, was there?"

You shook your head. You were very happy. You're a talkative man, a verbal man, but you said very little after we got out of bed. You touched my face and my body several times as we had drinks and nibbled on cold cuts from your refrigerator. I did most of the talking—about the Foundation, about myself.

But one thing you did say. "It was so *simple*. My God, after two long years, so very simple!"

I left a short while later. That was the last time I saw you as a patient, and I assumed you'd gone home the next day. By the time you finally returned to St. Louis, we had spoken on the phone once or twice, and you had received an okay from your agent to work up an outline and sample chapter of your experiences at the Foundation.

My story as a wife surrogate was a case longer before I decided to do the book—my last case, number nine. Everything, professionally and personally, changed quickly from then on.

Personally, it was fine. But professionally . . .

It was April Fool's Day when Gini and I first spoke about the patient I'll call Rick; and as it turned out, *I* was the fool for taking him on! Not that there weren't signs and portents from the beginning. Gini said he was an intense type, and added that he'd had some homosexual involvement. But I wasn't deterred. After all, that description might also have fit Larry, my third case, and he had turned out all right.

The briefing brought out a few disturbing facts that left me feeling, well, a little apprehensive. Rick was still in college—only twenty-one years old—and had just concluded a homosexual love affair with his erstwhile roommate. But relatively minor, I was assured. Also, he was here under duress. His father had insisted he come, or there would be grave consequences—such as no longer paying for Rick's education, which, with his currently low grades, would mean the draft.

An *unwilling* patient? How could I treat someone who didn't want . . . ?

I was assured Rick actually wanted to be straight, desired normalcy and girls and the approval of his father and his peers—but just wasn't willing to admit it as yet.

Okay. Willing, unwilling. I'd do my thing, and he would either be my ninth successful patient or my first unsuccessful one.

Somehow I had very little of Rick's background and

history. I guess—but it's only a guess—that he was local talent, and that the family was wealthy enough or important enough to feel threatened by anyone but Masters and Johnson knowing about their offspring. But you'd never know there was wealth or importance in *that* boy's background, not by looking at or talking to him!

I was to arrive at his apartment-hotel at seven, make myself comfortable, and wait until the patient arrived —which time could not be pinpointed exactly.

I did. There was liquor. Because I was beginning to feel a little nervous and not quite as tough as before, I had a stiff Scotch. Seven-thirty arrived, and passed, and I had another, even stiffer. Finally, at eight, there was a hard rap at the door. I went over and opened it, and what I saw almost floored me.

Remember when I said that David helped give me a more mature attitude in relation to men's looks, that I no longer was *quite* as tied to the handsome face and great body? Well, that maturity received a violent setback with Rick! I'm going to describe him just as he appeared to me, first standing outside the door, then entering the apartment and looking around.

The very first thing I saw was his hair. He had this enormous, guru head of black, greasy hair hanging literally below his shoulders! He was about six feet tall but looked even taller because he was—as I first put it to myself—quite lean. He was wearing a great big olive green maxicoat, and above that this huge head of hair, and under the hair a face so thin, with such big, buggy eyes. And his complexion, well, it was sort of yellow, an unhealthy, sallow, prison pallor.

That would seem to be enough, wouldn't it? But when I made myself smile and murmured come in, he simply brushed by me, his expression as down, as sour, as unfriendly as any I've ever seen on a man—and I don't see many! He took off his coat, tossed it across a chair, walked to the archway, and looked at the bedroom. He walked through a doorway to the kitchen, came back, put both hands on his hips, and stared at me. "Well?" he said.

Well indeed!

He'd been just awful-looking with that coat on, but

better on than off! I can't tell you how absolutely *cadaverous* he was—a sliver of a man, with a concave posture as he walked, sunk in about the middle and bent over, thrusting forward with that ugly head of hair. I was a sensitive girl again in an instant, and I didn't want to come within five feet of, not to say *touch,* this miserable creature!

"Well, what do we *do?*" he snapped, and I mean *snapped.* I felt the blood rush to my face and turned away to regain my composure. I took his coat and went to the closet with it. He said, "Just let it lie there."

I turned, startled.

"Let . . . it . . . lie . . . there," he said, spacing out the words as if addressing an idiot child. "Mommy taught you to hang everything up neat, did she? Well so did mine, but I no longer listen."

"My mommy is dead," I said, and dropped his coat on an armchair.

He sighed. He slumped onto the davenport. "Anything to drink around here?"

The only decent thing he'd said so far! "Yes, Scotch."

"I don't mean alcohol." His expression was full of contempt. "Coke, anything nonpoisonous."

There were Pepsis in the refrigerator. I poured one over ice for him, meanwhile praying for composure, professionalism, some way of bringing this thing into proper perspective. Prayer didn't help, so I poured my third Scotch of the evening.

We sat on the davenport, about a foot apart. He took a pull of his Pepsi. I took a pull of my Scotch. He fiddled around in his shirt pocket. The shirt was a heavily figured and patterned red silk production with big puffy sleeves, out of which hung his bony wrists and large skeletal hands. His trousers were overwashed blue-jean bells. His shoes were scruffy black stomping boots. He kept fiddling around in that pocket, and finally came out with what I first thought was a Bull Durham roll-your-own kit. Then he lit up, that special sweet smell filled the air, and I realized it was grass, pot—marihuana.

I said, "You can't do that!"

He took another deep drag. A remote expression began to move into his eyes. "You prefer that I drop acid?"

I stood up. "Dr. Masters will *not* allow any patient at the Foundation to use drugs. If I leave now and report this, you won't *be* a patient tomorrow."

He stared at me. I began to turn away. He quickly crushed out the joint in an ashtray. I sat down again beside him. We remained in absolute silence for about five minutes. Then he turned to me and said, "I don't want to be here. I don't like . . . women, and squares of either sex. And you're both. But we're going to be on each other's hands for quite a while—maybe two weeks, they tell me. Let's kill time as best we can."

I drank. I fought a powerful desire to get up and leave and never even *think* of surrogate work again. But there was my pride. And there was a patient who needed help.

I said, "You've been honest with me, so I'll be honest with you. I don't particularly like homosexuals, and I definitely don't like hippie types. And you're both. But I'm willing to bet two weeks of my life that you won't *be* a homosexual *if* . . ."

"If what?"

"If instead of *killing* time we *fill* it."

"How?" he said, smiling a thin, bitter smile. "Fucking? Sucking? Asshole plucking?"

I felt myself going white with rage. I gulped the rest of my drink, and remained seated. *If one of us ran, it wouldn't be me!* I was going to do my job! He could cut out anytime he chose!

"All right," I said. "Maybe that's as good a description of how we're supposed to use the time as any. But there has to be some *respect* between two humans— make that between two *bodies*—that are going to come into close and intimate contact. Some respect and some awareness of ground rules."

He went to a dresser and took out a pack of Luckies. He lit up, and sat down beside me. Then he said, "Do you know anything about me?"

"Very little."

"You know I lived with a boy for a year, in school, and that . . . I loved him?"

He said that word "loved" with complete and absolute conviction.

"I wasn't aware it went on that long and was that serious."

He got up and went to his coat. He took an envelope from the pocket and came back to the davenport and handed it to me. "An old one. He gave it back last month. But it'll help you dig our relationship."

I can't repeat the letter here. I don't remember it word for word. Besides, it could give my patient away to that other party, and perhaps to those who know something of their relationship. But I can say it was a love letter in the deepest sense of the word. It described the ecstasy of their being together, the beauty of the loved one's body, the tranquillity of days spent walking, talking, and evenings spent reading, studying. It ended with, "I'll always love you. I want to spend my life loving you. Please, never leave me, or my life will end."

Rick laughed a little, but it had nothing to do with humor. "He went off to Mexico with a little blond whore . . . well, not a whore in the legal sense. A *cunt*! A dirty, promiscuous bitch." He stopped himself. He cleared his throat and cracked his bony knuckles. He looked off across the room and spoke in a voice that matched his deathlike pallor. "A year, and he never really cared, never gave a damn. It was getting *blown*, getting *sucked*, that he cared about. A full year, and I never really knew a thing about him." Then he looked at me. "But I was wrong. My life didn't end. I'm here, ready to learn what he learned." Again he smiled, and now it was a terrible, hateful thing. Now he looked at me as if *I* had stolen his lover, as if *I* were the enemy; and I guess I was. *Woman* was the enemy for him. "Teach me," he said, his voice dripping venom. "Teach me to be *normal*, Valerie."

I said it was time to go out to dinner. I hated the thought of being in public with this man as much—no, *more*—than I had with poor little David. But the orders from up high were plain. Again, this was a patient who needed to learn the social as well as sexual way of being with a woman.

I chose a dingy little sandwich shop, and that suited

Rick just fine. "I haven't got much bread to spend," he
said, biting into a hamburger. "My dear old dad feels
that if I had more than fifty dollars, I'd catch a jet out
of this ugly town—maybe for Mexico." He grinned bit-
terly. "A joke. All I could do in Mexico is . . . kill
myself." He devoured the hamburger and gulped down a
Coke.

I said we should be getting back to the apartment. He
said he wanted to have a cigarette, and it *was* a cigarette.
I asked him to tell me about himself. He smiled that
bitter smile. "Not allowed to. Daddy's orders. It would
kill him if friends or relatives found out Sonny Boy is
gay."

Gay! What a misnomer for someone like Rick! This
was the least gay, most miserably unhappy personality
I'd ever met!

"I can tell you this," he said, looking down at his
hands. "I never had a sexual experience, homosexual or
otherwise, until I met my roommate." His eyes closed
briefly, in pain I believe. "He taught me how. I was just
a skinny, ugly, studious kid, and he turned me into a
skinny, ugly, unstudious cocksucker." The bitterness in
his voice, his expression, was far more shocking than his
words. "I did what he asked me to do . . . for a long
time without anything being done to me in return. I
worshiped him, that beautiful, popular athlete with the
oh-so-sensitive soul. And when he finally went down on
me one night, when he finally put his mouth to my
body—that body I hated—I achieved far more than an
orgasm. I became bearable to myself, and later I began
to love myself, the way a person should, because someone so wonderful loved me." Another laugh, another
drag, another gulp of Coke. "Now it's back to uglyville.
Now the lie is told. Now the joke is finished, the punch
line delivered. Beauty runs away with beauty. The beast
is left to . . ." His eyes rose. "Valerie. Lucky Valerie."

I shook my head. I didn't know what else to do. I felt
sorry for him, yes, but I was in deep trouble. My responses to this man were all wrong in terms of in-bed
therapy; the thought was growing that I wouldn't be
able to go through with it.

We returned to the apartment. I was on my own as

to whether to do anything physical this first time around. We sat on the davenport. His big, bulging eyes regarded me cynically. I forced myself to take his hand. It felt cold, sweaty, clammy in mine. *Nothing* was right for me with this boy! I released his hand. He looked at it, and again he smiled. His teeth were uneven and nicotine-stained.

Lord, Lord, could I find no area on which to concentrate where the turnoff wouldn't be *quite* so strong? Even Glenn, with his clothes off, had been acceptable in the genital area.

The genitals. They were my only hope—a purely physical, visceral, glandular reaction to them. For my sake —which meant for his sake too—I had to get down to genital play far more quickly than either the Foundation or I had planned. His penis couldn't possibly be as repulsive as the rest of him!

I began to speak, purely by rote, of what we would be doing in the next week or two. I explained that nothing could happen tonight, and as I said this I put my hand on his hand and rubbed my fingers over his fingers. I said that nothing could happen—or should happen— until it came about naturally, until he *wanted* it to happen. He laughed. *"That'll* be the day!" I almost pulled my hand away, but then I repeated to myself that if one of us ran from this thing, it wouldn't be me! I kept rubbing his fingers, and realized his hand had warmed, and that he was touching *my* hand in response. Whatever was going on in that bitter brain, the body was beginning to respond.

Against every natural instinct, I inched closer, still talking about the process of learning to touch a woman, to feel a woman, to respond to her touching and feeling him. Soon I was up against him, my breasts pressing his arm. Now our hands were turned into each other, clenching each other. Now the tense, angry look on his face had changed. Now he was confused, fighting his first positive reaction.

And what was *I* doing? I was keeping my eyes off him as much as possible, because nothing had changed for me. I still found him repulsive, and still didn't know if I was going to be able to go through with full therapy.

Finally, I closed my eyes and kissed him on the mouth —that bitter, bitter mouth, that mouth that had sucked cock. I kept my eyes closed, intensified the kiss, and dropped my hand to his thigh.

He jumped up, wiping his lips with the back of his hand. "Bitch!" he whispered, stalking away, shaking that wild head. "Filthy cunt!" Suddenly he whirled to face me. "You! She! Damned cunts . . . took him away."

I got up. It was over. I'd lost. I *was* going to be the one to run.

But then he said, "No . . . I didn't mean that. Not you . . . not you in *particular*. Look, let's cool it. I . . . I *must* try to . . . to work with you. I *must*, or my life . . . God . . . my life . . ."

I nodded. I hoped my smile looked more legitimate than it felt. I said this was all expected, all understandable, and that we'd do much better tomorrow.

"I *want* to," he whispered, "but I don't think so. I don't think we'll *ever* do better." And he grabbed his coat and rushed out of the apartment.

I agreed with him. I went right to the phone to call Gini, to tell her I couldn't spend two weeks with this . . . this pot freak!

But before I'd finished dialing, I hung up. I'd taken on the case. I had to maintain my objectivity, my viewpoint as a therapist.

I wandered around the apartment a few minutes, calmed down, and only then called in. I reported that there was considerable resistance, but that Rick *did* seem to have inner motivation to go on with the therapy. I was told to proceed toward touch-and-feel as quickly as possible.

I said I would, and hung up, and was proud of myself! But I didn't—I *couldn't*—think of tomorrow night.

It was nine-thirty. I could go home and read. (I had begun reading heavily lately, and enjoying it.) I could go to a movie; there was one I'd been planning to see, starring Brent Warren. But somehow I didn't want to do either. I made a call to a man who'd been asking me out regularly, and whom I'd accepted only irregularly. The background noise at his end was considerable, and he said that there was "a little party in progress." I could come if I wanted to.

About fifty men and women were jammed into his two and a half rooms. I got a drink and smiled my way through the mob and settled into a corner. I was content to be surrounded by people—normal if noisy people. I was content not to be alone. I knew that it wouldn't be too long before my friend came over and made passes, and perhaps tonight he would find me receptive. I didn't particularly want to make love, but if that was the price for a warm body next to mine, for someone to hold in my arms all night, someone to blot out fear and emptiness, it was little enough to pay.

My friend wasn't in luck. *I* was. Someone else came to my corner. He was in his early to mid-forties, with thinning pale-brown hair, a somewhat round and large-featured face, and a truly charming smile. His voice, when he spoke, was soft, his words right to the point.

"Could we cut out of this bedlam and find a place to sit, or lie, down?"

I looked at him. He wasn't nearly as good-looking as my host, nor as young, nor as well dressed. But that smile, and the calm way in which he waited for my answer . . .

We went to my apartment. We didn't talk much. We sat around watching an old movie on TV, and held hands. During a commercial, he said, "Do you insist on seeing the end?" I said no. He got up and turned it off. Then he said, "I'd like to stay." I nodded.

He went into the bathroom. I went into the bedroom. We met in bed, nude. We didn't make love that night. We held each other, and slept like the dead. Yes, at first he had a hard-on, but he didn't try to use it, and after a while it went away. I awoke about six the next morning, to find him looking down at me. He smiled and said, "You're not bad, even when you first awake." I began to get up, to fix my hair and brush my teeth and so on, but he stopped me, pulled me against him, kissed me. This time he *used* his hard-on.

He used it well. Nothing like Abner or Brent Warren, mind you. No wild, bizarre sex, or enormous cocks. Nothing but a man making love to me, finishing with a cry of delight and a whispered, "Better send me away right now, or I'm never going to leave."

We looked at each other. I felt a sudden wrenching inside, almost as if something were entering me to end the emptiness; and then I also felt fear. I didn't want love, if love ended as it had always ended for me. I preferred emptiness, and an occasional warm body beside me, rather than the anguish of lost loves.

I got up and said, "Well, you have to leave anyway . . . or don't you go to work?"

He washed while I made breakfast, and we ate together. He said nothing during breakfast except to thank me for the eggs and bacon, and nothing at the door but, "Good-bye, Val." I didn't know if I would see him again. I'd sent him away.

The second session with Rick began with chopped steak at a diner. The food wasn't bad, but I'll swear that at least a dozen people turned to stare at us when we entered, and as many more when we left. We were the oddest of odd couples, Rick and I! He never changed his outfit, except for the shirt, and I refused to compromise my taste in clothing. Along with the differences in our ages and general physical appearance, it helped make us stand out like sore thumbs!

Back at the room, I had myself a *big* Scotch, took a few *deep* breaths, and got to work. It took a while. First holding hands. Then kissing. (I kissing him, that is. He still made no move in my direction.) Then rubbing his thigh—and waiting for him to explode as he had last night. But even though he went into a state of rigid tension, he didn't break away. I worked my hand up quite far, pressing close to the crotch. He began to breathe heavily. This was a kind of physical love he'd experienced before—at the hands of a male. I rubbed his thigh, up and back, up and back, and kissed his mouth, my eyes shut firmly against the person who was my partner. And when I opened them briefly, I saw that *his* eyes were shut against me.

That I couldn't allow. He, as the patient, *had* to accept the fact that it was Valerie, a *woman,* who was making love to him. He couldn't be allowed to fantasize

that his beloved, a male, was doing the kissing and touching.

I stood up, and his eyes snapped open. I took him by
the hand and led him to the bedroom. For once, *I* was
trembling. I tried not to see him, and succeeded by
quickly turning my back as I removed my blouse. I asked
him to help with my brassiere. For a moment he did
nothing; and then his hands fumbled and finally got the
hooks open. I didn't turn. I couldn't *make* myself turn
and expose myself to those eyes that wanted to see a
different kind of chest. I couldn't make myself look at
that head, those eyes.

I fought my reaction. His cock would grow stiff, and
I would use it. His cock would satisfy me almost as
well as the one last night. . . .

Matt, his name was. I didn't want to think of him now,
here. But Matt was his name, and he had held me, and
I had felt the wrenching. . . .

I continued to undress, and my skirt fell to the floor,
and I asked Rick to take down my panties. I still hadn't
turned, and perhaps he read something in that, felt something, because he didn't move, and so I had to turn.

When I did, his eyes went to my breasts, and then
his lips twitched violently. I didn't know what was going to happen, and so I made myself smile and made my
voice soft and said, "A woman's body can mean pleasure, Rick. It can mean beauty and joy. Don't think of
anything but my body, a thing for *your* pleasure. Don't
think of anything but touching it, playing with it. No
personalities involved. No need to justify or explain or
love or do anything but touch me, touch me. . . ."

The twitch of the lips passed without the bitter words
I'd feared. He sighed deeply and came a step closer, and
bent, and slowly drew down my panties. He took them
off as I raised first one foot, then the other. He hesitated,
then straightened and stepped back without having
touched me. In a personal sense I was relieved; professionally, I was disappointed. But now another crisis
loomed—undressing *him!*

I came up close. He stood his ground, though there
was an involuntary leaning backward. I unbuttoned his
shirt and drew it off. There was a faint whiff of oniony

perspiration odor, but I told myself I was looking for faults. His undershirt was next, and revealed a chest in which ribs and bones were barely covered by flesh. And God, he *did* smell! And to complete the pretty picture, the same yellowish pallor of face was continued on the body, as if it had never been exposed to sunlight—which, with the sensitivity he'd shown about his physique, was probably true. He wouldn't be likely to get out much in a bathing suit!

Down came his trousers and his undershorts. But those shorts were too much. They were briefs, very tight-fitting, and of a pale violet color. And they were soiled. At first I thought that perhaps I was being too picky, but as I placed those shorts on a chair, the ripe odor of unwashed genitals filled the air!

I believe I could have walked out right then without provoking Dr. Masters' criticism, because he insists that his patients maintain a normal degree of cleanliness. And I almost did walk out. But then I wondered *why* Rick was dirty. He'd have had to be clean during his physical exam.

Then it struck me. Rick wanted to be dirty with me, because he hated women, hated me, would have liked me to run.

Well, I wouldn't run!

I still hadn't really seen his legs and genitals; I was so turned off by this time, I was simply *afraid* to look. I think that at that moment I believed his penis and testicles would also, somehow, be gaunt and yellow and repulsive.

We got into bed, and it was then I realized he was trembling.

That trembling was a hopeful sign. He was reacting in a way familiar to me—a way my other patients had reacted. He was becoming *involved*. I was getting through to him. Now, dear God, to see if he couldn't get through to *me* in some positive way, *any* positive way.

I looked at his legs. Skinny, of course, almost to the bone, and covered with hair. I looked at his genitals. He had such a large amount of thick black pubic hair that it reminded me of his *head*, and I almost burst out laughing! When I finally concentrated on his penis, I saw it lay stretched between his compressed thighs for a considerable length.

My God, he was actually turning on! Now, what could I do to join him?

He moved, stretched, and the odor was overpowering. I decided on drastic action. I didn't care how he took it. I went to the bathroom and soaked a towel in hot water and brought it, and a dry one, to the bedroom. I said, "Relax, Rick," as he stared at me. He smiled his bitter smile, and closed his eyes. "Mommy said cleanliness is next to Godliness, didn't she, and little Valerie is Mommy's pull-toy." I didn't answer. I began washing him, first under the arms and then around the genitals. "The TV commercials," he said, "tell little Valerie that it's un-American to smell normal, so she scrub-a-dubs all day long."

I finished and dried him. His eyes were still closed. I called his name. He looked at me and laughed, mocking me, hating me. "Your values," he said, "are deodorant values, TV values, organization values. . . ."

I nodded. "Yes, I guess so. You smell nice now, so I'm going to touch you. I want you to look at me as I do. If you'd like to, you can touch me, any part of me. Nothing can happen but our touching each other. Nothing can happen, *ever*, that you don't want to happen. But, Rick, look down at yourself. Go on, look."

He looked, and almost immediately closed his eyes again. He hadn't looked at his penis, which was what I'd meant him to do. (While I'd been washing and drying his genitals, the penis had lengthened even more.) He'd looked at his body. He said, "Charles Atlas, Dad used to call me. Ha-ha."

I had to do something. That skeletal body lay before me, topped by that bony face and greasy hairdo. It was the furthest from my ideal of male beauty I'd ever had to deal with. It was likely to be the furthest from most girls' ideal—and it was probably *knowing* this that had made Rick so susceptible to the first physical approach, male *or* female, that had come his way. His luck had been bad, and it had been male.

I told him he *was* thin, but that he could put on weight with the help of a good nutritionist, and muscle with a program of exercise. "But there's one area you don't have to build up at all, and that's what I wanted you to look at."

He understood then, and looked again. His penis had withdrawn a little, but was still semierect, and a damned good size. He said, "Every male has one of those," and looked away, but there was a change in his tone of voice, in his expression, that showed I'd gotten through to him.

I took a deep breath, and began to touch and feel and kiss his body. His penis grew into a state of full erection. I again suggested he touch me. He did—on the arm, lightly, and then on the side and on the hip. He seemed to like the feel of my hip; he stroked it, and he squeezed it a little. And then he went to my buttocks.

But there were two areas he stayed away from—my breasts and my vagina. And those were the two areas his lover couldn't duplicate: the two areas specifically female, even to the mind that might be fighting to superimpose a male image over the female form; the two areas he had to touch, had to enjoy.

I kept pushing my breasts into him, into his shoulder, his face—almost angrily. I kept angling so that he couldn't escape them. And all the time I was sickened by this boy.

I felt him touching my breast. His touch was inquisitive; he traced the curve of it, going underneath, as if to test how it supported its own weight; then he went to the nipple, and made me shiver, but not with desire.

I felt perspiration trickling down my sides, and it was quite comfortable in the apartment. I knew then what the expression "cold sweat" meant; *exactly* what it meant!

We touched each other. I blanked my mind. He was looking at me, and he was touching me, and I was smiling and sighing and touching him—acting all the way, but it worked, because his penis stayed up.

And I'd been right: it *was* the best part of him. It had the red, pulsing quality of a young man's cock, and when I reached down between his legs and grasped his testicles, they were large and hard, a nice handful. He gasped and began to close his eyes. I said, "Please look at me, Rick. It's important. I think you know why."

He opened his eyes. He looked at me, even when I took that stiff tool in my hand and stroked it. I continued to stroke, to pull, to caress, and suddenly he lifted his head, and his voice rose to a scream of hatred: "Cunt! Bitch! Dirty motherfucking . . . !"

I froze in shock, and he came off in my hand.

I ran to the bathroom and locked myself in. A while later, there was a tap at the door. "Valerie?" I didn't answer. I was sick. "Valerie, I'm sorry." His voice was dead. "It's . . . just in me." A long pause. "But . . . I did get pleasure out of it. I do want to go on."

He hated women. He hated me. But he was beginning to function with me, and through me with women. In time, the hatred would pass. And even if it didn't, completely, he could learn to control himself, learn to satisfy his body.

I opened the door. I nodded and smiled at him. "So much for being a homosexual," I said.

He struggled with himself. I could actually *see* him fighting not to answer. He turned and went back to the bedroom and lay down. Maybe I should have let it go at that, but the therapist in me knew everything had to come out. I followed him. I repeated, "So much for being a homosexual."

His eyes remained closed. "Bullshit," he said, voice strangled. "*Any* hand can do that."

"Yes, but it was *my* hand that *did*. And you can't confuse me with any man you know."

His eyes opened, and fixed on my breasts. He smiled a small smile. "No, I can't confuse you with any man I know." The smile changed. "How I wish I could!"

He was still in bed, eyes closed, mouth clamped shut in a bitter line, when I left.

On the way home, my insides churned; the old furies of guilt and shame and disgust were back.

I waited awhile before calling in to report. Then I spoke to Dr. Masters. I said Rick continued to fight me, but that he was coming along nevertheless. Dr. Masters said he was satisfied with Rick's interview sessions, his directive therapy, and that there was nothing in my reports to change that satisfaction. We were both silent a moment, and then he said good night.

I read until quite late and thought of Matt and of how he'd asked me to send him away or he would never leave, and of how I'd sent him away. But only because he'd made so strong an emotional pitch, so quickly. Only because he'd *pressured* me. Only because I'd grown frightened of feeling too much. I wondered if he would call again. I told myself he was bound to, after the good time I'd given him. He would want more of the same. Any man would.

I phoned my friend, the one who'd hosted the party. I asked about Matt.

"Matt who?"

I didn't know.

"There were so many gate crashers at that party, honey . . ."

I described him. It rang no bells in my host's mind. End of investigation; and if Matt didn't call me, end of relationship.

Perhaps it was just as well. It would lead to pain. All strong emotional affairs led to pain for me.

I was just coming out of the tub at eleven when the phone rang. I didn't rush to answer it. So some guy or other would be thinking of going out this week. I was busy with a greasy-haired horror!

It rang five times before I picked it up. "You're faster in bed," the quiet voice said.

It was Matt. I laughed and said, "You want breakfast again?"

"Yes. What time should I come over?"

"Now."

Twenty minutes later he was at my door. We talked a good deal more than we had last night, and we made love before going to sleep. In the morning, he cooked breakfast: cheese omelets, bacon, and coffee. I declared him the perfect mate for some lucky girl. He said, "I agree. I never thought to find the lucky girl . . . until now."

I laughed. He didn't. I stopped laughing, and said, "Let's keep it simple. I'm *not* lucky in love. I'll have to try cards."

"Remind me to stake you in Vegas."

"Vegas, Miami, New York . . . anyplace for a loving weekend or week. But no more weighty words, please?"

He nodded very somberly. He began to dress, and I went to the bathroom. When I came out, he was gone.

Dinner with Rick was at the diner again. He ate his hamburger and drank his Coke and smoked a cigarette. Then he said, "Let's forget the apartment tonight. Let's go out. I got a little bread to spare. We'll rap awhile. We'll dance. You dance, don't you? I mean rock."

It was the last thing in the world I wanted to do. But I said yes, I danced, and yes, we'd go out.

We went to a small dance joint in a not-too-good section of town, and most of the crowd was quite young, and some, not many, were hippie types, and I thought Rick would relax and enjoy himself. But even though we danced several times and he complimented me on my "movement," and even though he loosened up sufficiently to have a few Scotches, he seemed to grow more and more depressed. Finally he called for the check.

In the car, he sat slouched, low, staring out his side window. He sat that way until we were almost at the hotel, and then he spoke, his voice thick, low, shaky: "All those guys, all those chicks, having a ball. I . . . I don't know why I never . . ."

He stopped. I glanced at him. His head was turned away, his shoulders shook a little; I realized he was crying.

I said nothing. I had nothing to say. My role was to *do*, if I could. But sympathy, an awareness of his pain, came alive in me.

It helped, but not much. After our clothing came off, I was faced with my revulsion again. I drew him toward the bed. He said, "Wait . . . uh, just a minute," and hurried out of the room, looking like an animated skeleton. A moment later I heard water running. I moved quietly to the bathroom door. The shower was going!

I returned to the bed. He finished in record time and, hair still damp, joined me. He said nothing. I said nothing. But he had helped me, and I was able to go into touch-and-feel, as we had the night before. This time, when I touched his penis, I was careful to keep it *light*.

And I got him, finally, to touch my vagina. He seemed repelled at first, then murmured it felt soft and fingered it nicely. My purely physical response began, but it never got to the point where I could experience orgasm, not with *this* man.

Finally I climbed onto him. His eyes bugged out; his mouth sagged open; he gasped as I slid his tool inside me. His lips moved. He fought, and to a certain extent won, but I still heard the choked whisper: *"Bitch! Dirty cunt . . ."*

I blotted out his voice. I went to work. It *was* work. I was never before so purely mechanistic, but of course I sighed and moaned and groaned, and went through the motions of orgasm about a minute later, so as to be free to concentrate on *him*.

After a while—a long while, it seemed to me—he grabbed my waist and heaved upward, hurting me with his bony pelvic area, and whispered his hateful obscenities . . . and came.

I intended to go into male-dominant position tomorrow, and wanted to end it then, but I knew a few more sessions were called for.

I spoke to Gini. It was all going along well. They were satisfied; *more* than satisfied. I was too, professionally.

I went to bed early, but I didn't sleep. I waited for the phone to ring. I waited for Matt to call. He didn't.

I was edgy, short-tempered at work the next day. My superior finally remarked on it. I apologized, said I felt as if I were coming down with something, and left for home early. I took a long, hot bath, trying to soak the *ugly* feeling out of me—and at the same time ready to leap out and dash for the bedroom should the phone ring.

It did. I dashed. It wasn't Matt, but another man, and he got an unvarnished "no" when he asked for a date. He said, "Excuse me for daring to ask!" and hung up. I didn't blame him, but neither did I care.

Rick and I ate at the diner. The man behind the counter gave us a nod along with his quizzical look. He was getting to know us.

In the room, we undressed, and I sniffed the pleasant

fragrance of a man's cologne. In a sense, the worst was over!

I again had to do most of the work, most of the touch-and-feel, but Rick *did* come along toward the end. There was a point where, while kissing his stomach, I realized he was trying to maneuver his body in such a way that I would take his penis in my mouth.

No chance!

What he finally did was to kiss my breasts, my belly, my thighs, and then bury his face in my crotch. He stayed down there for quite a while, experimenting, and, I believe, examining by sight as well as by touch. And when he began to use his tongue, I put on my act, moaning, twisting, saying, "Yes, right there, more . . ." and so on. Sure, I felt *something,* but it was so little compared to what I'd felt with Matt. . . .

I had to stop thinking of Matt. I had to concentrate on my patient.

I went into the Big Orgasm, and then the Big Exhaustion, all part of the Big Act. Rick finally rose and looked at me. I murmured, "Thank you." He nodded, and stroked my body. I reached for his cock. It was hard and red.

I drew him over onto me. It went easy as pie. I put him in and hunched upward, and we began to move. When we'd passed a full minute without ejaculation or softening, I was able to close my eyes and shut him out and daydream a little. He worked well and long; and obscenities came . . . and so did he.

We lay side by side for a moment. I said, "What do you think now?"

He said, "I guess I'll try girls."

"Fine. But you'd better learn to control your . . . language."

He nodded briefly.

I dressed, and he asked if I wanted a Scotch. I was going to say no and run when I realized this was another first, so I said that *would* be nice. He had a Coke, and we sat on the davenport and drank. After a while he cleared his throat. "Dr. Masters said this might be my last night. Is it?"

So they *had* been aware of how rough this case was

on me! They'd decided that, if I managed to get Rick to male-dominant coitus tonight, and wanted out, they'd consider the case finished.

How I wanted to seize the opportunity and say, "Yes, it *is* the last night." My God, once the words were out, I'd be through!

I heard myself say, "I don't think so. I think we'll do it once more, tomorrow."

He was reaching into his shirt pocket for cigarettes, and he looked at me. He was wide-eyed-surprised. I said, "Well, why not? I enjoy it too."

I could see disbelief struggling with the will to believe, and I leaned over and put my hand on that sallow face and kissed his lips and murmured, "You're a man, Rick. You can satisfy a woman. I'm a woman as well as a therapist. Maybe I even turn on a little for your . . . rough treatment."

He never did smoke that cigarette. He took me in his arms, and I closed my eyes, and he kissed me and put his hands under my dress and on my breasts, and we ended up back in bed. This was the kind of sex act the Foundation most wanted—the one that came naturally, by inception of the patient. We didn't undress fully. He simply dropped his pants, pulled mine down, pushed me back on the bed, and made love. He did it well, and he almost swallowed his obscenities—and when he came, I wasn't *too* far from orgasm myself.

And still I was repelled, appalled, full of nausea on the way home!

My report to Gini was more in the way of a chat this night; a chat between two partners, with a third waiting to hear the results, all pleased with the way "business" was going.

Again I took a hot bath, and again I waited for Matt to call, and again I fell asleep alone—and beginning to be afraid. I'd neglected to get his last name, or his address, or any other information about him. When he was with me, it didn't seem important. But what if he *never* called again? What if I never had the chance to tell him how much I liked him?

I slept a worried sleep.

Rick and I had our farewell dinner at the diner. The

counterman recommended the pot roast, and Rick decided to splurge. And it was quite good.

In the apartment, he was anxious to get into bed, and
I was anxious to get *out* of it. Between the two of us, we
managed a good strong mating, though not a long one—
and I didn't catch a single obscenity. I then said good-bye,
and kissed him, but was careful not to arouse him again
as I had last night. I told him he had no problem at all
that I could see, and that he should keep trying until he
found himself a girl.

"Maybe my nutritionist will be a girl," he said, straight-
faced. I laughed. I would have liked to have countered
with, "And your barber."

He stopped me at the door. He touched my hand and
said, "You're . . . a hell of a good chick."

I left him there, and as I did, I actually *felt* his loneliness. I almost turned back, to say something, to tell him
he *would* find a girl, that every man could find a girl,
that the world was full of lonely people looking for each
other—and that now he had the method, the technique,
the capacity to satisfy women.

But I went on. He knew the important part—about being able to satisfy a woman. The rest would follow naturally. Besides, I was beset by my own loneliness.

I learned later that Rick went back to school and was
dating girls.

Again I didn't hear from Matt—for the third night in a
row. I decided it was no use sitting around and waiting,
so I called my host of the party and said, "Hey, watcha
doing?" and he said, "Thinking of a girl, any girl," and I
said, "Will this girl do?" and he said, "For what?" and I
laughed and said, "For dinner tomorrow night."

It was fun. We always did have a lot of laughs. He
wanted to come in when we got to my apartment, and I'd
planned just that, but I heard myself say, "Uh-huh . . .
wrong time of the month."

"Wait'll I see my astrologist. He said this was *not* a
sanguinary week!"

When ten days had passed without word from Matt, I
stopped hoping. Four nights later, the phone rang, and I
ambled over, still reading my novel, and said, "Yes?"

"The last time I asked it was *no*."

"Matt!" The name *burst* out of me! And then I was angry. "What do you mean, the last time you asked it was *no?* You've been here twice, and twice it was *yes!* And then you don't bother . . ."

"I'm not bothering now, either. I called to find out if you were all right, and to explain that I'm not interested in the kind of *yes* you seem to think is your great gift to mankind. That kind of yes is available for almost any ambulatory male. I'm forty-six, did you know that?"

I mumbled no, he'd seemed younger. He went right on in that quiet voice.

"I've had enough fun weekends in Vegas and Miami and New York. And in St. Louis too. I'm looking for a sweetheart, a lover, a wife."

Again, I was afraid, but I was also elated. And I wasn't going to sweat out any more two-week periods of silence. I asked his last name, and his address, and his telephone number. He asked if I were working for the Census Bureau, but he gave me the information. Only then did I say, "You move too quickly, Matt. I want to test more of your cooking before making weighty decisions. After all, one omelet doesn't make a marriage."

He came over. We made love and slept in each other's arms, and his pancakes were as good as his omelets. I was falling in love again, and I refused to accept it. I was sure that the moment I said, "I love you," he'd start looking for his sweetheart, his lover, his wife *somewhere else!* It never failed.

He slowed down his attack, thank goodness. We began to go together, more or less steadily. Less at first and more as time went on—until I was seeing no one else and he said he wasn't. You notice how I put that: "he *said* he wasn't." I wasn't going to be caught trusting a man again!

Four months went by. I was happy with things the way they were, but Matt began pushing for something more permanent. If not marriage, then he wanted us to live together.

I did too, desperately! But I didn't want to give in to the idea as yet. I was still bugged by the notion that something *had* to go wrong.

One night, just about the time Matt usually called, the

phone rang. I raced to it and said, "Yes?" and waited for that deep, soft voice. Instead I heard, "Valerie Scott?"

"Yes." The man sounded vaguely familiar. "Who is it?"

"Uh . . . are you alone?"

"No! And either identify yourself, or I'm hanging up!"

I'd had my share of nut and obscene calls, as does any single girl who's in the book.

"Wallace," he said. "Remember? Your patient . . ."

My second case. How had he learned my last name so as to look me up?

I asked him, and he muttered that he'd gotten the information while still my patient, and not in a very nice way, and he hoped I wouldn't insist on knowing. I did. He'd looked in my purse once when I was in the bathroom and found my driver's license.

Good God! And I'd *always* carried purse and identification to patients' rooms and apartments! *All* of them might know me!

I asked how he was. He murmured, "Not well. I mean . . . look, I'm not far away. Could I come over?"

I remembered that tall, gentle man; that successful lawyer; that patient who'd come along so nicely and seemed so secure at the end, though his treatment had lasted only four nights; that loving husband and father who had brought me those wonderful dinners. But if Matt called . . .

I said he would have to tell me what he had in mind.

He fumbled, he mumbled . . . and I finally got the drift. He wanted me to "treat" him without his going to the Foundation for further interviews. He would pay me the money, of course, and I would determine how many "sessions" were necessary.

"Are you failing again?" I asked.

"No, not really."

That caught me up short! "Then why . . . ?"

"I'm just not . . . enjoying it. I enjoyed it so with you. I want . . ."

I interrupted to say that perhaps what he wanted was a prostitute, and my voice revealed my growing anger. He quickly apologized. He rushed on, the words running into each other in his haste to explain. He said he'd never thought of me that way, and yet, an instant later, he added that he would pay whatever I thought appropriate; he bid higher and higher.

Whether he could admit it to himself or not, he was looking for outside ass, and had decided to start with me. I suggested, not unkindly, that he find a girl to *love* if things were falling apart at home.

"But . . . how can I? My wife . . ."

I said he had to make his own decisions there, and that he wasn't to call me again. "Good-bye, Wallace." I hung up.

The phone rang again a moment later. I took a deep breath, picked it up, and said, "Listen here . . . !"

"You going to fire me?"

It was Matt.

"No," I said, thinking of Wallace and his lack of pleasure with his wife, and of other men and their lack of pleasure with their wives, and of how time seemed to catch up with so many marriages, seemed to erode so many love affairs. And I felt time was running out, I was wasting the sweet and precious years, and I said, "No, I want to *hire* you."

He came right over, and brought a bottle of wine. He kissed me at the door and said, "Did you mean what I *think* you meant?"

I nodded. He opened the wine, and I got two glasses, and we sat at the table. He raised his glass. "To us," he said.

We drank.

He refilled the glasses.

"To us, forever," he said.

My insides began to tremble. There was something he didn't know, something that might make him leave me.

Not if he loved me!

What was this word "love" anyway? It had a million different meanings to a million different people. It was fire and fury one day, and cold ashes the next. It could make a man and women feel like *gods* together, and like death apart. And if one cooled, the other was left a legacy of pain that I, at least, had never seen fully or convincingly described.

"Val? Anything wrong?"

Matt was leaning across the table. I put down my

glass. I heard myself say, "Do you know anything about Masters and Johnson and the Reproductive Biology Research Foundation?" As he murmured, "Only what I've read in magazines," I was off and running, telling him everything . . . at least, everything but who the patients were.

He sat there, his glass of wine in his hand; sat there unmoving, eyes fixed on me; sat there that way for half an hour as I spilled my guts out. Sat there after I'd finished. Just sat there.

My heart was pounding and my mouth was bone dry. I felt I'd committed suicide. And yet, I was also relieved, free of a weight that had been growing heavier and heavier since the day I'd met him.

But he just sat there, staring.

I stood up and went to the closet to get his coat. It was finished.

He said, "Honey, wait."

I turned. He drank down his wine and poured another and drank that too. He came to me. He said, "I'm going to want to know more, when you're willing to talk more. It's fascinating."

I felt myself paling. Was he going to be another Greg, the man I'd thought was my true love, who had *turned on* for my being a surrogate?

Then I noticed how pale *he* was, and how his hands were trembling, and how hard he was breathing. And I realized he was controlling his true feelings by a tremendous effort of will. "But one thing," he said, putting those shaking hands on my arms. "No more cases, Valerie. I'm sure you wouldn't have told me if you didn't expect to stop. *No more, Val!*"

I placed my head on his chest and let the tears come.

That was the end of my work as a wife surrogate. But you'll just have to allow me a word about the academic snobs and so-called sex experts who have attacked Dr. Masters and Mrs. Johnson. I know what I know: in-bed therapy, combined with low-pressure, limited-range interview analysis, *succeeded* in eighty percent of the Foundation's cases. I, personally, had no failures while actually engaged in treating patients. Wallace, my second case, called two years after his treatment and reported a lack of real pleasure, so you can count that as a failure, if you wish (though, as I said, I think he was looking for out-side sex and decided to start with me). Brent Warren *did* fail to have successful sex after leaving St. Louis, and so my greatest success, in terms of the pleasure we gave each other, became my single failure, in terms of what he was able to take with him!

But even so, in my personal list of patients, I'm close to the Foundation's overall eighty-percent success factor. I wonder how many of the doctors and psychologists now engaged in shrugging off Masters and Johnson can match that record *using a two-week treatment period!*

EPILOGUE
by Herbert Lee

Valerie has given you my case in her eighth chapter, and I don't intend to repeat anything unnecessarily—just to tell it from my point of view.

After the first two sessions, covered in the Prologue, I was feeling quite confident. After all, I'd gained an erection, and after Valerie put it down, regained it again. And maintained it even after getting into my clothing. I wasn't wildly desirous, but I felt more hopeful, more like a male, than I had in two years.

At my third interview session on Friday, Dr. Masters said I had gone ahead even more quickly than scheduled, and that tonight, if the situation developed properly, I might have coitus. I nodded and smiled and, I'm sure, looked quite confident. But once I was out on the street, I began to sweat. Exam time tonight!

I knew that Valerie would relax me with the touch-and-feel process and with her spiel about nothing-having-to-happen. But I knew and she knew that we were going to try screwing.

Not only was I sweating with fear of failure, which could then inhibit me to the extent where the entire treatment, the whole two weeks, could fail, but I had begun thinking about Gail again. Valerie has given my thoughts and feelings on this point, *as I gave them to her,* but what she couldn't know was the *extent* of my compulsion to see and speak with Gail again.

I'm a great one for the *idée fixe,* having turned it to my

own benefit professionally, allowing some one idea to take over my mind, my total interest, until it grows to the point where it can sustain a book. Now it was working against me, and the idea was this: Valerie was forced-feeding; Gail was free-choice. I could never tolerate being *made* to do anything. Ergo, I could never be successful making love to Valerie.

Nice, huh? It had taken me just five days, and only two sessions with Valerie, to screw up a system that promised a way out of two years of agony. And all in *thought,* because in action I'd done exactly what Masters and Valerie had wanted me to do. Still, knowing the inflexibility of my inquisitor brain, I did the only thing I could, as I saw it: I walked toward the apartment house off Lindell, planning to speak to Gail, and to put her into proper perspective. I was going to show myself she was just another chick, offered nothing more than Valerie, and somehow get that damned *idée fixe* unfixed! And if she turned me down flat, I'd be left *only* with Valerie, and in a way *that* would solve the problem. . . .

Except that Gail didn't turn me down; she turned me *on.* We sat on her couch, and we went much further than we had on either of our two previous meetings. I had one hand inside her blouse, the other inside her pants, when she murmured, "No, please . . . stop, Herb."

I stopped. She was surprised, because it had been the very weakest of "Nos."

So why had I obeyed the letter and not the meaning of her request? I was frightened. I couldn't forget two years of varying degrees of failure just because I'd had an erection with Valerie. Besides, I *liked* this girl, felt good being with her, was *terrified* of failing with her and having her feel contempt for me.

I went to a bookcase and examined a set of leather-covered volumes. Gail was on a fellowship at a local college—one of the reasons her hours were so flexible, and her afternoons usually free. I said something about "handsome books," and my voice was shaky.

"Are you . . . upset?" she asked.

I answered rather sharply, to cover up. "No, of course not!"

She stood up, smoothing out her skirt. "I have some studying . . ."

I said I was sorry, and moved toward her. She shook her head. "You're uptight, Herb. I think it's time to say good-bye."

"For good?"

"That's up to you."

"Can I see you tonight?"

"I have a dinner date."

I'd communicated my agony, and she was upset by it, and she was going to drop me.

And I didn't want her to drop me. Not *this* girl!

"Afterward," I said. "Late."

She hesitated; then said, "I don't know. I'll call if I can get away."

I nodded. I wanted to say, *"Please* call. It's important. *We* can be important." And I wanted to explain why I was uptight, what lay behind the tension I'd communicated to her.

But how could I?

So I left, holding to the faint hope she would call.

That night, as Valerie has already stated, I was unable to function in the slightest. Like Pavlov's dog, a bell had to ring before my "head" could respond: a telephone bell, in my case. It didn't ring; Gail never called; I didn't respond. As Valerie noted, I wasn't surprised, and therefore didn't appear too upset. I hadn't expected to function.

But inside, of course, I was dying. I spoke of Gail to Valerie and worked out the reasons for my failure, but I didn't speak of my fear that she would never call me, and that it was already too late for me to get anything at all from in-bed therapy.

I switched areas of tension, as I always had, to books: I tried the concept of a book on Valerie. And I grew calmer, stronger, and decided that if I didn't hear from Gail by tomorrow, I would again try to see her.

Masters had given me the day off (in terms of an interview session) Saturday, so I was able to sleep late. In fact, I slept past noon, drugged by depression, by unwillingness to face another day of failure. Then I had a glass of juice in the luncheonette off the lobby, and went out.

It was clear, beautiful, and far warmer than it had been all week. I walked, and of course went down Lindell toward that apartment house, telling myself I wouldn't go in—and entered the moment I reached it. Gail wasn't home. I used my pen and a page torn from the notebook I always carry. I asked her to call me, no matter what time. And I wrote what I hadn't been able to say: "Please It's important. *We're* important."

Valerie has already described Saturday night. I was without desire, until Gail called. While talking to her, I gained an erection, and Valerie took over from there with hand and mouth. It felt good, but not great. Yet, as I said before, I sensed the problem was on its way out, if not yet completely vanquished.

Gail came to my suite at eleven-thirty, half an hour late. I was beginning to sweat by then, and asked what had kept her. She began to tell me something about her brother-in-law's car stalling, then stopped and shook her head. "I'm always late," she said. "I'm sorry, Herb."

Looking at her, I forgot what I'd been worrying about; forgot everything but her being here. She wore a white coat, a short, furry thing that might have looked stupid on most girls but looked perfect on her. Under the coat she wore a cream-colored mini-suit, and her blond hair rolled to her shoulders and her eyes held mine and we kissed.

We talked until almost four Sunday morning. We sat on the couch and talked and held hands. I never knew hand-holding could be so exciting, tender, erotic! Then we went to bed. We didn't make love. It just didn't happen. Perhaps residual fear had something to do with my not pressing the issue. But I don't think so, because I was hard as soon as her warm, fragrant body came against me.

We played with each other; then she murmured, "It's been such a long day," and kissed my cheek, little-girl fashion, and fell asleep.

So there I was, wanting her, but not quite wild for it, because of Valerie's attentions earlier in the evening. Still, there I was, finally unafraid and with a girl I liked, a girl I was perhaps beginning to love. There I was, and it was funny, wasn't it, after those two horrible years, and I laughed to myself and drew her even closer, and after a while, a long while, fell asleep.

I awoke to hear water running in the bathroom. I stumbled in there, bleary-eyed, because it was only nine, and I'd had about four and a half hours' sleep. Gail was singing in the shower. What a voice! High and thin and weak and quavery—and beautiful to my ears. I pulled back the sliding door. She squealed and began covering herself, then laughed and said, "Come in, Herbie!"

Herbie . . . I hadn't been called that since my teens.

We washed each other, and dried each other, and went back to bed. I never thought of failure. I didn't have time. I wanted her too much, and she wanted me too much, and it happened very quickly. Only after she raked my back with her nails, crying out, and I felt myself approaching orgasm, was there one instant when my mind tried to panic, tried to tell my body it was going to fail. But by then it was too late, though it *did* cut down on the intensity of my orgasm.

That was rectified after a room-service breakfast. Back to bed, and a long, tender period of touch-and-feel, as Valerie had shown me, and kissing, and telling Gail (and myself) that nothing *had* to happen, that we would play and play. . . .

We made love again, and for the first time in two years it was right: it was better than right, it was *perfect!*

When we finally dressed, it was almost three—and Valerie was due at four. I told Gail a business appointment would soon be here. She said she was going to take her little niece out for hamburgers at Steak and Shake, a Midwest drive-in chain. But first she wanted me to take her for a brief walk in Forest Park.

It was another beautiful day, and I had this beautiful girl, and before I knew it the time was four-fifteen. I put her in a cab and ran back to the hotel, getting there at four-thirty. Valerie was waiting in the lobby.

I didn't think we would make love; not after I told her about Gail. But we did, and it was excellent—and it was *important.* Valerie was right: I *didn't* need love with a capital L, a deep feeling, a special woman, to have sex.

It brought me back to where I'd been before the prostatitis and my inquisitor brain imprisoned me. It gave me back the male values, the male strengths.

And it made Gail even *more* important, because it made her even more special!

I went to the Foundation the next morning, and confessed Gail to Dr. Masters. He felt it was a mistake, but said I had received as much from surrogate-wife therapy as most patients get. I disagreed. I told him that Valerie was not my type and that I wanted to try another surrogate for the remaining week.

Masters instantly rejected my suggestion. He said they were not here to provide patients with a choice of women. Then he rose to terminate the meeting—and my treatment at the Foundation. We shook hands. I began to leave, then stopped and told him I was sorry about Gail—about breaking the rules, that is—but that it was unavoidable, given my mentality, my life style.

He nodded. I said I would like to come back in a month or two and see him again. He said we'd see, and that we would be talking every so often. The receptionist would give me a date, a time, and a telephone number. Contact would be maintained for five years, if I was intelligent enough to utilize the advice the Foundation could offer.

As I prepared to leave, he said, "You'll be all right. It'll get better as it goes on."

I believed him. I'd felt that myself, but I needed to hear him say it. And I also felt something else. Despite the brevity of my treatment, of my stay at the Foundation, I'd never gotten more for my money, medically, in all my life.

I spent ten more days in St. Louis, at the Forest Park Hotel. Gail was consistently late the first five days. The sixth day she was on time, and my, "I don't *believe* it!" brought forth delighted peals of laughter.

She was on time the remaining days too . . . and *early* that last sad, beautiful evening.

I was right. Dr. Masters was right. It got better and better. *Because* of Dr. Masters, and Mrs. Johnson, and the system, the seemingly simple system, they'd devised.

And because of Valerie, and the way she'd learned to apply her portion of that system.

Valerie has said it all. I can only add "Amen" and think ahead to Gail's next visit.

A Nationwide Bestseller!

The utterly candid guide to becoming fabulously female

The Sensuous Woman by "J"

Every woman has the ability and the right to be fully sensuous. But most women never learn how. And those who have discovered their wonderous female potential generally do not reveal their secrets.

Now "J", one of those fabulous females, reveals her secret, step-by-step program that allows every woman to free her body, train her senses and become a maddeningly exciting modern Aphrodite!

THE SENSUOUS WOMAN—the first how-to book for the female who yearns to be all woman.

Soon to be a major motion picture

A DELL BOOK $1.25

If you cannot obtain copies of this title from your local bookseller, just send the price (plus 15c per copy for handling and postage) to Dell Books, Post Office Box 1000, Pinebrook, N. J. 07058. No postage or handling charge is required on any order of five or more books.

A nationwide bestseller!

*The most
intimate novel
a woman
ever wrote*

Such Good Friends

by Lois Gould

Julie Messinger, age thirty-one and mother of two, is going through a kind of personal hell. It begins when her husband, Richard, enters a hospital for a simple operation, which turns into a medical disaster that eventually causes his death. Hunting through his desk for insurance papers, she comes across his diary which, if she reads the symbols correctly, means he has had several affairs over the past few years. His most recent mistress, it turns out, is one of Julie's best friends and the woman she turned to when Richard became ill.

"An important, believable book." *Saturday Review*
"A superb book . . . and hauntingly unforgettable reading experience." *Los Angeles Times*

A forthcoming major motion picture

A Dell Book $1.25

If you cannot obtain copies of this title from your local bookseller, just send the price (plus 15c per copy for handling and postage) to Dell Books, Post Office Box 1000, Pinebrook, N. J. 07058. No postage or handling charge is required on any order of five or more books.

Not since SEVENTH AVENUE!
The new blistering bestseller

The Value of Nothing

by John Weitz

From Seventh Avenue to Fifth Avenue is a short but savage journey.

John Weitz, one of the world's great fashion designers, tells a powerful story of the world of high fashion and low morals, of money and power and sex. It is a world where young Philip Ross, through a sexual arrangement that provides him with his first big break, crawls onto the lowest rung of the fashion ladder and begins the great climb, over backs and bodies, from couturier's assistant to nationwide fame as an avant-garde American designer.

"John Weitz has a true, storytelling gift."
Hollywood Reporter

"Authentic and fascinating"
San Antonio Express

"Only the names are changed"
Chicago Tribune

A DELL BOOK $1.25

If you cannot obtain copies of this title from your local bookseller, just send the price (plus 15c per copy for handling and postage) to Dell Books, Post Office Box 1000, Pinebrook, N. J. 07058. No postage or handling charge is required on any order of five or more books.

How many of these Dell bestsellers have you read?

DELL Bestseller List

1. **SUCH GOOD FRIENDS** by Lois Gould $1.25

2. **THE SENSUOUS WOMAN** by "J" $1.25

3. **DELIVERANCE** by James Dickey $1.25

4. **BALL FOUR** by Jim Bouton $1.25

5. **MARY QUEEN OF SCOTS** by Antonia Fraser $1.50

6. **GOING ALL THE WAY** by Dan Wakefield $1.25

7. **THE ANDERSON TAPES** by Lawrence Sanders $1.25

8. **DOCTORS AND WIVES** by Benjamin Siegel $1.25

9. **THE DOCTOR'S QUICK WEIGHT LOSS DIET** by Irwin Maxwell Stillman, M.D. and Samm Sinclair Baker   95c

10. **PLEASE TOUCH** by Jane Howard $1.25

11. **MILE HIGH** by Richard Condon $1.25

12. **THE TERRITORIAL IMPERATIVE** by Robert Ardrey $1.25

13. **THE ANDROMEDA STRAIN** by Michael Crichton $1.25

14. **THE POSEIDON ADVENTURE** by Paul Gallico $1.25

15. **THE $20,000,000 HONEYMOON** by Fred Sparks   95c

If you cannot obtain copies of these titles at your local bookseller, just send the price (plus 15c per copy for handling and postage) to Dell Books, Post Office Box 1000, Pinebrook, N. J. 07058. No postage or handling charge is required on any order of five or more books.